Old Age and the Welfare State

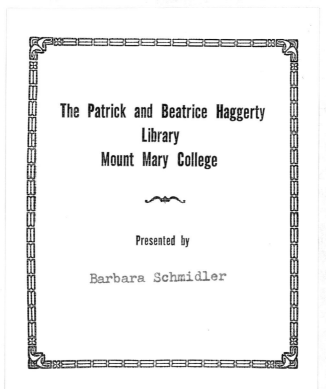

Old Age and the Welfare State

Editor
Anne-Marie Guillemard

 SAGE Studies in International Sociology 28
sponsored by the International Sociological Association/ISA

For information address

SAGE Publications Ltd
28 Banner Street
London EC1Y 8QE

SAGE Publications Inc
275 South Beverly Drive
Beverly Hills, California 90212

SAGE Publications India Pvt Ltd
C-236 Defence Colony
New Delhi 110 024

British Library Cataloguing in Publication Data

Old age and the welfare state — (Sage studies in international sociology; 28)
1. Ages — Social Conditions — Congresses
1. Guillemard, Anne-Marie
305.2'6   HQ1064.G7

Library of Congress Catalog Card Number 82-42835

ISBN 0-8039-9784-1

ISBN 0-8039-9759-0 (pbk)

Printed in the United States of America

CONTENTS

II.   THE SOCIAL IMPACT OF
OLD AGE POLICIES

PREFACE

The chapters in this book have come out of the original contributions
to and subsequent discussions during the Round Table on Public
Social Policies and Aging in Industrialized Countries. This round
table was organized in Paris from 8 to 10 July 1981 under the auspices
of the Research Committee on Aging and with the benevolent
support of both the Fondation de la Maison des Sciences de l'Homme
(Paris) and the International Sociological Association. Thirty-five
researchers from eight industrialized countries thus had the
opportunity to meet.

Plans to hold a round table took shape in August 1978 during the
World Congress of Sociology in Uppsala, Sweden. During one of the
sessions organized by the Research Committee on Sociology of
Aging, which had just been created within the International
Sociological Association, approximately ten researchers from
several countries discovered affinities while comparing work on the
theme of old age policy. Critical of a certain academic gerontology,
they wanted to develop what some termed a 'political economy of
aging', which would decipher relationships between sociopolitical
structures and the social organization of old age. Because of the
importance of the theoretical and political questions under
discussion, participants asked for a seminar in order to further and
deepen exchanges. Shortly thereafter I was elected president of the
Research Committee on Sociology of Aging. I thought that this
committee could give no better proof of its vitality than by holding a
meeting between congresses in order to sustain the discussions begun
at Uppsala.

I would like to thank all those who have participated in the
preparation of this book. Many authors agreed to significantly revise
the papers which they had submitted to the round table, so as to take

into account comments and criticisms that came out of the discussions. In particular, my gratitude goes to Isabelle Baszanger who assisted me throughout preparations for this volume. She not only accepted the post of round table secretary but has also helped in editing the chapters herein. The book in your hands owes much to my numerous discussions with her.

Anne-Marie Guillemard
June 1982

INTRODUCTION

Anne-Marie Guillemard

Centre National de la Recherche Scientifique, Paris

Public action on behalf of the elderly in the industrialized nations has grown prodigiously since the Second World War. Public old age policy first developed in the form of pension systems, then diversified as specific facilities and services were set up. The sum of transfers toward the elderly out of public expenditures is an indicator of the extent of these developments. At the start of the 1970s, old age pensions made up an average of 63 percent of the volume of social transfers in member countries according to the Organization for Economic Cooperation and Development. This percentage nevertheless underestimates the share of total public expenditures on the elderly. In particular, it leaves out major sums spent for the aged out of health and social service appropriations. As a consequence, the so-called welfare state is first of all a welfare state for the elderly.

Nowadays, as the future of social policies comes into question, the analysis of public old age policy is more crucial than ever. But in order to evaluate the present and anticipate the future, it is necessary to understand both the origins and development of the 'providential' welfare state, whose ambivalences are captured by Octavio Paz's expression, 'the philanthropic ogre'. Besides what it teaches about attitudes toward old age in industrialized societies, the study of policy development in this field raises broader questions about the very nature of the welfare state. Modern capitalistic states now in a

---

Translated from the French by Noal J. Mellott.

worldwide economic crisis, have implemented a variety of alleviatory social measures which, ironically, have exacerbated the crisis in old age policies. A case in point is the decision by many countries to push aging workers out of the work force in order to palliate employment difficulties.

Oddly enough, sociologists have more or less neglected this field of research, in spite of the theoretical and political lessons to be learned from inquiry into the origins and development of old age policies. Only a few researchers, isolated within their national frontiers, have dealt with this matter. A look at the relevant North American research, which is somewhat more voluminous because of the attention given to gerontological studies in the United States, gives rise to two remarks. First of all, these works principally examine specific political measures in the context of a sociology of decision making. They do not provide a global interpretation of the meaning of the whole set of composite and sometimes contradictory government interventions that, at a given moment, form public policy on old age. Secondly, they are dominated by a pluralistic approach to power that gives priority to an atomistic analysis of policy making. Such studies focus upon pressure groups and decision makers and generally fail to establish the relationship between the policy making process and the larger class structure or the nature of the state apparatus.

This book brings together essays that analyze public interventions on behalf of the elderly from both a global and a macrosociological perspective. It thus contributes toward defining a new area of research that should arouse both political and theoretical interest. Such research is crucial as industrial nations examine the past and scrutinize the future in order to find ways of dealing with the current crisis of the welfare state. From a global perspective, the chapters herein treat all aspects of old age policy — policies concerning both standards of living and ways of life, as well as employment policies. They principally aim at analyzing the ways in which the state regulates relations between aging and society. From a macrosociological perspective, they arise out of a common endeavor to interpret relationships between economic, social and political structures and the social treatment of old age resulting from policy implementation. In fact, some authors have advocated the establishment of a political economy of old age.

In spite of the preceding shared points of view, the chapters herein take their inspiration from various theories. For the same object of study, they propose approaches ranging from structural functionalism to neomarxism while omitting neither a type of analysis deriving from that of Michel Foucault nor the historical dimension. The reader thus has the opportunity to confront different theories in order to better evaluate each one's heuristic contribution.

Chapters are arranged according to the major question which they try to address. The first section, entitled 'Social Conditions in the Making of Old Age Policies', brings together texts that reflect upon both the formation of public old age policy and policy reorientations during the present economic crisis. Chapters in the second part, 'The Social Impact of Old Age Policies', examine the effects of existing policies upon the behavior of the elderly and upon societal conceptions of old age.

Social Conditions in the Making of Old Age Policies

All chapters under this heading more or less explicitly reject the conventional explanation for the formation of social policies for the elderly and, in particular, retirement policies. In the conventional view, the origins of the welfare-states-for-the-elderly are to be found in the aging of demographic structures which accompanied economic development in the industrialized nations.

John Myles' text is both theoretical and empirical. It evaluates various currents of thought about the welfare state and appraises their pertinence to social policies for the elderly. For the author, treating theories as though they apply to different levels of social reality is of more interest than trying to establish the superiority of one over the other. The chapter's empirical contribution comes from its presentation of available sources and types of data on social policies for the elderly. The possibility of proceeding from these data to cross-national studies is discussed. He concludes with an appeal to the scientific community to seek and obtain appropriate information for understanding these policies.

During the discussion that followed his contribution to the round table, Myles attempted to identify the factors that explain the extraordinary development of the welfare state in the industrialized nations during the 20th century. Why have these welfare states been organized primarily around providing support to the elderly? His answer opens with a criticism of Wilensky's (1975) functionalist theory. Wilensky explains the expansion of the welfare state in terms of changing needs — more old people to support — and increasing resources to meet new needs produced by economic growth.

For Myles, this interpretation can be refuted in two ways. In the first place, a comparative historical analysis does not clearly establish regular concomitant relationships between, on the one hand, growth in the size of the elderly population and, on the other, increasing public expenditures on behalf of the elderly. Pension systems for the elderly were introduced prior to population aging in many Western nations. Secondly, the functionalist argument reverses the order of causality. It assumes that in the past, as in the present, the elderly were economically dependent persons. But it is only in recent times, and especially since the Second World War, that the majority of the elderly have withdrawn from productive activity in advance of physiological decline, i.e. retired. The creation of a new social category — retirees — is the effect and not the cause of the extension of the welfare state and old age pensions.

The dominant idea defended by Myles and a few other authors of the chapters herein is that the establishment of the welfare-state-for-the-elderly must be understood in terms of the specific forms of class struggle in advanced industrialized nations during the 20th century. He characterizes class relationships in terms of the agreement between capital and labor to restrict the field of conflict to wage issues. Consequently, company heads have had their hands freed to rationalize job processes and control the composition of the labor force. Relying upon Graebner's study (1980), Myles sees in the spread of Taylorism and Fordism as a decisive influence upon the institutionalization of retirement. These two new trends logically eliminated the least productive segments from the labor force, including elderly workers, while also arousing in them the aspiration to retire. By virtue of losing control over the way work was to be done, workers also lost control over who would be eligible for work. In the reorganized labor process which followed the introduction of scientific management and the assembly-line, older and slower workers soon became redundant. The result was the retirement movement and the establishment of retirement pensions.

The institutionalization of retirement was slow and gradual. Until the Second World War, pension fund benefits were limited, and the ideology of retirement was more widespread than its practice. The final impetus came from the postwar principle of income replacement. Old age benefits no longer provided minimal relief; rather, they represented deferred income. This principle defined a new framework for wage negotiations between capital and labor and positively stimulated the expansion and orientation of welfare states toward the elderly.

Myles' argument, that modern retirement policies originated mainly in the dual rationalization of work by Taylorism and Fordism, has not gone unquestioned. Some researchers have found it convincing only inasmuch as liberal capitalism in large-scale industry had no other means for ridding itself of older workers and thus had to invent retirement. As several studies have shown, however, workers over 45 were chased out of factories in the early days of large-scale industry, and had to take shelter in precapitalistic branches of the economy. They were not retired but moved. Pensions have become a means for controlling the ejection of older workers from the labor force only within modern, extensive capitalism. Many researchers do agree, however, with Myles' refutation of the functionalist demographic explanation. Ephraim Mizruchi, Eugene Friedmann and Donald Adamchak also propose alternatives to this demographic explanation. In effect, sociologists cannot accept the reduction of a social problem to an economic or demographic one.

Mizruchi attempts to furnish demographic equilibria with a social content through the concept of abeyance. Given transformations in its demographic structure, a social system suspends certain groups on the basis of age. The purpose of abeyance is to regulate the population's demands and adapt them to the limited number of available occupational slots. Abeyance is a process of withholding individuals and of suspending time for the social system. Both the invention of schools for teenagers and the institutionalization of retirement for the elderly can be analyzed with this single concept.

This approach raises several questions. If abeyance throws some light upon the social system's treatment of youth, it takes on a totally different hue for old people who are not held in reserve until granted jobs but pushed aside until death. The theoretical model has to incorporate the idea of death. Furthermore, it is based upon a Parsonian vision of social systems being able to regulate themselves in the face of major transformations, such as those brought about by demographic change. This view is problematic since it leaves abeyant other contributions to our round table that dealt with the making of old age policies as the result of new institutions being created at a given moment in response to contradictory demands from various social forces.

Friedmann and Adamchak formulate other criticisms of analyses that only consider the size of the elderly population or its economic costs. For these authors modern welfare states are based upon income transfers; this mode of functioning poses problems in narrow economic terms. The major problem has become the costs to active producers and the limits that these costs fix on distributional policies. This logic has led to a questionable utilization of the notion of a dependency ratio. Introducing the latter into long-term population projections has resulted in alarming statements about the unbearable burden of the nonworking elderly in certain countries toward 2033 (President's Commission, 1980). Such declarations are obviously not neutral, for they shake the public's trust in the welfare state. They consequently clear the way for renegotiating the system of social protection, which could end up by being slashed or cut. For the authors, defining a better dependency ratio is of major political importance even though, unfortunately, few researchers have tackled this problem.

Friedmann and Adamchak propose a more relevant dependency ratio than the crude one currently used that divides the 'dependent' population over 65 years old by the 'productive' one between 18 and 64. They suggest a more sociological approach to replace this narrow demographic/economic one. The dependency ratio must incorporate intergenerational exchanges that take place outside the marketplace. The outcome of demographic projections calculated with such a ratio does not sound a cry of alarm as did the US President's Commission. A much more radical criticism of dependency ratios comes from Alan Walker who challenges the very idea that old age problems can be treated in such terms. These ratios imply outright acceptance of old age dependency as an incontrovertible fact, and thus ignore that it is a socially created phenomenon in capitalistic, industrial societies.

In line with Myles' queries, my chapter on the making of old age policies suggests a general outline for the analysis of the formation and evolution of French policy since the Second World War. This outline takes shape around two distinct efforts: on the one hand, a reconstruction of successive old age policies so as to identify their operations, and, on the other, an analysis of the most influential factors which led to the change from one system of operations to another.

The recent history of the manner in which public policy has assigned responsibility for old age matters has been reconstructed around both the major stakes involved in the development of this responsibility and the system of actors in conflict over these stakes. This reconstruction marks off three main periods in the history of public interventions in France since 1945. Each is characterized by a specific dynamic related both to the major issues at stake and to contending social forces. Moreover, each period has produced a social reconstruction of old age, from retirement to senior citizenship (in French, 'third age') and finally, to 'unjustified' employment.

One question often raised during the round table was: what does 'old age policy' cover? In reply, my chapter raises several points. The expression 'old age policy' does not merely juxtapose distinct, real objects: retirement policy (with which various participants at the round table dealt) and provision of services and facilities for the elderly. In French, old age policy often refers to the latter, particularly since the 1962 Laroque Report. Starting from the principal issues that serve as bases for change in responsibility for the elderly, my analysis traces the controversial relationships among debates about retirement benefits, standards of living and ways of living during the later years of life. Concrete old age policy represents only the resultant of these controversial relationships at a given moment.

The second aspect of my chapter is an effort to understand the specific configurations of social relations that explain the changing dynamics in responsibility for the elderly. Four major factors are proposed. To the two determinants that other participants have brought to light (the impact of socioeconomic structures as well as the forms and intensity of social conflicts), two others must be added: the cultural model of old age and its contradictions, including misfits or lags in relation to other aspects of the social matrix; and the specific forms of state intervention as well as the autonomy of the state in relation to civil society.

Rolande Trempé, in her chapter, draws up a prehistory of pension systems in France through her account of labor disputes in the mines from 1848 to 1914. As early as 1848, miners were aware of the need for retirement; they related the notions of rest at the end of life to wear and tear at work. They therefore demanded the right to retirement as a function, not of age, but of years of service (25 years). Mining companies also had the exhaustion of workers on their minds inasmuch as productivity was affected. Out of a paternalistic logic, they set up the Caisses de secours et de retraite minières, a relief and retirement fund. But this solution hardly met workers' expectations. The latter harshly criticized irregularities in operation and shortcomings in services. These funds, which should have been a source of labor peace, actually stirred up trouble between the miners and the companies. Conscious of their lack of power over the management of these employer funds, miners organized so as to bring pressure to bear on the government through both legislative circuits and general strikes, with the aim of regulating employer/employee relations in this matter. In response, the companies united to prevent government intervention. In 1914, this dispute was settled by the creation of an autonomously managed retirement fund. Miners thus opened a breach in economic liberalism. Their recourse to the government fore-shadowed the movement toward social security. Trempé has high-lighted the impact of social conflicts upon the formation and public management of retirement institutions, at least within one key industrial branch before the First World War.

In 'Old Age as a Risk', François Ewald does not so much analyze the origins of French retirement policies as search for the new conceptions of security and mutual liability underlying them. These made it possible to set up worker retirement programs and to implement the 1910 law on old age pensions for farmers and workers. Throughout the 19th century in France, from a policy of protection or relief to one of insurance and security, the problem of retirement benefits was a major cause of rationalizing institutions that covered all social risks. Consequently, various risks were separated, and those of old age, taken over by state institutions. The government could not, however, intervene effectively without making insurance mandatory. Proof had come from the failure of a century-old policy of individual protection. In 1903, for instance, the Caisse Nationale des retraites, a non-mandatory system, only covered two percent of the working class population.

The principle of obligatory insurance could only be adopted once a new idea — that of social insurance — had been defined. Ewald finds the first formulation of a new system of liability in debate about work-related accidents and occupational hazards (the Act of 9 April 1898). It broke completely with the prevailing liberal policy of individual protection. This transformation of the system of liability opened the way to a new conception of old age as a social risk, as embodied in the 1910 law on old age pensions for farmers and workers. In this new perspective, and according to the concept of social debt embodied in Leon Bourgeois' theory of 'solidarity', each individual's problems of insecurity became the responsibility of the whole society. As a counterpart to this new duty, society obtained a new right: it could oblige the improvident to anticipate the future in spite of themselves. This new legal conception of risk and security was formed out of the propitious juncture of several events. Among these were the birth of sociology with its new ways of conceiving social problems, the inception in France of the Republic that needed a solid basis, and the rise of socialism. Ewald has brought up a new point for reflection with respect to old age policies. He has helped unravel the complicated links between social conflicts, which set employees and employers at odds over retirement programs, and changes in the 'insurance mentality' with its conceptions of risk and security as well as related rationalities and practices.

In his analysis of the British case since 1945, Chris Phillipson sketches what he terms a political economy of retirement. He shows that old age and retirement policies, as well as ideologies, have varied directly as a function of capitalism's manpower requirements. Two principal phases can be distinguished during the period under study. At the beginning of the 1950s, in spite of progress toward institutionalizing retirement, the state encouraged aging workers to prolong their activities. This policy must be understood in terms of manpower shortages at that time. The myth of retirement as trauma, and work as therapy, was also created during this period; it obfuscated the enlarged right to retirement. Since the 1970s, a reversal can be observed in both retirement ideologies and employment policies adopted for aging workers. Because of the economic crisis and the introduction of new technology, the government has launched a new theme that can be summarized as 'Give your place to the young'. This has been applied politically through the job release scheme, which will speed up the withdrawal of older workers from the labor market.

For Phillipson, retirement is merely a concession made by capitalism which is continually adjusted to the politicoeconomic juncture. Hence the idea of flexible retirement must be questioned. Given the strong trends revealed by his historical analysis, flexible retirement schemes risk being subject to labor market needs and employer interests. Their development would only increase insecurity among older workers. Contrary to a widely held view, Phillipson affirms that older workers would be better protected by setting definite age criteria that would grant inalienable retirement rights. This stand is made along with criticism of both radical and conservative gerontology, which has always argued for voluntary age limits. Gerontology has two shortcomings. In the first place, its findings are at odds with sociological research. In particular, it overlooks the sociology of work and studies of worker alienation. Secondly, gerontology bases most analyses upon a middle class vision of work and retirement. These analyses leave aside a question that should have priority: is the working class, faced with large-scale unemployment and premature exclusion from the labor force, adopting new behaviors and attitudes toward retirement?

Phillipson's view of old age and retirement policies is not shared by all researchers. Walker, in particular, defends the idea that a formal age of retirement is one of the most influential factors in social disparagement of the elderly. He argues that, as long as an individual's job is a central element in his identity and social integration, a fixed age of retirement, which is nowadays being lowered, tends to make the elderly more dependent upon and peripheral to society.

THE SOCIAL IMPACT OF OLD AGE POLICIES

Walker's analysis of the consequences of policies in Great Britain emphasizes their implicit role in making old age into a social status consisting of relationships of dependency and domination. He sees three principal factors in this social creation of dependency. The first is the importance of the age criterion in labor market operations, which exclude older workers at ever lower ages and, in turn, reinforce their dependency upon the state. The second factor is the pension system and the limited resources supplied to retirees. Thirdly, the role of professionals has developed from the implementation of a specific old age policy; and these professionals, by their practices, contribute toward creating a dependent age group.

The chapters by Carroll Estes, Danilo Giori and Hilde von Balluseck provide global evaluations of policies in the United States, Italy and West Germany, respectively.

Estes endeavors to show that formulations of the old age problem, as well as its political solutions, reflect the social system's economic and political structures. She describes the relations between the problem of old age and America's economic and political structures during the last thirty years, and particularly under the Reagan administration. Actions in this policy field spring from two dominant approaches which the author evaluates. The first is based on the concept of a fiscal crisis, which has made it possible to initiate the retrenchment of major federal programs by transferring responsibility from the federal to state and local governments. The elderly poor will be hit hardest. The second approach perceives aging as an individual rather than a social matter. Interventions consequently apply a policy of providing services to individuals. An 'aging enterprise' has thus come into being. To survive, it must accentuate the segregative nature of the policy underlying it.

Estes concludes by drawing attention to the danger of adopting 'separatist' solutions during a period of austerity. These can turn against the group in question, as it becomes a scapegoat whose increasing needs are eventually perceived as a source of the deepening fiscal crisis. Within the study of old age policy, she has cleared the way for a sociology of knowledge by indicating the mutual legitimation of dominant theoretical constructions and political practices.

Giori's appraisal of the Italian case resembles some of Walker's conclusions concerning the dependency generated by social policy on behalf of the elderly. The central mechanisms of a capitalist society, fixated on productivity, relegate the elderly to its fringes, like all other persons who do not enter the productive sphere or the labor market. This trend is all the stronger in Italy inasmuch as management of this segment of the population is widely entrusted to the private sector. Moreover, the main response to demands for help is still institutionalization. Giori remarks that the development of disability pensions at the end of the 1960s constituted one of the principal means for stimulating consumer demand, especially in central and southern Italy. It also consolidated a new political clientele around a power block. Furthermore, the application of disability or early retirement programs indirectly contributed to the growth of illegal employment. After 1972, inflation forced older workers, who had retired but a few years earlier as a result of these pensions, to go back to work. Private industry saw in this age group a reserve of rather cheap manpower for jobs in the underground economy.

Von Balluseck has surveyed 130 years of German history from the origins of social policy on behalf of the elderly to present-day trends. Her inquiry develops along three lines: the manipulation of the labor market and establishment of social security; the formation of a specific social policy for the aged; and health policy in old age matters. The implicit functions of these policies are pointed out. They have had a double goal, namely to stabilize and extend the mass of wage-earners and also to fasten down women in nuclear families. In this way, the difficulties of a growing fraction of the population, socially defined as unproductive, are explained as consequences of social and sexual divisions of labor. In the case of medical care, the author analyzes how the very functions of social policy hinder both a correct delimitation of the elderly's needs in health matters and the discovery of adequate responses.

Nick Bosanquet has pragmatically questioned the relevance of a unified policy that overlooks the diversity among the elderly. He has dealt with the very old age group and its needs, for which a specific social policy must be conceived. Such an adapted policy would combine in-kind benefits with a particular type of service.

The texts herein will enable readers to grasp the diverse approaches to contemporary explorations of old age policies as well as the multiple questions that arise out of their comparison. By bringing together original material and studies about the century-old development of old age policies and their social effects in six advanced industrialized countries, the United States, Canada, Great Britain, Italy, West Germany and France, this book aims at provoking reflection from a comparative viewpoint. This is still largely lacking. It is my hope that the debates and inquiries arising out of this book will stimulate this field of research, which sociologists have overlooked. Many lessons are to be learned as we now face the unavoidable question of the welfare state and its future.

REFERENCES

Graebner, W. (1980) *A History of Retirement* (New Haven, Yale University Press).
Laroque Commission d'Etude des Problèmes de la Vieillesse (1962) *Politique de la Vieillesse* (Paris, La Documentation Française).
President's Commission on Pension Policy (1980) *Demographic Shifts and Projections, Implications for Pension Systems* (Washington, DC, Government Printing Office).
Wilensky, H. (1975) *Welfare State and Equality* (Berkeley, University of California Press).

I

SOCIAL CONDITIONS IN THE MAKING OF OLD AGE POLICIES

1

COMPARATIVE PUBLIC POLICIES FOR THE ELDERLY:
Frameworks and Resources for Analysis

John Myles
Carleton University, Ottawa

Within the field of social gerontology there has been a growing shift of interest during the past decade away from the study of aging individuals as such, and their problems of adaptation to the conditions and experience of growing old, towards the study of those social institutions and arrangements to which the elderly must adapt. In a general way this reflects a shift away from the analytical concerns and focus of the social psychological tradition within sociology towards the more macro perspectives and theories which address problems of social structure and social organization. Thus, for example, an adequate social gerontology requires not only an account of how aging individuals adjust or fail to adjust to the loss of income associated with retirement and aging but also an account of the social, economic and political processes which produce the typical pattern of income decay associated with old age. Similarly, a political sociology of aging requires not only an analysis of how or whether political behavior is altered by the aging process or the role of 'grey lobbies' in the political process but also analyses of the political processes that produce the political outputs which most directly affect the experience of growing old — public pensions and social services for the elderly. The elderly themselves have played only a marginal role in the production of these outputs of the political process in the advanced capitalist countries, and as a result, the development of a 'political sociology of aging' requires going far beyond the gerontologist's traditional concern with the elderly as such and extending the traditional boundaries of the discipline to include those social groups and institutions which produce the social policies that do shape the experience of growing old in contemporary societies.

This does not mean, however, that such a political sociology of aging must now be created *ex nihilo*. Although the number of national and comparative studies of social policies for the elderly is still restricted (Aaron, 1967; Heclo, 1974; Estes, 1979; Guillemard, 1980; Derthick, 1979; Bryden, 1974), the larger body of both theoretical and empirical research which subsumes such policies is now vast indeed. For at least two decades the various analytical frameworks of political theory have been applied with regularity and diligence to the study of what in the postwar period has come to be called the welfare state and public consumption expenditures on the elderly are but one, albeit the single largest, component of welfare state expenditures in the advanced capitalist countries (OECD, 1976). It is from within this broader tradition in political and social theory that any analysis of the 'politics of aging' must perforce begin.

The purposes of this paper are twofold. The first is to provide an overview of the major theoretical perspectives and debates which have emerged from the analysis of the welfare state in the past two decades and to evaluate their relevance for the study of social policies for the elderly. The second is to identify and evaluate major extant data sources for the study of social policy for the aged. The intent is to provide a background paper for the growing number of social gerontologists who are now attempting to pursue this line of research. This review has two major limitations. The first is that the primary emphasis is on the relevance of both theory and data for *comparative* studies of social policy for the aged. The second is that among the three major forms of state expenditures on the elderly — income transfers, in-kind transfers of goods, and social services — only the first will be considered in detail and the last will be virtually ignored. Finally, my intent in this review is not to be exhaustive of the available theory and research but simply to indicate the various types of theoretical frameworks and data sources available for the analysis of public policies for the elderly.

THEORETICAL PERSPECTIVES
ON THE WELFARE STATE

My intent in this section is to present some of the major perspectives which have been applied to the study of the welfare state and to give some indication of their strengths and limitations with respect to the analysis of social policy for the elderly. There exist several excellent overviews of such theory (Mishra, 1977; Gough, 1979) which the reader can consult for more detail and additional references. The reader should be forewarned, moreover, that the classification of theories presented below in no way captures the diversity or richness of work in this field. No single author can be as easily classified as the presentation might suggest. The best analyses are more nuanced than any single classification scheme can capture and authors may adopt different positions in different works or even with the same work. Nonetheless, these categories do capture broad theoretical positions and points of view which characterize the major debates in the analyses of the modern welfare state.

Equilibrium Models of the Welfare State

One important class of models that attempts to account for the emergence of the welfare state is that which I shall refer to as equilibrium models. This general class of models can be found in theories which are derived from a variety of major theoretical perspectives in sociology, both marxist and nonmarxist. Such theories tend to be held by functionalist theorists of a variety of theoretical persuasions who see modern societies as having moved from one point of historical equilibrium to another. Since the nonmarxist versions of this perspective will be more familiar to many readers, we shall begin with these.

Structural-Functionalism and the Industrialization Thesis

The authors whom I shall identify as equilibrium theorists of a nonmarxist variety are those who are usually designated by the term 'structural-functionalist' in the sociological literature. They are so denoted because they view society as an integrated structural whole and explain the existence and change of social institutions — the parts — in terms of their functions for the whole; that is, in terms of their contribution to the survival and efficient operation of the social organism we call society. Particularly prominent in this tradition is the Parsonian view of social evolution as characterized by a continuous process of differentiation and integration. As societies become more complex — i.e. differentiated — new mechanisms of coordination and social cohesion are required if the newly differentiated parts are to continue to function as a whole and hence for a society to survive (see Mishra, 1977, Chapter 4 for an extended discussion). As Giddens (1976, pp. 716-722) has argued, however, it is not these purely formal concepts which differentiate 'structural-functionalism' from 'marxism' but rather the substantive content of the approach which Giddens calls the *theory of industrial society*. The modern era is to be understood not in terms of the transition from feudalism to capitalism, as in the marxian paradigm, but in terms of the transition from agricultural to industrial society (Kerr et al., 1964, p. 14). It is the 'logic of industrialism' which moves and changes modern society. Social institutions, including welfare institutions, emerge in response to the imperatives of the technological requirements of industrial production and the increased capacity to respond to new needs as a result of the increased wealth created by economic growth. With industrialization come the requirements for an educated and mobile labor force and the disruption of traditional familial bonds of social support and solidarity. Urbanization creates new health problems, as well as transportation and housing requirements for the population which inhabits the factories and office buildings of industrial societies. This highly complex and differentiated social order requires coordination and integration to maintain order and consensus. All of these factors generate an expanded role for the state to *maintain the work force and achieve coordination and consensus*[1] in society (Kerr et al., 1964, pp. 22, 152ff.) The logic of industrialism therefore impels all industrial societies along a similar evolutionary path and the 'ideological' conflicts of earlier periods decline as this logic draws them to adopt similar forms of social organization in the pursuit of efficiency. Thus, governments in all states, communist or capitalist, have created a variety of welfare measures — workmen's compensation, old age insurance, sickness and unemployment benefits — and the major ideological cleavages of the advanced industrial countries account for little in explaining variations in the scope and development of the welfare state (Pryor, 1968; Wilensky, 1975, pp. 15-49). The expansion of welfare provisions is facilitated by the new wealth and expanded surplus available from increased productivity. In turn, this expanded wealth may create additional needs which require welfare efforts; for example, by enabling individuals to live longer, the relative size of the aged population may increase (Wilensky, 1975).

The Logic of Capital Accumulation

A quite similar version of the development of the welfare state can be found in traditional marxist accounts of this phenomenon. Consistent with marxist theory, these accounts emphasize the social form (feudal, capitalist, socialist) in which production is carried out rather than simply the material content (agriculture, commerce, industry) of production. The new needs which accompany industrialization are not due to industrial production as such, but are shaped and molded — given content — by the relations of production peculiar to industrial capitalism. Old age becomes a problem, for example, because of the commodification of labor and, hence, the dependency of the mass of the population on the wage relation and the labor market for survival. For those who do not have access to the labor market, such as the aged, survival becomes a dilemma. Their survival is also a dilemma for capitalism. On the one hand, this mode of production requires that most of the people most of the time have little or no alternative but to deliver their services for sale on the labor market and, thus, the availability of alternative forms of subsistence has to be eliminated or greatly restricted. State provision of a livelihood — public welfare — is generally viewed by capital as an obstacle and unwarranted restraint on the 'free play' of market forces. At the same time, a minimum level of social cohesion and stability must be maintained for production to go on and such stability is unlikely to be a characteristic feature of capitalist societies if most people are faced with the threat of impoverishment when they are sick, old, unemployed, etc. A major task of the capitalist state, therefore, is to manage this inherent contradiction between the *accumulation requirements* of capital on the one hand and the *legitimization* of this mode of production on the other (O'Connor, 1973). The *welfare state*, in this view, is simply an *effect* of the *capitalist state* which must develop policies and programs necessary to sustain and reproduce capitalist social relations (Offe, 1972).

The conceptual equivalent for economic development in the marxian model is the shift from competitive to monopoly capitalism which results from the increasing concentration and centralization of capital characteristic of all advanced capitalist societies. Indeed, the welfare state is the child of the monopoly sector which '. . . depends on the continuous expansion of social investment and social consumption projects that in part or in whole indirectly increase productivity from the standpoint of monopoly capital' (O'Connor, 1973, p. 24). Monopoly capital both requires and is generally successful in having the state absorb more and more of its real costs of production including a substantial portion of the wage bill through such devices as socialized health care and social security programs.

The welfare state, then, is little more than the *effect* of the capitalist state exercising its necessary — if contradictory — functions for the expanded reproduction of capitalism. Moreover, the primary beneficiary of the welfare state is capital not labor. In creating the conditions necessary for private capital accumulation, few, if any, benefits derive to labor. Despite the emergence of the welfare state, poverty persists amidst affluence; little if any genuine redistribution occurs; and, at best, there is the creation of 'socialism in one class' whereby redistribution largely occurs *within* the working class — from healthy workers to sick workers, from young workers to old workers and from the employed to the unemployed. Within this view, a preoccupation with cross-national differences in welfare state expenditures is to be taken in by 'appearances' and misses the underlying fundamental reality of the contradiction between production for profit and human need which persists in all advanced capitalist countries (Offe, 1972).

On both theoretical and empirical grounds both of the equilibrium models of the welfare state — marxist and nonmarxist — discussed above are of limited utility in explaining cross-national variations in welfare state development in general or social policy for the elderly in particular among the advanced industrial or capitalist nations. A first and very important reason for this arises from the historical scope at which such theories frequently tend to be pitched. The scope of historical explanation in such theories is extremely broad. The intent is to make sense of changes which have occurred across major historical periods. Structural-functionalist theory, for example, is often directed at explaining the major shifts which occurred in the transition from preindustrial to industrial societies or from early to advanced stages of industrialization. Similarly, marxist analyses tend to focus on the shift from precapitalist to capitalist modes of production or from early competitive capitalism to advanced monopoly capitalism. The variations which occur *within* any one of these broad social-historical categories tend frequently to lie outside the scope of the theory. The intent is to sketch out the structural limits of major historical types; not to account for variations which occur within these limits.

In other formulations, however, lack of attention to variations within broad historical types is not simply a matter of theoretical oversight but an explicitly adopted theoretical position; that is, variations within types (e.g. advanced industrial or advanced capitalist economies) are essentially viewed as being nonsystematic (i.e. random) and hence inherently uninteresting for further investigation. The *essential* identity between different instances of a social type is affirmed and the differences between such instances defined as accidental or epiphenomenal. For example, the authors of *Industrialism and Industrial Man* (Kerr et al., 1964) have much to say about the variations in state policy during the early period of industrialization but as industrialization proceeds and the logic of industrialism increasingly imposes itself on all societies, initial differences disappear and, it would seem, history comes to an end. Marxist equilibrium theorists frequently adopt a similar position. Thus, Claus Offe (1972, p. 380), commenting on differences in current welfare state policies in Europe and North America, considers these differences '. . . as simply different manifestations of the same institutional structure — i.e. the economic, social, and political mechanism of advanced capitalism'. All advanced capitalist states operate in essentially similar fashion — to fulfill the functions necessary for the reproduction of capitalism.

On purely theoretical grounds both the 'logic of industrialism' school and the 'logic of capitalism' school tend to be undermined by the functionalist logic of their argument. As Gough (1979, p. 50) has pointed out, the fact that some function is required of the capitalist state or the industrial state tells us nothing about *how* or *when* these functions are fulfilled or even *whether* they are fulfilled.

In assessing such theories Gough (1979, p. 9) suggests that while they can explain the historical growth and the emergence of similar social policies in all advanced capitalist countries, such theories cannot deal with '. . . the immense diversity of social policies which any comparative survey will reveal'. Furthermore, to the extent that it can be demonstrated that such differences are systematic both in their origins and their consequences, the empirical underpinning required for the theoretical dismissal of such differences is removed. There are numerous studies which attest to the systematic character of such diversities within the advanced capitalist countries with respect to economic policy and welfare expenditures in general (e.g. Cameron, 1978; Stephens, 1980).

Perhaps the best way to summarize the positions on this perspective is to distinguish between strong and weak versions of the 'logic of industrialism' and 'logic of capitalism' theses. In their weak form these are important for distinguishing between broad historical categories. However, variations *within* these broad historical types simply escape or lie outside the scope of the theory and hence are of limited utility for comparative analysis. The proponents of such theories, however, more often than not present a strong version in which the within-group variations are considered to be nonsystematic. These strong versions simply do not stand up to empirical analysis.

Nonetheless, such theories are of singular importance in drawing our attention to the limits within which the state in capitalist and/or industrial societies is free to maneuver. The state in capitalist societies, for example, is continuously constrained by the requirement to create an environment in which capital accumulation is possible and investments profitable. And its social policies will tend to reflect this constraint. Thus, as William Graebner (1980) has argued, retirement policy and income provisions for the retired are also a strategy of labor force management which emerged when they were perceived as potentially enhancing efficiency and corporate profitability.

Democracy, Social Democracy and the Class Struggle

The second broad grouping of theoretical perspectives which I shall now discuss adopts a rather different view of the emergence of the welfare state. These theories once again include marxist and nonmarxist versions but tend to share certain common assumptions. Of particular importance is the role of human agency in producing social change. Without denying the structural determinants (capitalism/industrialism) of the modern welfare state, these theories place considerable emphasis on the role of human agency and human intervention. Men may not make their own history exactly as they please, but they do make it nonetheless.

Democracy, Equality and the Welfare State

The view that the rise of universal suffrage and mass democracy would bring with it a great levelling of existing inequalities is a view which goes back to the 19th century and was shared by radicals, conservatives and liberals alike. The fundamental fear/hope of 19th century observers was that with mass enfranchisement, the impoverished majority would seize control of the state and use it as an instrument to counteract the inegalitarian effects of the market. A similar if somewhat modified view can be found in numerous contemporary theories which address the issue of inequality and the welfare state.

Among the most frequently cited examples of what Hewitt (1977) has called the 'simple democratic' hypothesis is that originally outlined by Lenski (1966). The critical elements of Lenski's argument (for our purposes) are as follows:

(1) '...the appearance of mature industrial societies marks the first significant reversal in the age-old evolutionary trend toward ever-increasing inequality' (1966, p. 308).

(2) Among the reasons for this are:
2.1. the growing knowledge base of subordinates and the dependency of the ruling elite on this knowledge; and
2.2. the rapid growth in productivity and wealth which permits the elite to trade relative advantage for absolute gains.

Propositions 2.1 and 2.2 are simply restatements of the industrialization argument discussed previously. In addition to these preconditions, however, an important and independent effect is due to:

2.3. the spread of democratic theory and practice which enable the many to

'...combine against the few and even though individually the many are weaker, in combination they may be as strong or stronger' ... Where democracy has taken hold, the many have combined in varying degrees to use the state on their own behalf (Lenski, 1966, pp. 318-325).

In effect, although neither capitalism nor industrialism are over-thrown, political democracy permits the many to alter the distribu-tion of life chances through their own political struggles and efforts. Industrialization *as such*, '...creates conditions favorable to the growth of democracy (and hence the welfare state) but does not make it inevitable' (Lenski, 1966, p. 317). Where political democracy has taken hold, it has tended to result in significant shifts towards equality via the instrumentality of state policies. To use a phrase from an author who holds a similar view, the relationship between industrialization and the emergence of the welfare state is mediated by the 'democratic class struggle' (Lipset, 1960).

The simple democratic hypothesis, then, views the welfare state as an effect of successful political struggles and demands imposed on ruling elites which are made possible by the establishment of democratic political forms. Carried to its extreme (which Lenski avoids), this view is expressed in the pluralist thesis which asserts that the modern state is a neutral instrument of rule which simply referees and adjudicates among the various interests of the citizenry of the advanced capitalist countries. The liberal democratic state is a state which is inherently responsive to the needs and preferences of its citizenry and the welfare state is but one expression of the responsiveness. Hence as the number of elderly persons grows and their participation in the labor force declines, this new interest group, along with its allies, exerts political pressure through normal democratic channels and over time a series of policies begins to emerge in response to these demands.

In its more extreme pluralist version, human agency comes to dominate all else and structural limits are virtually eliminated from the analysis. A democratic society is a political marketplace where political outcomes are determined by and large by the values and preferences of its citizenry; the only 'uncaused' cause in this view is *culture,* the aggregate of individual values and preferences. Explanations of variations in state policy outputs would turn largely on differences in national cultures or the distribution of particular sets of values and preferences across societies (e.g. Americans are more individualistic in their values than Germans or Swedes).

Some early support for this view of the singular importance of formal democratic institutions was presented in the analyses of Cutright (1965, 1967a, 1967b) but subsequent analyses (Jackman, 1975; Hewitt, 1977) have tended to disconfirm it. The critical problem for this position is that among the eighteen or so advanced capitalist countries of Western Europe, North America and Oceania there is in fact little difference in the level of development of formal democratic institutions (see Bollen, 1980) despite wide divergence in the development of welfare state provision and social policies for the aged. Since many who hold to this position view the United States as the most democratic of nations, the relative underdevelopment of welfare policies in that country constitutes a difficult negative case. Moreover, historical case studies of the development of social legislation for the elderly (Heclo, 1974; Derthick, 1979) indicate a relatively minor role for the elderly or their organized representatives who, in the pluralist framework, ought to play a decisive role in the generation of legislation in favor of the aged. It is only *after* such legislation has been passed that the elderly become a distinctive object of state policy-making and only then do the elderly begin to appear as a distinctive political constituency to be reckoned with. It is nonetheless true, however, that at later stages of development the aged have emerged as a distinctive constituency in the political marketplace and with the aging of all the developed societies cannot be considered a trivial political force with respect to current and future developments in old age policies.

Class Struggle, Social Democracy and the Welfare State

Marxist interpretations of the role of political democracy in capitalist society have varied considerably over time. Early *bourgeois democracy* in which rights to vote and/or hold office were contingent on ownership of property and by and large excluded the working class were of course seen as highly compatible with a capitalist economy. However, with the expansion of mass democracy and the removal of class, sex and race as obstacles to political participation, it was anticipated that political democratization would lead rather quickly to a political victory by the working class and the quick demise of capitalism. Even Marx and Engels saw democratization as necessarily leading towards socialism (see Przeworski, 1980, pp. 21-22).

As it became apparent that universal suffrage was not about to lead to the overthrow of capitalism, however, another interpretation quickly emerged. Rather than a threat to capitalism, Lenin saw democracy as 'the best possible political shell' for its survival, a view which has been shared by many subsequent marxists. By creating the *appearance* of equality in the political arena (the superstructure), political democracy effectively *obscures* the inequality and authoritarian character of economic relations under capitalism. This is the view of the democratic process which tends to prevail among those marxists characterized previously as equilibrium theorists. There is no inherent contradiction between democratic polities and capitalist economies and, in the end, the interests of capital (perceived or not) dominate and determine the democratic political process, reproducing the subordinate status of the masses.

A rather different view is held by those theorists who emphasize the role of *class struggle* in explaining social change (Esping-Anderson, Friedland and Wright, 1976). Minimally, the tension between political equality and economic inequality is seen as a source of strain for the capitalist state. While emphasizing the limits of democracy, Przeworski (1980, pp. 30-31) observes that democracy:

> ...is a mechanism by which anyone as a citizen can express claims to goods and services which have expanded because a part of the societal product was withheld in the past from the immediate producers. While as immediate producers, wage earners have no institutional claim to the product, as citizens, they can process such claims through the democratic system...This opportunity is limited but nonetheless real. It is the opportunity to influence the rate of accumulation to mitigate the operation of the market, to escape the competition for wages, to equalize individual access to some services, to gain some security for old age.

Thus, there is a growing tendency among recent marxist theorists to emphasize the role of political democracy in accounting for the growth and expansion of the *citizen's* wage (Bowles and Gintis, forthcoming) and the welfare state.

Unlike the 'simple democratic hypothesis', however, the marxist version of this theory does not see political democracy *as such* as a sufficient explanation either for the development of or for variations in welfare state expenditures in the advanced capitalist countries (Martin, 1973, p. 14). As Hewitt (1977, p. 451) observes:

...the crucial matter is what the mass electorate *does* with the franchise and other democratic procedures. Only if the lower classes use their votes to elect socialist governments will democracy result in more equality.

In order for democracy to be an effective instrument of redistribution, it is necessary that the democratic process become organized around explicit class lines — that workers organize as a class and become represented in the political process as such. In sum, the degree to which democracy leads to equality depends on the level of class formation and in particular *political* class formation which develops within the democratic 'political shell'. The welfare state, in this view, is an *effect* of class struggle (Gough, 1975, 1979) and variations in the development of the welfare state a reflection of variation in the power achieved by the working class as a consequence of their struggle. While not transforming capitalism, the welfare state constitutes a set of genuine if limited victories for the working class.

Scholars who have adopted some variant of this perspective have produced an impressive volume of quantitative cross-national studies and historical case studies during the past decade (for example, see Stephens, 1980, and for a review of this literature see Shalev, 1980). Not all of these authors adopt a formally marxist or neomarxist perspective but all converge in their focus on the role of class forces in the generation of social change and the production of cross-national variations in state outputs. Terms such as 'class struggle' may be replaced by 'the bargaining power of labor' but the emphasis is similar throughout.

Gerontologists may initially be at a loss to see the relevance of this perspective for explaining differences in social policy for the aged, particularly in view of the emphasis in the gerontological literature on conflict between age strata, that is between the elderly who are not in the labor force and workers in the productive age groups. But as historical analyses have made clear, the primary actors in the generation of old age legislation in the 20th century have not been the elderly but the young. It is the AFL-CIO, not the Grey Panthers, which has been the major advocate of expanded Social Security in the United States throughout the postwar period. The reason for this is rather simple. Social policies for the elderly are also social policies for the young. Economists are generally agreed that pensions for the elderly, including public pensions, should be viewed as a deferred wage which is negotiated between employers and employees while workers are still in the labor force,

rather than as social benefits which are extracted by the elderly
from the larger society after retirement.

As a result, the critical factors explaining cross-national differences in the development and growth of the 'deferred wage' are
variations in the structure and organization of the larger wage
struggle between capital and labor during the 20th century and
variations in the role of the state in organizing and mediating that
struggle. A common strategy in containing wage pressures in
postwar Europe, for example, was that of exchanging current real
wage gains for a promise of more state expenditures on social
services and income maintenance programs, especially for the
elderly. In sum, real wage demands were lowered in exchange for a
promise of an expanded deferred wage to be delivered after
retirement, usually by the state. This phenomenon generally
reflects the much greater strength of organized labor and labor-
based political parties, especially in Northern Europe, and the level
of wage pressure workers were able to exert in the postwar years
(Panitch, 1981) and goes far in explaining the more generous and
highly developed social policies for the elderly formed in those
countries than in North America.

Smart Capitalists and Mass Turmoil:
Some American Variations

There are numerous interpretations of the rise of the welfare state
which are not captured by the preceding discussion. Two views
which have acquired particular importance within the American
context are the corporate liberal theories of authors such as
Domhoff (1970) on the one hand and the mass turmoil theory of
Piven and Cloward (1971) on the other.

The corporate liberal thesis is frequently exemplified by analyses
of the American New Deal and the Social Security Act of 1935.
Whereas in the traditional view Roosevelt brought in his reforms
on a wave of popular support and against strong opposition from
American business, the corporate liberals attribute Roosevelt's
reforms to the direct intervention and support of a group of
farsighted capitalists who were able to see that such reforms were
necessary to *save* capitalism. These enlightened or 'smart'
capitalists (mostly from the increasingly dominant monopoly sector
of the economy) engaged in a preemptive strike against more
fundamental social, political and economic reforms by moving

quickly to introduce a series of economic and social policies necesary to stabilize capitalism.

The corporate liberal thesis may be seen as a particular version of what has come to be called the instrumentalist variant of a marxist theory of the state (see Gold, Lo and Wright, 1975). This view finds its roots in a variety of important statements by Marx in which the state is characterized as the executive committee of the ruling class The state does what it does (including the making of social policy) because it is directed to do so by representatives of the ruling class. In this sense the state is an *instrument* in the hands of capital.

An alternative view, which also relies to a large extent on reanalysis of the New Deal as well as of the 'welfare explosion' of the 1960s in the United States is to be found in Piven and Cloward's *Regulating the Poor*. At first glance, the Piven-Cloward thesis appears to resemble the 'class struggle' perspective discussed above. Welfare expansion in this perspective is not the result of intervention by 'smart capitalists' but rather a response to outbreaks of mass turmoil (strikes, riots, demonstrations) which occur in the face of economic downturns and mass unemployment. When stability returns, welfare is retracted again to encourage and ensure the return of the masses to the labor market.

While on the face of it these two theories appear remarkably different, in other respects they are remarkably similar. First of all, like the democratic and class struggle theories discussed above, both emphasize the importance of human agency in explaining state outputs and welfare reforms in particular. For the corporate liberals the important agent is the group of enlightened capitalists who plan and provide the critical support for such reforms; for the 'mass turmoil' thesis it is the actions of the popular masses which account for the level of welfare state outputs. On the other hand, both perspectives are essentially equilibrium views of social change; for both, the end result of expanded welfarism is the restabilization and reproduction of the existing (capitalist) social order. The capitalist class is ultimately the winner in all social confrontations and experiences no contradictions or long term losses. The working classes or the masses are little more than the passive recipients of capitalist rule and in this respect both theories more closely resemble the static power elite models of Pareto, Mosca and Michels than the dialectical models of class struggle found in traditional marxism. The 'smart capitalists' thesis has been severely criticized in recent debates (e.g. Skocpol, 1979), as have all

conspiratorial types of theorizing, but remains a useful corrective
to some of the more extreme versions of the class struggle theories
by reminding us that big business has not always been the unalloyed
opponent of welfare state reforms and frequently took positive
action to advance such reforms. This is clearly illustrated by
William Graebner's (1980) analysis of retirement and social
security policy in the United States, a work which must surely stand
as a benchmark in future studies of the 'politics of aging'.

There is a nascent body of as yet unpublished empirical studies
which indicates that the Piven and Cloward 'mass turmoil' thesis
may be of some value in accounting for welfare state expenditures
in the United States (Griffin et al., 1980) and cross-nationally
(Swank, 1981), but its utility for explaining the expansion of social
policy for the elderly is limited (for an assessment of the
applicability of Piven and Cloward's thesis to American Social
Security, see Achenbaum, 1980). Unlike welfare expenditures for
the poor and unemployed, old age security has not tended to
expand and contract in relation to growth and decline in social
unrest or mass turmoil. Rather they have consistently grown in all
advanced capitalist countries and, once granted, benefits for the
elderly are withdrawn only with great difficulty. Moreover,
throughout the postwar years, the most generous social polices for
the elderly have been established in countries with the least amount
of social unrest (Sweden, Holland) while in countries with more
social unrest (the United States, France, Italy) social benefits for
the elderly have developed less quickly.

The Bureaucratic Elite:
Civil Servants and Public Policy

A further theoretical strand which can be found throughout the
public policy literature is one which finds its intellectual roots in
Weber, and emphasizes the predominant role of modern state
bureaucracies in shaping the evolution of modern societies.
Scholars who have engaged in extremely detailed historical case
studies of particular social policies for the elderly (Heclo, 1974,
Derthick, 1979) seem particularly prone to adopt such a view. Civil
servants in various policy-making branches of government become
advocates for the expansion of their particular program areas since
such expansion enhances their own power and prestige.
Simultaneously, bureaucratic capacities impose restraints on the

type of policies which can be introduced at any particular point in time. Thus, the reason Britain did not follow Germany in the adoption of a wage-related pension system in its initial legislation of 1909 and adopted a flat-benefit system instead was due to the relative under-development of the British state bureaucracy and the administrative difficulty of managing a wage-related program (Heclo, 1974). Wilensky (1975) also views the tendency towards 'bureaucratic incrementalism' — the tendency of government programs to expand but not contract — as a key factor in explaining cross-national differences in welfare state effort. Those countries which began their programs sooner have simply been subject to this 'bureaucratic imperative' for a longer period of time. A recent attempt to explain the growth of welfare expenditures in Britain, Germany, France and Italy (Hage and Hanneman, 1980) could be construed as providing some support for this organizational perspective. However, while public officials are frequently key actors in the generation of new policies and in particular in the choices made among competing policy strategies, they too work within constraints which are not of their making or subject to their control (Block, 1977; Lindblom, 1977). They too must be sensitive to the imperatives of capital accumulation since ultimately the revenues upon which their programs depend (taxes) reflect the success of the economy as a whole. And indeed, in many instances it is not the welfare branches of the state bureaucracy which are finally responsible for the formation of social policies for the elderly (that is those officials most directly involved in serving the elderly) but rather those branches of government responsible for managing the economy as a whole. The expansion of pension benefits for the elderly and the manner in which they have been distributed have more often been determined by macroeconomic policies such as Keynesian demand management or neocorporatist solutions to wage pressure than by the rational calculation of the requirements of the elderly or the pressures from the old-age lobby inside the state bureaucracy (see Myles, 1980).

Competing Theories or
Multiple Levels of Analysis

This is not the place to provide a detailed critical synthesis of the various theoretical perspectives outlined above. To do so would require an assessment of the entire corpus of social and political theory which has addressed these topics throughout the postwar period. Rather my intent is to indicate to the interested reader the various strands in political and social theory which bear directly on our understanding of the growth and variation in social policy for the aged. But one may point to at least two different strategies in dealing with the differences between these alternative perspectives.

A common strategy is to view them as competing theories of social reality and to set about disproving one or the other or showing the superiority of one over the other (e.g. which one can 'explain the most variance'). But a second strategy is to recognize the different *levels* of social reality at which each is directed. There is no doubt, for example, that the *interest groups* so dear to pluralist theory are active in the policy-making process and at various times and places have to be appeased to a greater or lesser degree. But interest groups must operate within a policy-making structure (a state system, including the bureaucracy) that is not of their own making which imposes limits on the alternatives open to them and the strategies which will be effective. Moreover, their own fate as a collective actor in the system is frequently dependent upon those very agencies they are struggling to influence — they may be banned, subjected to repression of various sorts or alternatively provided with state subsidies to pursue their interest group activities. The *officials* who actually prepare the legislation are in a key position to affect the direction and timing of policy development but they too must work within the constraints and limits of the larger political economy. The limits imposed by the larger *political economy* of a society are the ultimate constraints which shape the degrees of freedom within which social actors pursue their objectives but these limits can, themselves, be pushed back and even transformed by human intervention, otherwise there would be no history. But the modern state does have a history and social policies for the aged are no exception. The task for a political sociology of aging and aging policy is to document and explain this history.

RESOURCES FOR COMPARATIVE
POLICY ANALYSIS

While there is no shortage of elegant theories which can be readily applied to the study of social policies for the aged, there is a dearth of adequate sources of data on cross-national differences in such policies which would make such analyses feasible. As indicated at the beginning of the paper, I shall not attempt to deal with data sources on social services for the elderly (but see Teicher, Thursz and Vigilante, 1979 on this) but will focus primarily on old age pensions and other income maintenance programs for the aged.

What Should be Included?

In order to make any sort of reasonable comparisons among national systems for the elderly it is necessary to first decide upon what it is we wish to compare. Do we want to make comparisons among national pension systems or national income maintenance systems? The two are far from being identical since in some countries only part of the income flows directed toward the elderly are actually distributed through the pension per se whereas in other countries virtually all of the income directed toward the elderly comes in this form. A major portion of Danish expenditures on the elderly, for example, is in the form of housing subsidies, the expenditures for which do not show up in comparative tables on social security benefits for the elderly.

A second way in which some countries choose to allocate income to the elderly is through tax expenditures. Rather than raising benefit levels for the elderly by increasing the size of the monthly social security check, the elderly are simply allowed to retain a higher percentage of that check as a result of taxing these benefits at a lower rate than other income or by taxing the total income of the elderly at a lower rate than that for the younger population. For example, according to a study conducted by the Union of Swiss Banks (1977) income replacement ratios *before taxes* for an average retired wage-earner with a dependent spouse were virtually identical in Canada and the Netherlands — 53.1 percent in Canada and 55.5 percent in the Netherlands, in 1975. After taxes, however, the real income replacement ratio in the Netherlands was 80.4 percent while in Canada it was only 62.1 percent.

In comparing national pension systems should we compare the pension system as a whole — both public and private pensions — or simply compare the public systems? Most comparative studies of public policy direct their attention to public sector pensions since it is public policy — what is done by the state — which is under consideration. But what is public and what is private is not always easy to determine. Should the pensions for state employees be included in the public sector? Expenditures data routinely published by the International Labor Organization (ILO) include pensions for state employees while the Organization for Economic Cooperation and Development (OECD) accounts (OECD, 1976) do not. It is argued that such pensions are similar to occupational pensions in the private sector and hence should be excluded when the object is to determine how well the state provides for the elderly population as a whole. Cross-national variation in expenditures which include pensions for state employees may simply be measuring differences in the relative economic well-being of retired government workers.

Even more troublesome, especially from a North American point of view where the public-private distinction is sharper than in Europe, is the existence of mandated pensions in several West European countries. Rather than increase state pensions, these countries have addressed the problem of providing old age security by means of laws which force employers to participate in pension schemes that are not officially state administered and do not appear in the accounts of the government but which nonetheless should be considered policy outputs or an 'effect' of the political system on the economic well-being of the elderly. In Japan and the United Kingdom, employers may opt out of the public system if they provide a pension equivalent to that provided by the public system (see Torrey and Thompson, 1980, p. 26). But even in the United States and Canada, 'private' occupational plans receive large subsidies from the state in the form of tax exemptions.

Such complexities in national pension systems can and do result in a wide array of estimates for the same countries when different criteria are used. There is no easy way to resolve these discrepancies, but it is important to be aware of such differences when considering any single set of comparisons on any given dimension of the various national systems.

Types of Data Sources for Comparative Policy Analysis

There are essentially three types of data which can or have been used in comparative studies of income maintenance for the elderly — income surveys, public expenditure data and policy data. Each of these types of data has its own strengths and weaknesses with respect to their quality and availability on the one hand and their utility for addressing specific substantive issues on the other.

The most important but least used source of data for comparative purposes are data derived from national income surveys. Such surveys typically provide extremely detailed information on income by source, including income from government programs, which can then be analyzed to determine how the elderly in general and specific segments of the elderly population in particular (e.g. widows) benefit from government policy. In the long run, these are probably the only data which can satisfactorily answer the typical questions which are of interest to most gerontologists in comparing the 'generosity' or effectiveness of income maintenance programs for the elderly in the advanced industrial nations, since it is only from such data that we can utlimately determine not only *how much* is spent on the elderly but also how that which is spent is *distributed* within the elderly population. Moreover, it is only from such data that we will ultimately capture state expenditures on the elderly which derive from programs not explicitly directed at the elderly (e.g. public assistance programs and other forms of state subsidies which are not directed at the elderly per se). To date there has been only one cross-national study of the incomes of the aged based on survey data (Wedderburn, 1968). This was done for three countries (the United States, the United Kingdom and Denmark). During the 1970s a growing number of countries began to launch national surveys designed to provide detailed information on the distribution of income but these remain a major untapped source for cross-national empirical analysis. In some instances, differences in survey methodologies render these national studies of little use for comparative analysis but the Nordic countries, the United Kingdom, the United States, Germany and Canada all now have income surveys of reasonably quality which can be exploited for this purpose.

A second and more commonly used type of data on income maintenance programs for the elderly is public expenditure data; that is, state budgets which report expenditures on the elderly under its various programs. Data of this type are routinely gathered and reported by a variety of international agencies such as the ILO, the OECD and the European Economic Community (EEC). Such sources provide data on total expenditures but not on how these expenditures are distributed. Thus per capita expenditures may be higher in one country than in another but disproportionately allocated towards those with already high incomes, about which such data are silent. Data of this type suffer from additional defects which limit their use for comparative purposes. First there is no country which has an accounting system so well developed that it can in fact report all public consumption expenditures received by the elderly. Further, politicians and bureaucrats have various motives which lead them to conceal or reveal the true level of such expenditures. In some forums they may wish to demonstrate their zeal in providing for the elderly while at other times they may seek to conceal the true level of state expenditures. Moreover, comparative data are usually collected by international agencies by means of questionnaires sent out to be filled in by officials of the various national governments. There is an attempt to standardize categories for reporting purposes but it is not always apparent that the same words even when well understood have the same meaning across countries. Finally, these categories rarely if ever conform exactly to those which the researcher may wish to employ. A complete accounting of the citizen's wage provided to the elderly would ideally include all benefits provided in kind (housing, medical care, home services) as well as those provided in cash (pensions) and also capture all provisions made for the elderly which come out of other programs not designed specifically for them (public assistance, tax expenditures). Comparable data of this level and quality are simply unavailable and any attempt at comparison must be prepared to live with considerable measurement error.

The third type of data and perhaps the most commonly used are what I shall call 'policy' data. These are measures not of what the system does but of what it is *supposed* to do. Thus, we know from existing legislation the minimum benefit which a retired worker *should* receive, the level of income replacement which the average worker can expect and so forth. As various studies have shown, the gap between what the system is supposed to do in principle and what it does in practice may be considerable (e.g. Fox, 1979 on replacement ratios). In large measure this is because in the real world the average worker seldom lives up to the hypothetical work and earnings history expected of him, individuals do not collect all the benefits to which they are technically entitled and so forth. Despite its weaknesses this type of data also has its advantages. Many of the differences observed with even the most accurate income survey or public expenditure data will reflect differences which from the point of view of the researcher are little more than historical and demographic accidents. Thus, two countries with identical policies and with equally effective means of administering such policies will produce very different total levels of expenditure as a result of different age and sex structures, patterns of migration, occupationally-specific mortality rates and the like. Policy-based measures permit the investigator to assess what would happen to identical individuals as a result of two different sets of policies. An elegant example is the study of Schulz et al. (1974), in which estimates are made of what the income profile of the American elderly would be like had the United States introduced social security legislation like that of Germany or Sweden.

Policy data have also been fruitfully exploited to develop indices of pension quality. Various attributes of the pension system — degree of coverage, level of indexing, income replacement ratios for different levels of preretirement income, etc. — are combined in a weighted index based on the specific theoretical concerns of the investigator. The first systematic attempt to develop an index of pension quality in this way is that of the demographer, Lincoln Day (1978). As a demographer, his interest was in developing an index of the extent to which national pension systems differed in the degree to which they assure individuals of economic security in their old age since it is hypothesized that fertility is related to the extent to which there is a perceived need for additional children to provide such security. Using information published by the United States Department of Health, Education and Welfare in *Social Security Programs Throughout the World* he devised a weighted index of pension quality based on eight separate indicators. A similar strategy has recently been followed by Maguire (1981) in a comparative study of ten West European nations.

For purposes of comparative analysis, however, all of these data sources suffer from major shortcomings, the most important reason for which is the fact that they were not originally gathered or published with the intent of addressing the questions which researchers in the field of aging policy had posed. But in the decades which lie ahead, the growing interest in the economic consequences of aging population are likely to make national data collection agencies increasingly responsive to requests to gather information in a form which will be appropriate for understanding social policies for the elderly. It remains for the community of researchers to pose their questions and then to make them known.

NOTE

1. Compare this with the marxist discussion of the accumulation and legitimization functions of the state discussed below.

REFERENCES

Aaron, Henry (1967), 'Social Security: International Comparisons', pp. 13-48 in Otto Eckstein (ed.), *Studies in Income Maintenance* (Washington DC, Brookings).

Achenbaum, Andrew (1980), 'Did Social Security Attempt to Regulate the Poor?', *Research on Aging,* Vol. 2 (December), pp. 470-488.

Block, Fred (1977), 'The Ruling Class Does not Rule: Notes on the Marxist Theory of the State', *Socialist Revolution,* Vol. 33 (May-June), pp. 6-27.

Bollen, Kenneth A. (1980), 'Issues in the Comparative Measurement of Political Democracy', *American Sociological Review,* Vol. 80 (June), pp. 370-390.

Bowles, Samuel and Herbert Gintis (forthcoming), 'The Crisis of Liberal Democratic Capitalism', *New Left Review.*

Bryden, Kenneth (1974) *Old Age Pensions and Policy-Making in Canada* (Montreal, McGill-Queen's University Press).

Cameron, David (1978), 'The expansion of the Public Economy: A Comparative Analysis', *American Political Science Review,* Vol. 72 (December), pp. 1243-1261.

Cutright, Phillip (1965), 'Political Structure, Economic Development and National Social Security Programs', *American Journal of Sociology,* Vol. 70, pp. 537-550.

Cutright, Phillip (1967a), 'Inequality: A Cross-National Analysis', *American Sociological Review,* Vol. 46, pp. 180-190.

Cutright, Phillip (1967b), 'Income Redistribution: A Cross-National Analysis', *Social Forces,* Vol. 46, pp. 180-190.

Day, Lincoln (1978), 'Government Pensions for the Aged in 19 Industrialized Countries', pp. 217-234 in R. Tomasson (ed.), *Comparative Studies in Sociology* (Greenwich, Conn., JAI Press).

Derthick, Martha (1979), *Policy Making for Social Security* (Washington DC, Brookings Institution).

Domhoff, G. W. (1970), *The Higher Circles* (New York, Vintage).

Esping-Anderson (1976), Gosta, Roger Friedland and Erik Wright 'Modes of Class Struggle and the Capitalist State', *Kapitalistate,* Vol. 4-5, pp. 186-218.

Estes, Carroll L. (1979), *The Aging Enterprise* (San Francisco, Jossey Bass).

Fox, Alan (1979), 'Earnings Replacement Rates of Retired Couples: Findings from the Retirement History Study', *Social Security Bulletin,* Vol. 42 (January) pp. 17-39.

Giddens, Anthony (1976), 'Classical Social Theory and the Origins of Modern Social Theory', *American Journal of Sociology,* Vol. 81 (January), pp. 703-729.

Gold, David, Clarence Lo and Erik Wright (1975), 'Recent Developments in Marxist Theories of the Capitalist State', *Monthly Review* (October-November), pp. 29-51.

Gough, Ian (1975), 'State Expenditures in Advanced Capitalism', *New Left Review,* No. 92, pp. 53-92.

Gough, Ian (1979), *The Political Economy of the Welfare State* (London, Macmillan Press).

Graebner, William (1980), *A History of Retirement* (New Haven, Yale University Press).

Griffin, Larry, Joel Devine and Michael Wallace (1980), 'Accumulation, Legitimation, and Politics: Neo-marxist Explanations of the Growth of Welfare Expenditures in the United States since the Second World War', mimeo, Indiana University.

Guillemard, Anne-Marie (1980), *La Vieillesse et l'Etat* (Paris, Presses Universitaires).

Hage, Jerald and Robert Hanneman (1980), 'The Growth of the Welfare State in Britain, France, Germany and Italy: A Comparison of Three Paradigms', pp. 45-70 in R. Tomasson (ed.), *Comparative Social Research* (Greenwich, Conn., JAI Press).

Heclo, Hugh (1974), *Modern Social Politics in Britain and Sweden. From Relief to Income Maintenance* (New Haven, Yale University Press).

Hewitt, Christopher (1977), 'The effect of Political Democracy and Social Democracy on Equality in Industrial Societies: A Cross-National Comparison', *American Sociological Review,* Vol. 39, pp. 29-45.

Jackman, Robert (1974), 'Political Democracy and Social Equality: A Comparative Analysis', *American Sociological Review,* 42 (June), pp. 450-464.

Jackman, Robert (1975), *'Politics and Social Equality': A Comparative Analysis* (New York, Wiley).

Kerr, Clark, J.T. Dunlop, Frederick Harbison and Charles Myers (1964), *Industrialism and Industrial Man* (New York, Oxford University Press).

Lenski, Gerhard (1966), *Power and Privilege* (Toronto, McGraw-Hill).

Lindblom, Charles (1977), *Politics and Markets* (New York, Basic Books).

Lipset, Seymour Martin, *Political Man* (Garden City, NY, Doubleday).

Maguire, Maria (1981), 'Pensions Policy: An Overview of Patterns of Development and the Impact of Party'. Paper presented at the meetings of European Consortium for Political Research, Lancaster, Great Britain, April.

Martin, Andrew (1973), *The Politics of Economic Policy in the United States: A Tentative View from a Comparative Perspective* (Beverly Hills, Sage Publications).

Mishra, Ramesh (1977), *Society and Social Policy* (London, Macmillan).

Myles, John F. (1980), 'The Aged, the State and the Structure of Inequality', pp. 317-342 in J. Harp and J. Hofley (eds.), *Structured Social Inequality* (Toronto, Prentice Hall).

O'Connor, James (1973), *The Fiscal Crisis of the State* (New York, St. Martin's Press).

OECD (1976), *Public Expenditure on Income Maintenance Programs* (Paris, OECD).

Offe, Claus (1972), 'Advanced Capitalism and the Welfare State', *Politics and Society,* Vol. 2, pp. 479-488.

Panitch, Leo (1981), 'Trade Unions and the Capitalist State', *New Left Review,* No. 125 (January/February), pp. 21-43.

Piven, F.F. and R.A. Cloward (1971), *Regulating the Poor: The Functions of Public Welfare* (New York, Vintage Books).

Pryor, Frederic L. (1968), *Public Expenditures in Communist and Capitalist Nations* (Homewood, Ill., Irwin).

Przeworski, Adam (1980), 'Material Bases of Consent: Economics and Politics in a Hegemonic System', pp. 21-66 in Maurice Zeitlin (ed.), *Political Power and Social Theory,* Vol. 1 (Greenwich, Conn., JAI Press).

Schulz, James, Guy Carrin, Hans Krupp, Manfred Peschke, Elliot Sclar and J. Van Steenberge (1974), *Providing Adequate Retirement Income — Pension Reform in the United States and Abroad* (Hanover, NH, Brandeis University Press).

Shalev, Michael (1980), 'Socialism and the Welfare State in Democratic Politics: The Limits and Possibilities of a Class Conflict Interpretation'. Paper presented at the Sapir Conference on Social Policy Evaluation, Tel Aviv, December.

Skocpol, Theda (1979), 'Political Response to Capitalist Crises: Neo-marxist Theories of the State and the Case of the New Deal'. Working Paper Series No. 8, Department of Sociology, University of Toronto.

Teicher, Morton, D. Thursz and J. Vigilante (1979), *Reaching the Aged. Social Services in Forty-Four Countries* (Beverly Hills, Sage Publications).

Torrey, Barbara and Carole Thompson (1980), *An International Comparison of Pension Systems* (Washington, DC, President's Commission on Pension Policy).

Union of Swiss Banks (1977), *Social Security in 10 Industrial Nations* (Zurich, Union Bank of Switzerland).

Wedderburn, Dorothy (1968), 'The Financial Resources of Old People', pp. 347-423 in E. Shanas et al. (eds.), *Old People in Three Industrial Societies* (New York, Atherton).

Wilensky, Harold (1975), *The Welfare State and Equality* (Berkeley, University of California Press).

2

ABEYANCE PROCESSES, SOCIAL POLICY AND AGING

Ephraim H. Mizruchi
Syracuse University

Little attention has been directed, in the gerontological and sociological literature, to the processes by which persons in certain social categories are manipulated in and out of occupational and other positions. This is especially true with respect to age categories. The point of these brief remarks is to conceptualize and sensitize the student of age-related processes to what I call abeyance (Mizruchi, 1982, 1983).[1]

Abeyance is a holding process. When a society is faced with too few or too many people in relation to the availability of certain kinds of status vacancies, i.e. unoccupied positions, certain mechanisms come into play which contribute to the temporal solution of the problem. While efforts to move personnel into and out of contexts which enhance either absorption or expulsion of a given population may be conscious and intentional the process is, for the most part, unintentional and occurs at a less than conscious level. In sociological terms it is latent rather than manifest.

In order to articulate my conceptualization I will focus, briefly, on three aspects of abeyance, *time, normative enhancements* and *statutory devices* used in the United States.

TIME AND ABEYANCE

Abeyance is a time suspending process. At the organizational level large masses of people may be 'warehoused', to use a similar term, until status vacancies become available in other organizations. At the personal level impulses, motives and desires are postponed until both opportunity and normative justification allow goals to be attained. This process, viewed as the time-rate of absorption at the organizational level and the time-rate of personal attainment of goals at the individual level is essential to the effective functioning of society. Because it is essential, abeyance is typically associated with institutionalized patterns. How does the process work and what are some of the typical patterns associated with it?

Socialization and Patterning

In order for abeyance processes to work it is necessary first to socialize persons in ways which enhance these processes and to reinforce the socialization process with group and organizational activities. The most general and useful descriptive concept with respect to socialization for abeyance is the Deferred Gratification Pattern (DGP), originally formulated by Schneider and Lysgaard (1953). While the DGP was most closely associated, in the sociological literature, with variations by social class, there is ample observation of ethnic patterns which suggests that other variables are similarly associated. Not only do people in the middle classes in the United States tend to control their impulses to a greater extent than those in the working and lower classes with respect to sex, spending, and aggression but, according to my hypotheses, they are better at waiting in all contexts and at anticipating future conditioning (Schwartz, 1975). With the help of a whole array of values and norms like, 'keep at it, success is just around the corner', Americans are taught to hold *themselves* in abeyance. When asynchronization in the system occurs, these patterns play a role in the capacity of persons to cope with the holding process. Religious explanations, for example, including notions about life after death, tend to reinforce patterns of deferring gratification among some segments of the population of elderly in Judeo-Christian societies. Sometimes, under extreme conditions, the holding pattern fails or another is too late in emerging and a higher probability of rebellious collective action results. At still other times, as with the Calvinist experience, a rigorous system emerges which controls time and abeyance in an extremely effective manner. All of these examples attest to our assumption that societies do not allow for the random expression of impulse and that the patterns which exert control enhance the abeyance process.

However, since socialization alone is incapable of controlling behavior it is necessary to explore the organizational patterns which reinforce the DGP. Glaser and Straus' concept of transitional status suggests statuses and roles which reinforce holding patterns. Transitional status denotes

> ...time in terms of the social structure. It is a social system's tactic for keeping a person in passage between two statuses for a period of time. He is put in a transitional status, or sequence of time that determines the period of time that he will be in a status passage. Thus the transitional status of the initiate will, in a particular case, carry with it the given amount of time it will take to make a non-member a member — a civilian is made a soldier by spending a given number of weeks as a basic trainee; an adolescent spends a number of years 'in training' to be an adult (1967, p. 85).

It is safe to hold that all interaction involves impulse control, but engagement in organizational activities which include complementarity and reciprocity, coordination and integration, yields greater increments of reinforcement than do informal social relations. The articulation of normative and cognitive expectations, the potentially greater symbolic impact of more impersonal social interaction as size and complexity of organization or group increases tend to enhance awareness of one's need to be patient, that in time one will be able to pursue desirable goals. For these patterns to effectively reinforce there must be supports in the larger social structure. In a relatively complex society there may be pressures exerted which inhibit the process.

Timing, Spacing and Status Vacancies

It is important to keep in mind that a substantial portion of societal members consciously and intentionally behave in ways which enhance the cushioning of asynchronization between status vacancies and personnel. A substantial body of literature based on demographic and survey research has been accumulating for at least twenty years on timing of pregnancy and child spacing.[2] This should come as no surprise to the social scientist since one of the most conspicuous variable social patterns in American society is the delay of marriage by relatively higher class persons. But the motivation, and thus the constancy and predictability of the pattern, is probably explained not only by the structuring of life styles — including greater concern and opportunity for extended educational and career involvement — but also by personal motives. Relative affluence allows for greater opportunity to 'sow one's wild oats', to take time to decide what to do with one's life. It is sufficient to remind ourselves, in this context, that normative, cognitive and idiosyncratic factors must be explored in order to explain the connections between personal behavior, group expectations and societal synchronization and asynchronization.

We are not suggesting, in this context, that there is a one-to-one correlation between apparent societal needs and the behavior of persons and groups. The structuring of behavior in a society may create strains in the system which contribute to severe imbalances between personnel and status vacancies. The classic study is of Irish countrymen, as Arensberg and Kimball (1937) called them, in which it was observed that the unwillingness of the aging father to relinquish control and ownership of his farm to his son until quite late in life led to relatively late marriages between persons whose fertility levels were in decline. The result was a low reproduction rate which, from some points of view, limited personnel for status vacancies in the agricultural sphere. It is well to note that from still another value perspective, that of stability, there were no strains. One more example, related to cognitive motivation, suggests how asynchronization may emerge out of reproductive patterns. During the early part of the 19th century in England, when the factory system was expanding, it was economically feasible to have many children. The more children working, the greater the income for the family as a whole. As factory methods changed and fewer workers, i.e. children, were employable a surplus population emerged. Without work and without school, children roamed the streets panhandling and committing diverse crimes. Engels (1845), in his study of the British working class, provides a description of the scene much like one would derive from a reading of Dickens. This particular imbalance was directly responsible, as Musgrove (1964) shows, for the rise of mandatory education and child labor laws.

The most conspicuous population being held in abeyance in the United States is the elderly. The descriptions of unattached youth roaming the streets in London during the early part of the 19th century call to mind the many elderly who can be found wandering aimlessly through the downtown areas of America's cities. They too are without work and without school.

NORMATIVE ENHANCEMENTS
AND STATUTORY DEVICES

To hold that the elderly are the most conspicuous of the surplus populations of contemporary America is not to explain how they come to be superfluous. What is clear is that at least one source of this large category of persons is the increased longevity which we in the Western societies enjoy as a result of improved living standards. But biological factors aside there are good sociological and economic explanations for too many unintegrated persons in American society.

If we view the social structure of any society as dynamic, as possessing the potential for expansion, contraction and change as societal needs are altered, alternative and additional explanations emerge. Ordinarily and historically, as population pressures have increased so have the number and types of economic and social activities to absorb and control these populations. The monasteries, medieval urban communes, the public schools and the diverse Works Progress Administration (WPA) projects performed these functions. But since the Middle Ages there has been increasing concern with the occupational structure as the main absorber of personnel. This is related, I suggest, to the increasing domination of the societal structure and values by the economic institution.

The conception of the capacities of the occupational structure which seems to have emerged is that there is a finite number of positions which can be filled at any one point in time. Furthermore, this finite number is to be made available to selected segments of the population, categorized by age, gender and race, to name but a few of the factors determining eligibility. While this pattern has been showing signs of weakening other signs suggest that discrimination along these lines will continue for some time.

In order to enhance the process by which a presumably limited number of jobs is distributed to those selected from a *relatively* unlimited population society uses some subtle and sometimes not so subtle devices. Two normative devices which *are* subtle are the lay and professional conceptions of *adolescence,* on the one hand, and *senility,* on the other. One concept justifies holding the youthful population out of the labor market, the other legitimates expulsion of the mature from the labor market.

Adolescence, a time of postponed maturity among other characteristics, was invented in the latter part of the 18th century. And it is probably no accident that the emergence of the idea and its proliferation throughout Western societies came at a time when there were more children than there had been earlier. Child mortality rates had declined and the numbers of young people who were physically capable of assuming employment increased accordingly. By the latter part of the 18th century the demand both for factory laborers and what we now call white collar workers increased. The advantages of having more children, suggested earlier, coupled with the lower mortality rates encouraged the growth of population.

But the devices for injecting or holding back personnel from the occupational market, particularly the apprenticeship system, were now incapable of controlling the process. Men could no longer be detained by those who wanted to restrain their m̐ovement. Statutes to encourage mobility to places where labor was needed now had to attack the matter in oblique and surreptitious ways. The later Enclosure Acts forced people from the land and into the cities by contracting opportunities in one sphere while advertising the availability of others in another setting. The era of Bridewells and anti-vagrancy statutes was coming to an end.

The idea of adolescence was timely. Here was an abeyance device which could be used to control the flow of personnel into the market. With apprenticeship on the decline and no other alternative holding system in sight creating a new conception of the person provided the start of a more subtle device for abeyance and social control. And this idea, probably more than any other, provided legitimation for the emergence of the new system to control, withhold and infuse society with personnel as status vacancies expanded and contracted. Compulsory education, justified in part by the idea that children were not sufficiently responsible to assume full-time employment, is a device which until now has effectively limited the number of persons eligible to enter the labor market.

While the concept of senility has not yet received the scholarly attention it deserves our imagination and experience both tell us that characterizing the elderly and not-so-elderly as senile is an effective device for forcing people out of the labor market.

In both cases, it is interesting to note, adolescents and the presumably senile aged are characterized as incapable of caring for themselves or performing ordinary occupational roles. In the case of both there is subtle and explicit suggestion that these times — before entering the labor market and after retirement — are times when young and old should enjoy themselves, should take advantage of the so-called opportunities which exist *outside* of the constraints of paid employment.

While the school system holds back youth there are other devices which enhance the process of shrinking the age-range of the economically employed. Child labor laws and encouragement to join the armed forces enhance the process. The social security system[3], private pension funds and alternative health-care plans — alternative to those sponsored by employers — also encourage premature withdrawal from the labor market.

Thus both normative changes and statutory inducements enhance the process of limiting, by age, the numbers who are eligible to enter the labor market. Policy makers and researchers need to be more attuned to these devices if we are to expand the opportunities for integrating and sustaining those who are indeed capable of effective contributions to society at large. The abeyance concept sensitizes us to this aspect of societal processes.

NOTES

1. My first explicit usage of the term 'abeyance' appears in 'Bohemianism, Deviant Behavior and Social Structure', a paper read at the Annual Meeting of the Society for the Study of Social Problems, San Francisco, 1969. The idea appears in some of my earlier work. Cf. e.g., *Success and Opportunity: A Study of Anomie* (New York, Free Press, 1964), p. 75.

2. Recent examples of this type of research include: R.M. Stolzenberg and L. Waite, 'Age Fertility Expectations and Plans for Employment', *American Sociological Review,* Vol. 42 (1977), pp. 769-781; H.B. Presser, 'Perfect Fertility Control: Consequences for Women and the Family', pp. 133-144 in C.F. Westoff et al. (eds.), *Toward the End of Growth: Population in America* (Englewood Cliffs, NJ, Prentice-Hall, 1973).

3. I thank Gordon Streib for the Social Security suggestion. Daniel F. Dowd, one of my students, is researching the connection between the notion of senility and similar concepts and unemployment rate fluctuation.

REFERENCES

Arensberg, C. and S.T. Kimball (1937), *The Irish Countryman* (New York, Harcourt, Brace, Jovanovich).

Engels, F. (1845), *The Condition of the Working Class in England,* trans. and ed. by W.O. Henderson and W.H. Chaloner (New York, Macmillan, 1958).

Glaser, B. and A. Straus (1967), *The Discovery of Grounded Theory* (Chicago, Aldine).

Mizruchi, E.H. (1982), 'Abeyance Processes and Time', pp. 112-118 in E.H. Mizruchi, B. Glassner and T. Pastorello (eds.), *Time and Aging: Conceptualization and Application in Sociological and Gerontological Research* (Bayside, NY, General Hall).

Mizruchi, E.H. (1983), *Regulating Society: Marginality and Social Control in Historical Perspective* (New York, Free Press and London, Collier-Macmillan).

Musgrove, F. (1964), *Youth and the Social Order* (Bloomington, Indiana University Press).

Schneider, L. and S. Lysgaard (1953), 'The Deferred Gratification Pattern', *American Sociological Review,* Vol. 18, pp. 142-149.

Schwartz, B. (1975), *Queueing and Waiting: Studies in the Social Organization of Access and Delay* (Chicago, University of Chicago Press).

3

SOCIETAL AGING AND INTERGENERATIONAL SUPPORT SYSTEMS

Eugene A. Friedmann
Donald J. Adamchak
Kansas State University

> . . . instead of the economy being embedded in social relations, social relations are embedded in the economic system. (Karl Polanyi, *Origins of Our Times: The Great Transformation.*)

WELFARE AND THE RISE OF THE MARKET ECONOMY

Polanyi analyzed the emergence of the market economy in Europe in the 16th century, which was to grow to its full stature by the 19th century. In the process it was to break free of and ultimately subjugate the network of social relationships — e.g. family, kin group, tribes, city-state, church, village, or feudal order — which had formerly contained and regulated reciprocity of exchange relations and the redistribution of goods and wealth. A new group identified as the 'poor' first appeared in England in the 16th century who '. . . became conspicuous as individuals unattached to the manor or to any feudal superior, and their gradual transformation into a class of free laborers was the combined result of the fierce persecution of vagrancy and the fostering of domestic industry. . .' (p. 108).

The rise of industrial production demanded a free market for labor no longer bound to their parish by law or protected by the institutional support systems of rural society. The worker now was paid in wages with wage levels set by the 'market', and without protection against the contingencies of unemployment, illness or old age. To be without a source of work income meant poverty. Titmuss in tracing the development of the concept of welfare cites Disraeli's observation that 'poverty was declared a crime by industrialism'. Laws about poverty became associated with laws about crime. Eighteenth and 19th century poor laws which required work as a condition of assistance were a direct reflection of the new market economy. The poor law concept of welfare was to be supplemented and ultimately supplanted by direct assistance programs defined in terms of specific needs and with strict rules of eligibility as stipulated by the state. Titmuss maintains its role '....was to support industrialism and....establish a completely competitive, self-regulating market economy founded on the motive of individual gain. It thus had to create a great many rules of expected behaviour; about work and nonwork, property, savings, family relationships, cohabitation, men-in-the-house and so forth' (p. 189).

Welfare in the pre-industrial setting had been part of the obligation of the social network. No matter how meager, it was essentially without stigma. However, the early income redistribution schemes which emerged to offset the negative effects of industrialization were to create a new status — that of the 'poor'. The new programs drew hard lines between 'poor' and 'non-poor', 'eligible' and 'ineligible', and even 'worthy' and 'unworthy'. Titmuss argues that these systems began to break down in the 20th century because they were inefficient, discriminatory and could not function effectively in a time of rapid social change and crisis (p. 190). They were to be supplemented and then supplanted in the 20th century by redistribution programs that were universal in character, providing services and benefits (e.g. education, medical care, retirement pensions, family allowances) without distinction as to income, race or class. Wilensky and Leboux (1965) have described this as a transition to an 'institutional' approach to welfare in providing the social infrastructure needed by the modern industrial state.

Many observers have related the phenomenon of population aging to the rise of industrialization and the emergence of systems of income transfer which characterized the contemporary welfare state. Wilensky (1975) contends that economic growth and not population aging per se is the independent variable in this historical process, but that the aged are among the first recipients. He further states that social security systems established to meet their needs have expanded rapidly and have become the impetus for providing for a range of needs for the larger population. He also notes the developing revolt against the rising costs of welfare systems, as well as against the costs of newly added concerns of environmental protection which we first began to address on a major scale in the 1970s. Viewing the counter movement from the perspective of California in the early 1970s he identified it as a revolt of the 'middle masses' who felt they were carrying a disproportionate burden for providing for programs which benefited the poor, while the rich escaped through the use of tax shelters; and he predicted that the revolt would develop throughout the United States, and could be detected in other Western industrial societies as well.

Events of the past several years in the United States have seen the controversy intensify. There is now a dialogue on the viability of the concept of the welfare state, the limits of 'income transfer' from one group to another, and the extent of the 'dependency' load which can be placed upon the working age population. This presentation will focus on the dialogue by examining some of the concepts implicit in the rhetoric employed. In particular, it will seek to contrast conclusions that might be drawn when using the definitions of 'dependency ratio' and 'income transfer', as they are derived from the construct of 'market economy', with conclusions that might be drawn when they are defined in the context of social networks.

RETIREMENT AND INTERGENERATIONAL SUPPORT SYSTEMS

The United States has seen in the past few decades a rapid growth in the acceptance of retirement at or before age 65 accompanied by a rapid growth in coverage and benefit levels of Social Security as well as supplementary employment relation pension programs. Retirement was becoming 'institutionalized' as a normative expectation and a right earned after a lifetime of work (Friedmann and Orbach, 1974). Withdrawal from labor force participation by workers 65 and over has been dramatic — declining from 55 percent in 1950 to 20 percent in 1980, with a growing proportion opting for 'early retirement' before reaching the age of maximum social security entitlement at 65 (Friedmann, 1979). By the late 1970s the implications of this historic shift were entering the dialogue on the welfare state with questions being raised as to how large a proportion of nonworkers a working population can be expected to support.

In May 1980 the President's Commission on Pension Policy (appointed by President Carter) released a report titled *Working Paper, Demographic Shifts and Projections, Implications for Pension Systems.* This called attention to the rapid and continuing increase in proportion of population of persons 65 and over: from 4 percent in 1900, to 8 percent in 1950, 11 percent in 1980 to their projection of 23 percent in 2035; and to the increase in 'dependency ratio' of population 65 and over to those in the 18-64 age group from 18 percent in 1980 to 39 percent in 2035 based upon the specific projection assumptions they employed. This immediately sounded a cry of alarm which literally swept the nation. On 18 May 1980 the *New York Times* ran a series of five articles on the consequences of these projected demographic shifts that was reprinted in several regional newspapers and a number of major news and business magazines also ran lead stories on the implications of these shifts. All focused on the increasing 'burden' represented by a decline in proportion of 5.5 persons in the 'productive' age group (i.e. 18-64) in 1980 to each member of the 'dependent' age group (65 and over) to 2.5 persons in 2035.

And they all showed concern over the concluding observations of this 'demographic' working paper which stated:

> Historically, there has been an implicit social contract that working generations help support the retired and disabled either privately or publicly. But the contract may have to be renegotiated if the future size of the retired and disabled more than doubles relative to the size of the working age population (p. 38).

Unfortunately, this document contains fundamental errors of assumption and analysis. But even if it did not, the conclusions calling for a possible renegotiation of the 'social contract' that has emerged as the societal support system for a market economy are startling. These errors represent more than just an aberration of a single report, they are now central to the current dialogue to which social scientists have thus far made only limited, contradictory and often confusing inputs.

'Dependency' as viewed in terms of generational transfers was also to be transformed with the onset of industrialization. In the family and kin centered production units of pre-industrial society both children and the aged contributed in greater or lesser degree to the family enterprize. Only the very young or the invalided old could be regarded as noncontributing 'dependents' in a system in which transfers of goods and services were regulated in the context of social network. Industrial society, in contrast, was to regard 'producers' as 'job-holders' participating in the wage system of the market economy. As the Presidential Committee's *Working Paper* and similar discussions illustrate, those persons who are not wage-earning job holders are arbitrarily defined as 'nonproducers' and 'dependents'. This is done without regard to the contributions they may make to family or community in the form of services or cash payments drawing upon accumulated capital and earned pension rights.

DEPENDENCY RATIOS AND SUPPORT NETWORKS

In the earliest stages of the Industrial Revolution when children entered the labor force as young as six and the old remained for as long as they were physically able, without any financial resources for retirement, there probably was a high degree of congruence between exclusion from labor force participation and 'dependency'. The removal of able bodied potential producers, however, was to begin with the enactment of child labor laws which prohibited employment of children under the age of nine in England in 1833, with the concept spreading to other Western European nations in the 19th century, and the United States in the early part of the 20th century. The age of entry was increasing steadily in the 20th century to fourteen, sixteen and now eighteen in some industrial countries as a consequence of child employment legislation, compulsory education requirements and the need for more extended periods of training prior to labor force entry; while in the same period the age of labor force withdrawal has steadily been lowered through the progressive development of retirement as previously noted. Historical comparisons and future projections of the size and composition of generational 'dependency' (or conversely for contributions made) by persons outside of the 'working age' population group.

Dependency ratios, as they are variously employed, express numerical relationships between the 'productive' and 'non-productive' or 'dependent' components of a population. Shryock and Siegel (1973, p. 235) have noted that there is no standard definition of 'the economic dependency ratio'. Generally, the comparison is between the combined numbers of 'dependent young' and 'dependent old' and those in the 'working age' segment of the population. The 'productive age' component may be based broadly upon a categorical assumption as to the productive status of specific age groups (e.g. numbers of persons aged 18-64 compared to those under 18 and 65 and over) or they may focus more specifically upon the labor force component and define a dependency ratio as a relationship between persons participating in the labor force and those who are not. And, finally, we can note the use of what might be best termed a *segmental dependency ratio* which may deal with one of the 'dependent' components (e.g. the young or the old), relating its numbers to the total 'working' or 'productive age' population. This latter is a restricted comparison and care should be taken that it is not represented as a statement of an overall societal or labor force dependency ratio.

We would offer two major categorizations of dependency ratios based upon differing sets of assumptions:

1. *Societal dependency ratio.* This is sometimes termed a 'crude' ratio which is stated in terms of age-group relationships describing a generational interchange between those in the 'productive' age groups and the young and the old who are dependent upon them. Broadly conceptualized it can be regarded as a generational transfer of goods and services whether produced in the market economy or produced within the family or other nonmarket societal transfer networks.

2. *Labor force dependency ratio.* This would refer to a transfer of goods and services produced in the market economy by labor force participants.

Forecasting involves assumptions as to both growth and composition of the 'productive' and 'labor force' components. We will refer to forecasting models that assume no change in composition over time as *static* and those that assume compositional changes as *dynamic*, and examine selected forecasts as to future dependency ratios making use of the concepts and definitions we have introduced.

Segmental Dependency Ratio —
Changing Ratio of Retired to
Working Age Population

The report of the President's Commission on Pension Policy, discussed above, is an example of the use of a segmental dependency ratio. It projects changes in the population 65 and over and compares them both to population in the 18-64 age group and to the labor force through the year 2035. It correctly notes that the proportion of persons in the retired aged group would double in this period in relation to the numbers of 18-64 year olds. It concludes that existing mechanisms for transferring income from wage earners to Social Security retirees would be placed under severe strain by this demographic shift. The conclusion draws upon a segmental dependency analysis and is appropriate for examining a Social Security benefit program for retirees based upon a specific funding mechanism which was established under a set of demographic assumptions which are no longer valid. However, in suggesting that the social contract may need to be 'renegotiated' it implies that the doubling of the proportion of aged will exceed society's (or the economy's) capacity to support its dependent population. Yet no data are given on changes in total dependency ratio, including both young and old in this period of time. It is unfortunate that the report chose to dramatize this latter unsupported inference in its conclusions and that this undocumented assertion has become the focus of a national debate.

Clark and Spengler in their recent book (1980) offer a similar set of inferences which states:

> The capacity of a population to support its retired population depends upon its age structure and the ratio of persons eligible for benefits (approximated by those aged 65 and over) to those of working age (say 18-64) and in the labor force (p. 155).

They conclude that the 'transfer burden' of supporting these retirees can be met when their proportion increases either by '....greatly diminishing pensions....or by deferring retirement until a later age' (p. 155).

Both of these analyses treat the aged/working group segmental ratio as a closed system and infer that changes in the ratio represent changes in the ability of the society to carry its dependency load. This places intergenerational support relationships solely within the context of the market economy. By arbitrarily excluding one dependent group (those under 18) from their calculations they present their case *reductio ad absurdum*.

Policy matters of this magnitude require more adequate data for their consideration and require at the minimum:

(a) data on changes in the total as well as segmental dependency ratios in the period discussed;

(b) an approximation of the relative support or transfer costs of each dependent segment (i.e. young and old);

(c) an evaluation of the inputs which a nominal 'dependent' retiree makes to the economic and social system.

Labor Force Dependency Ratio

Dependency ratios expressed in terms of ratio of all persons not in the labor force to those in the labor force are not presented in either of the discussions reviewed above. Surprisingly, although a great deal of attention has been given to the segmental ratio of retired to employed, there has been very little analysis of changes in the total labor force dependency ratio which will occur in the United States during its period of accelerating population aging over the next sixty years. Sheppard and Rix (1977) address this question drawing upon the projections of Marc Rosenblum (Sheppard and Rix, p. 20) who projects a decline in the total number of nonworkers per 100 workers from 114 in 1980 to 103 in 2010, but does not project for the period of rapid growth of the retirement age population between 2010 and 2040. He supplements these (p. 21) with some 1972 projections of Dennis Johnson which state the ratio as 112 for 2020 and 115 for 2040. This would give a sixty year labor force dependency ratio shift from 114 in 1980, to 103 in 2010, to 115 in 2040; or practically no change as historical trends are calculated.

Labor force projections are always hazardous undertakings since they make assumptions about variables which may not be borne out. We have attempted in Table 1 to update these projections on a more current set of assumptions. These are based upon assumptions as to future labor force made by Fullerton (1980) which yield a larger labor force because he assumes a higher percentage of female and minority populations employment in his projections than did earlier projections. Table 1 projections are also based upon Series II birth rate assumptions (essentially replacement level) and also give figures for two different retirement age assumptions — age 65, and age 68 which is now being discussed as a possible Social Security change.

Under these assumptions we would project a progressive *decline* in total dependency ratio from 127.0 in 1980 to 85.5 in 2050 if Social Security eligibility age remains at 65; and a decline from 127.0 to 76.8 in 2050 if Social Security age for full retirement benefits is increased to 68.

The relationship among columns 2, 3 and 5 of Table 1 helps explain why the labor force dependency approach is meaningful. If normal age at retirement for full Social Security benefits is maintained at age 65 the total labor force dependency ratio (column 1) will continue on a small but steady downward spiral from 1980 to 2050. And beginning in 2010 our projections indicate that there will be more people in the labor force than not (the ratio dips below 100). Even though the aged dependency ratio (column 3) increases from 22.0 in 1980 to 33.4 in 2030 (the peak year) for an increase of 51.8 percent, the child ratio (column 2) decreases 25.2 percent and the adult (nonaged) ratio (column 5) decreases 65.5 percent, both for the same time period. In other words, there will be 51.8 percent more people aged 65 and over between 1980 and 2030; however, this increase will be more than compensated by a 25.5 percent decline in youth dependency, and a 65.5 percent decline in the number of nonworkers in the labor force age group, 18-64. There will be more elderly, less youth and more workers, resulting in a declining total labor force dependency ratio. The so-called Social Security problem is not necessarily a 'demographic' problem, it is an 'economic' problem or perhaps an 'economic transfer' problem. Resources from the declining youth segment must be transferred to the increasing aged segment. With an increasing labor force (paying into Social Security) and the transfer of resources from the youth to the aging segment it would appear that the Social Security system could be maintained. However, there are two exogenous forces that plague the system that are not taken into consideration in our projections or any previous projections. One is unemployment which has two detrimental factors on the Social Security system: first, the loss of contri-

TABLE 1
Labor Force Dependency Ratios — United States, 1900-2050
(with Projection Comparisons for Retirement at
65 and 68 Years of Age)

	1 Total	2 Child	3 Aged	4 Aged- -Child	5 Adult (Non- Aged)
1900	166.6	86.2	6.9	8.0	76.6
1910	149.6	75.0	7.1	9.4	70.0
1920	153.4	75.7	8.1	10.7	72.3
1930	151.7	69.0	9.4	13.7	76.4
1940	148.4	57.7	13.0	22.6	80.9
1950	151.9	64.6	15.7	24.3	75.2
1960	156.6	75.9	19.2	25.3	64.4
1970	147.7	75.5	20.5	27.2	53.8
1980 *	127.0	63.2	22.0	34.7	43.2
Series II	**Normal Retirement Age — 65 Years**				
1990	103.2	54.0	22.2	41.1	27.6
2000	101.3	53.3	22.2	41.7	26.4
2010	98.5	48.8	23.0	47.0	27.3
2020	98.0	48.8	28.4	58.3	21.3
2030	95.0	47.1	33.4	70.9	14.9
2035	92.8	46.1	33.2	72.1	13.8
2040	90.5	45.7	31.9	69.8	13.2
2045	88.0	45.5	30.06	67.3	12.2
2050	85.5	45.0	30.07	68.2	10.0
Series II	**Normal Retirement Age — 68 Years**				
1990	96.1	52.2	17.9	34.4	26.2
2000	95.4	51.8	18.7	36.0	25.2
2010	90.8	46.9	18.2	38.7	25.9
2020	87.9	46.3	21.9	47.2	19.9
2030	85.2	44.7	26.7	59.7	14.0
2035	84.4	44.1	27.4	62.1	13.0
2040	83.2	43.9	26.9	61.1	12.5
2045	80.3	43.6	25.2	57.8	11.5
2050	76.8	42.9	24.6	57.3	9.5

* The 1980 dependency ratios are Series II projections. They were included in the top panel in order to facilitate Series II comparisons between normal age at retirement at 65 and 68 years of age.

Note: Labor force age was defined as 14 years and over from 1900 to 1960; 16 years and over in 1970; and 18 years and over from 1980 to 2050. Normal age at retirement was defined as 65 years and over for the top and middle panels, and 68 and over for the lower panel. However, those active in the labor force past these ages were included in the labor force. None of the youth dependent population was included in the labor force.

TABLE 1 (continued)

Ratio definitions:

column 1   Total dependency ratio = $\dfrac{\text{total pop. not in labor force}}{\text{total pop. in labor force}}$ 100

column 2   Child dependency ratio = $\dfrac{\text{youth dependent pop.}}{\text{total pop. in labor force}}$ 100

column 3   Aged dependency ratio = $\dfrac{\text{aged pop. not in labor force}}{\text{total pop. in labor force}}$ 100

column 4   Aged-child dependency ratio = $\dfrac{\text{aged pop. not in labor force}}{\text{youth dependent pop.}}$ 100

column 5   Adult (non-aged) dependency ratio = $\dfrac{\text{pop. 18-64 not in labor force}}{\text{pop. 18-64 in labor force}}$ 100

Assumptions:
Percent annual increase in labor force:

1970-1980 = 2.45%	2020-2030 = 0.5%
1980-1990 = 1.56%	2030-2035 = 0.5%
1990-2000 = 0.765%	2035-2040 = 0.5%
2000-2010 = 0.70%	2040-2045 = 0.5%
2010-2020 = 0.55%	2045-2050 = 0.5%

According to Fullerton (1980) there will be an increasing labor force participation among women and minorities in the future. Based on Fullerton's labor force projections to 1995 and used as a base line, women and minorities' participation increases were taken into consideration for our projections.

Percent aged 65 and over and 68 and over in the labor force:

	65 +	68 +
1990	11.6	5.8
2000	9.6	5.2
2010	8.6	4.3
2020	7.6	3.8
2030	6.6	3.3
2035	6.6	3.0
2040	6.0	3.0
2045	6.0	3.0
2050	6.0	3.0

Sources: US Bureau of the Census, *Historical Statistics of the United States, Colonial Times to 1970* (Bicentennial edition, Part 1, Washington, DC, 1975), Washington, DC, US Bureau of the Census, *Current Population Reports,* Series P-25, No. 704, 'Projections of the Population of the United States: 1977-2050' (Washington, DC, US Government Printing Office, 1977). (Note: Series P-25, No. 704, single years of age were obtained from the Population Projections Branch, Population Division, US Bureau of the Census.) The following Censuses of the United States were used: 1900, 1910, 1920, 1930, 1940, 1950, 1960, 1970. Fullerton (1980).

butions put into the system by the unemployed, and secondly, the resources via government expenditures to support workers while unemployed. The second force plaguing the system is uncontrollable inflation which has its greatest effect on the fixed income population. Based on the above the Social Security problem is, we see, first an 'economic' problem, and second an 'economic transfer' problem. Without unemployment and inflation the Social Security system appears to be keeping ahead of itself based on our projections. Therefore, the changing demographic structure of American society does not appear to be the problem and there is no need to change full retirement benefits from 65 to 68 years of age. The problem appears to be economic in nature based on inflation and unemployment. Perhaps the culprit is our inflexible governmental bureaucracy that is willing to change age at retirement for full Social Security benefits rather than change the system itself. We should be moving from 'the system is the solution', to 'the solution is in changing the system'.

If labor force dependency ratio is a meaningful measurement of the total dependency load a society must bear, none of the projections examined suggests that the load will increase with a possible doubling in proportion of retirees in the population, nor do they in themselves suggest a compelling need for increasing Social Security full benefit age to 68.

Societal Dependency Ratio

Societal dependency ratios approach a truer approximation of intergenerational support or transfer networks. These are frequently expressed as static ratios for historical comparison or projection since relatively few assumptions need to be made about the changing composition of component groups over time. However, in Tables 2 and 3 we present four alternative projections of the societal dependency ratio based on differing assumptions as to the age composition of the 'non-dependent' or 'productive' age population.

Column 1 of Table 2 presents the ratio from 1900, and projected from 1980-2050 based on the definition of the productive age group as 15-64; this is the figure usually employed in historical analysis and occasionally used for projection. It shows a dependency ratio of 62.4 in 1900 falling to a low of 46.6 in 1940 rising to a high of

67.4 in 1960 dropping to 50.8 in 1980 and rising to 60.8 in 2040. The total dependency ratio as projected to 2040 will not exceed its historical ratio and does not substantiate the alarming increase in dependents to working age population which segmental ratios of retired to working age populations might seem to indicate.

The second, alternative set of projection assumptions in column 5 of this table switches to 18-64 as the age boundaries of the 'productive' age group in projecting for 1980 and beyond, reflecting the later age of labor force entry for youth, and a more limited age span comprising the 'productive' ages. The third set of projections in column 9 uses this same entry date but extends the retirement age to 68 as might occur under one of the options being considered for Social Security revision. Under the former assumption the dependency ratio would increase from 64.3 in 1980 to 71.8 in 2040; under the latter, assuming an increase in Social Security eligibility age, the ratio would be 64.2 in 2040. While the age 68 eligibility assumption would see no increase in societal dependency ratio by 2040, the age 65 assumption would produce only a relatively small increase and ratio which would be well below those we maintained throughout the 1900 to 1970 period.

Societal ratios calculated in this manner relate to labor force but are more than just 'crude' ratios of labor force size. They do at least implicitly recognize productive contributions made outside of the market sector such as that by housewives not in the labor force.

Table 3, reflecting our fourth alternative set of assumptions, attempts to expand the concept of contributions to the societal support network made by persons outside of the labor force. It extends the 'productive age' group to include persons aged 65-74, not because of a change in assumptions about future ages of labor force participation but to explore the premise that persons in this age range can be considered part of the 'productive' component of the population even though not part of the labor force. It is an attempt to recognise a distinction now being made between the 'young-old' (aged 65-74) and the 'old-old' (aged 75 and over), reflecting the active and able bodied adult status of the large majority of 65-74 year olds, even if retired. Table 4 shows that only 27% percent of the men and 5 percent of the women in the 65-74 age group are physically unable to carry on any of their major activities, 96 percent of the men and 91 percent of the women live independently in households in which they or their spouse are the head, and less than 2 percent are institutionalized. The societal

TABLE 2

Societal Dependency Ratios — United States, 1900–2050

| | Dependent Population 0-14 and 65 + | | | | Dependent Population 0-17 and 65 + | | | | Dependent Population 0-17 and 68 + | | | |
	1 Total	2 Child	3 Aged	4 Aged-Child	5 Total	6 Child	7 Aged	8 Aged-Child	9 Total	10 Child	11 Aged	12 Aged-Child
1900	62.4	55.8	6.6	11.9	79.9	72.6	7.3	10.1	76.4	71.3	5.1	7.2
1910	57.2	50.4	6.8	13.5	73.2	65.7	7.5	11.4	69.5	64.3	5.2	8.2
1920	57.2	49.9	7.3	14.6	72.0	64.0	8.0	12.4	71.7	65.9	5.8	8.8
1930	53.1	44.8	8.3	18.5	67.8	58.6	9.1	15.6	64.0	57.5	6.5	11.4
1940	46.6	36.5	10.0	27.4	59.7	48.8	10.9	22.4	55.2	47.5	7.7	16.3
1950	54.0	41.4	12.5	30.3	64.4	51.0	13.4	26.3	57.6	48.9	8.7	17.8
1960	67.4	52.0	15.5	29.7	81.6	64.9	16.8	25.8	74.9	62.6	12.3	19.7
1970	61.4	45.6	15.8	34.7	78.0	60.6	17.5	28.8	72.4	59.1	13.3	22.5
Series II												
1980	50.8	33.9	16.9	49.9	64.3	45.8	18.4	40.2	57.9	44.1	13.9	31.5
1990	53.5	34.8	18.8	54.0	63.5	43.5	20.0	46.0	57.0	41.8	15.3	36.5
2000	51.8	33.2	18.5	55.8	63.2	43.2	19.9	46.1	49.7	36.0	13.7	38.0
2010	49.3	30.4	18.9	62.1	59.4	39.2	20.2	51.4	52.8	37.6	15.2	40.7
2020	56.8	32.4	24.4	75.2	67.2	41.2	30.0	63.1	58.1	38.9	19.1	49.1
2030	62.0	32.4	29.7	91.8	73.8	42.0	31.8	75.9	64.0	39.6	24.4	61.7
2035	61.7	32.1	29.6	92.4	73.1	41.1	31.7	76.6	54.5	39.3	25.2	64.0
2040	60.8	32.2	28.6	89.0	71.8	41.2	30.6	74.3	64.2	39.4	24.8	63.0
2045	60.1	32.4	27.7	85.6	70.9	41.3	29.8	71.6	82.9	39.4	23.5	59.6
2050	60.7	32.5	28.3	87.1	71.9	41.7	30.2	72.5	64.6	39.5	23.2	59.1

$$\text{Total} = \frac{(0\text{-}14)+(65+)}{(15\text{-}64)} \cdot 100$$

$$\text{Child} = \frac{(0\text{-}14)}{(15\text{-}64)} \cdot 100$$

$$\text{Aged} = \frac{(65+)}{(15\text{-}64)} \cdot 100$$

$$\text{Aged-Child} = \frac{(65+)}{(0\text{-}14)} \cdot 100$$

$$\text{Total} = \frac{(0\text{-}17)+(65+)}{(18\text{-}64)} \cdot 100$$

$$\text{Child} = \frac{(0\text{-}17)}{(18\text{-}64)} \cdot 100$$

$$\text{Aged} = \frac{(65+)}{(18\text{-}64)} \cdot 100$$

$$\text{Aged-Child} = \frac{(65+)}{(0\text{-}17)} \cdot 100$$

$$\text{Total} = \frac{(0\text{-}17)+(68+)}{(18\text{-}67)} \cdot 100$$

$$\text{Child} = \frac{(0\text{-}17)}{(18\text{-}67)} \cdot 100$$

$$\text{Aged} = \frac{(68+)}{(18\text{-}67)} \cdot 100$$

$$\text{Aged-Child} = \frac{(68+)}{(0\text{-}17)} \cdot 100$$

Sources: US Bureau of the Census, *Historical Statistics of the United States, Colonial Times to 1970* (Bicentennial Edition, Part 1, Washington, DC, 1975), US Bureau of the Census, *Current Population Reports*, Series P-25, No. 704, 'Projections of the Population of the United States: 1977 to 2050' (Washington, DC, US Government Printing Office, 1977. (Note: Series P-25, No 70 single years of age were obtained from the Population Projections Branch, Population Division, US Bureau of the Census.) The following Censuses of the United States were used: 1900, 1910, 1920, 1930, 1940, 1950, 1960, and 1970.

TABLE 3
Societal Dependency Ratio — United States, 1990-2050
(Dependent Population = (0-17) + (75 +);
'Productive' Age = (18-64))

	Total Dependency Ratio
Series II	
1990	46.1
2000	47.1
2010	43.0
2020	43.9
2030	46.8
2035	48.2
2040	49.3
2045	49.3
2050	48.6

$$\text{Total dependency ratio} = \frac{(0-17) + (75+)}{(18-64)} \times 100$$

Source: US Bureau of the Census, *Current Population Reports*, Series P-25, No. 704, 'Projections of the Population of the United States: 1977-2050' (Washington, DC, US Government Printing Office, 1977). (Note: Series P-25, No. 704, single years of age were obtained from the Population Projections Branch, Population Division, US Bureau of the Census.)

TABLE 4
The 'Young-Old' and the 'Old-Old': Selected Characteristics of
Population 65-74 and 75 and Over by Sex, 1978

	Men		Women	
	65-74	75 and over	65-74	75 and over
Functional Capacity: Unable to carry on a major activity	26.6	36.4	5.5	14.5
Marital Status: Married, spouse present	78.1	68.2	46.2	21.6
Living Arrangements: Household head or spouse of head	95.9	85.5	91.1	71.0
Living Arrangements: In institutions	1.6	6.8	1.5	10.3

Source: Beth J. Soldo, *Population Bulletin: America's Elderly in the 1980's*, Population Reference Bureau (Vol. 35, No. 4), November 1980.

'dependency' sometimes associated with old age does not set in for most aged until after 75. If the 'nondependent' and, we might speculate, societally potentially productive group can be defined as 18-74 we would then have a 'dependency' ratio of only 46.1 in 1990, rising to 49.3 in 2040. It will also help us to frame questions of how to define and measure transfers of goods and services in a societal context which we will be addressing next in our concluding section.

SOCIAL POLICY AND INTERGENERATIONAL TRANSFER SYSTEMS

While the projected demographic shifts we have discussed should not represent any significant increase in the total proportion of groups outside the 'productive' components of the population, there will be a major change in representation of young vs. old in this group. For example, column 8 of Table 2 which defines the two dependent groups as 65 + and 0-17 shows the ratio of 'old dependents' to 'young dependents'[1] increasing from 40.2 in 1980 to 72.5 in 2040. Table 1 (column 4), which defines 'dependents' in terms of labor force participation, projects an increase in the ratio of aged not in the labor force to young from 34.7 in 1980 to 69.8 in 2040, assuming Social Security full benefit age remains at 65; and an increase in ratio to 61.1 in 2040 assuming full benefit age is increased to 68.

Sheppard and Rix (1977) who have dealt with the labor force dependency ratio noting that it will not increase in the decades ahead, as we have earlier discussed, still warn against assuming the decline in the youth component of the ratio will automatically offset the support costs represented by the increasing proportion of retirees. In support of their warning that aged dependents may represent a greater per capita cost than young dependents they cite a study by Clark and Spengler (1978) which concludes that 'about three times as much public money is spent, on the average, per aged dependent than is spent on a younger one (1978)'. Clark and Spengler also note that private spending is more important for the support of youth than the elderly and state that '. . . . when private expenditures on clothing and food are included, the total cost of an elderly dependent is only 50 percent higher than that of a younger one'. And finally they note that much of the spending on youth, unlike spending on the elderly, '. . . increases their earning capacity in adulthood'.

James Schulz (1980) questions the adequacy of current information on the relative costs of young and old dependents as well as the Clark and Spengler inferences; Schulz cites a study by Hilde Wander (1978) which finds that in West Germany the total cost of rearing a child to 20 is one-quarter to one-third higher than is needed to support a 60 year old for the rest of his life (cited in Schulz, p. 1).

Concerns about relative 'costs' of young vs. old in the United States and other industrial nations not only reflect the need for more and adequate data on this poorly understood matter, but also raise questions about the utility of the analytic concepts employed. As our analysis has shown, whatever the reasons for the revolt against the alleged increases in 'dependency' loads resulting from population aging and the institutionalization of retirement it cannot be justified by a demonstrable increase in dependency load based upon any appropriate measure — whether labor force participation or more broadly conceptualized societal transfers between generations, or whether static or dynamic measures are used for time series comparison. As social scientists concerned with policy issues we are confronted with a not uncommon problem of scientific inference in which the answers obtained are no better than the questions asked. Economic questions require societal perspectives for analysis, and sociological concerns in this issue must have economic reference points as well. Political decision making requires social science inputs that are independent and of a scope appropriate for the issues considered.

In this paper we have attempted to refute the narrowest economic construction of changes in the dependency load and income transfers which will occur with an increase in the proportion of retirees in industrial society. Perhaps the problems which prompted this recent outburst of concern in the United States are situational and of short duration, e.g. the problems which our Social Security now faces could be significantly alleviated by a reduction in unemployment level or by a broadening of the participation of women and minorities in the labor force, without increasing retirement age or reducing benefits. Some aspects of the problem may be resolved by using general taxation revenues for meeting the needs represented by the changing age composition of the 'dependent' groups rather than relying so heavily upon an already overburdened Social Security system designed in an earlier era. Lastly, our inflationary economic system is controlling us at the same time as our government is unwilling to entertain systemic change.

But the current dialogue also points up the needs for more adequate data and relevant analytical inputs into policy decisions concerning the aged. The societal network which has evolved as a support system for the market economy is a prerequisite for the modern industrial state. Policies affecting the one cannot be made without examining their consequences for the other. The necessary information for policy decisions deals with changes in industrial society itself and requires comparative analysis for its investigation. Specific questions for cross-national investigation which this paper has sought to raise include:

1. How do dependency ratios vary in magnitude and composition with population aging in industrial societies?

2. How do changing societal norms influence 'dependency' status as well as contributions made by age and sex groups?

3. Should only public funds be considered in the calculation of dependency ratios as is sometimes done, or should intra family and other private source fund transfers also be included in the 'income transfer' total as well? And as John Myles' paper suggests,[2] should pension and Social Security pension payments be properly regarded as life cycle rather than generational income transfers, in which a portion of wages are withheld during working life to be paid upon retirement?

4. How do we quantify the value of societal transfers of goods and services which occur outside of the market nexus? The economist is only now beginning to try to estimate the value of services performed within the family household context such as those performed by the 'wife-mother', and discovering that cost-benefit calculations are incomplete measures at best. How do we estimate the value of support services contributed by children to parents outside their own households or by parents to their children's household?

5. How do we conceptualize and devise measures for the broad network of unpaid services which are important to the social infrastructure of communities and states? Labor force projections for the United States indicate that up to 80 percent of adult women

will be in the labor force by the end of the century. This group formerly represented a major reservoir of unpaid service contributions vital to many community activities. Will they be replaced by the active retired (i.e. the 'young-old') and if so, how do we value their contribution?

6. How can we measure indirect as well as direct costs and benefits assignable to a population segment? Thus, the cost represented by a retiree may be partially offset by the elimination of unemployment cost of a younger worker filling the job in times of high unemployment; or by the contribution to morale and work efficiency of opening up the promotion ladder for employees within an organization.

7. How is net cost of a retiree to be reckoned? The old, to a much greater extent than the young, are likely to be contributors to as well as receivers of transfers of incomes, goods and services within the social network.

NOTES

1. Valaroas (1950) has defined this ratio of 'old' to young in population as the *index of aging*.

2. See John Myles, Chapter 1, this volume.

REFERENCES

Clark, Robert L. and Joseph Spengler (1978), 'The Implications of Future Dependency Ratios and Their Composition', pp. 55-89 in Barbara Pieman Herzog (ed.), *Aging and Income* (New York, Human Sciences Press).

Clark, Robert L. and Joseph Spengler (1980), *The Economics of Individual and Population Aging* (Cambridge, Cambridge University Press).

Drucker, Peter (1976), *The Unseen Revolution: How Pension Fund Socialism Came To America* (New York, Harper and Row).

Friedmann, Eugene A. (1979), 'Changements des Rapports entre Travail et Loisir dans une Perspective de Retrait', *Gerontologie et Société*, No. 10, pp. 6-19.

Friedmann, Eugene A. and Harold Orbach (1974), 'Adjustment to Retirement', pp. 609-647 in Silvano Arieti (ed.), *The Foundations of Psychiatry,* Vol. I,

American Handbook of Psychiatry (2nd ed., New York, Basic Books).

Fullerton, Howard N., Jr. (1980), 'The 1995 Labor Force: A First Look', *Monthly Labor Review* (December), pp. 11-21.

Polyani, Karl (1945), *Origins of Our Times: The Great Transformation* (London, Victor Gollancz).

Schulz, James H. (1980), *The Economics of Aging* (2nd ed., Belmont, Calif., Wadsworth Publishing Co.).

Sheppard, Harold L. and Sara Rix (1977), *The Graying of Working America — The Coming Crisis of Retirement — Age Policy* (New York, Free Press).

Shryock, Henry and Jacob Siegel (1973), *The Methods and Materials of Demography* (US Department of Commerce: Bureau of the Census).

Titmuss, Richard M. (1968), *Commitment to Welfare* (London, George Allen and Unwin).

Valaoras, V.G. (1950), 'Patterns of Aging of Human Populations', pp. 67-85 in *The Social and Biological Challenge of an Aging Population: Proceedings of the Eastern States Health Education Conference, 31 March-1 April, 1949* (New York, Columbia University Press).

Wander, Hilde (1978), 'ZPG Now: The Lesson from Europe', pp. 41-69 in Thomas Espenshade and William Serow (eds.), *The Economic Consequences of Slowing Population Growth* (New York, Academic Press).

Wilensky, Harold L. (1975), *The Welfare State and Equality* (Berkeley, University of California Press).

4

THE MAKING OF OLD AGE POLICY IN FRANCE: Points of Debate, Issues at Stake, Underlying Social Relations

Anne-Marie Guillemard
Centre National de la Recherche Scientifique, Paris

In the last three decades, old age management in most industrialized countries has become progressively socialized. Old age, which for many years had been considered a private, family issue or in extreme cases one which was to be dealt with through traditional channels of aid to the poor, has given rise to the definition of a whole series of specific governmental orientations and actions.

The growth of state policy in this field is no doubt part of the general pattern of social policy growth that has taken place since the Second World War.

In the field of the elderly as in other social areas, the expansion of public social action has been interpreted as an inescapable march forward, brought on by a double movement: on the one hand, that of the system of production, which engendered new demands and new tensions, and on the other, that of a demand, brought about in turn by the latter, for increased state action. This evolution was to come to its end only when economic conditions began to tighten, which brought on, in the middle of the 1970s, a crisis in the welfare system.

The above approach appears limited, in our view, in two ways: firstly, it reduces social questions to economic considerations, and secondly, it is based on a technocratic conception of the state as an independent actor above society and capable of autonomous action.

At the base of the research on old age policy we have been carrying out over the last few years is the study of the successive modes of old age management insofar as they simultaneously represent an attempt to redefine old age socially, on the one hand, and a specific set of practical policies, on the other, both being viewed in the light of the social relations that engender them.

From this standpoint, social policies appear to engender new cultural categories — the salient trait of which is more often than not presented as 'natural' or even 'naturalized' by administrative practice (hence old age, illness) — as well as to engender specific sets of political and administrative decisions. In this respect, the emergence of a new 'territory' of social policy, cannot be analyzed independently from the new social category — the elderly — which that policy presupposes as existing, and which views aging citizens in society as constituting a coherent and autonomous entity requiring the creation of a specific mode of management.

In this paper, we will seek to put forward an interpretative framework for the study of the making and evolution of old age policy in France, using a number of research works, some completed and some not,[1] as our base. The present work represents an attempt to develop a political economy of old age policy. A series of empirical observations on the development of old age policy complements the main body of this work, the goal of which is to bring into focus the specific possibilities for further research that the proposed analytical framework provides.

First of all, we will seek to recompose the history of old age care by delimiting modes of functioning and by observing their dominance according to the time period. Secondly, we will strive to decipher the specific configurations of social relations capable of explaining the shift from one functioning mode of old age management to another and to outline an analytical framework for understanding the origins of the successive modes of old age care.

OLD AGE POLICIES AS SUCCESSIVE
SIDES OF A TWO-TIERED DEBATE

The socialization of old age management may be recomposed by taking into consideration three basic elements:
— the major issues around which that socialization has developed;
— the systems of social actors in conflict over these issues;
— the polemical relationships that are fostered and maintained by

the issue-determined controversy.

The historical outline of the major issues and of the social actors involved in them which we have drawn up is based on an analysis of a body of original documentary work according to the three above-mentioned elements. This body of documentary work is composed essentially of the following·

1. a close examination of articles dealing with questions of old age and retirement published in the French daily newspaper *Le Monde* from 1946 to the present;

2. an analysis of the main trade union publications for the same period;

3. an examination of the records of debates held on these subjects in the French Assemblée Nationale and Conseil Economique et Social (Parliament and Council of Economic and Social Advisors, respectively). Not all aspects of this documentary work have been completed and some supplementary materials, in particular interviews with the social actors involved and direct observational reports (participation in the committee work of the Commissariat du Plan), have been added to the main body of the work.

Two Major Issues, Two Systems of Actors

At the present state of research, it appears that the debate on the old age question has revolved essentially around two major points or issues: the 'standard of living of old people' and the 'way of life of old people'. The former is at the core of the debate on retirement pensions and on the age at which one is to retire, a debate which started as far back as the 19th century and which is still going on today.

Without going into a discussion of the origins of retirement plans and of the emergence of the social security system in France, it can be said that these policies reflect the social relations created between capital and labor, or to be more precise, between certain elements of these two forces.

The social actors at odds over this issue, given the institutionalization of work conflicts, are the trade unions and management, while the state for the most part simply enforces by law the settlements negotiated by the other two.[2]

The second issue has to do, not with the standard of living of the aged, but rather their way of life and their social integration. The opening of this sort of debate occurred, at least as far as its essential elements are concerned, in the early 1960s and pre-supposed that old age should represent, from the standpoint of social conditions, something more or less identical to everyone, that old age should be identifiable, thus enabling it to become the object of specific public action, is precisely the development of retirement schemes that made possible such representation and identification of old age. By redefining the limits and content of this the last stage of life, the extension of retirement conferred a homogenous dimension on old age — namely, that of being inactive and a pensioner — whereas old age had previously presented the extremely varied traits of individual family heritage. [3]

The main social actors involved in the second issue may be defined as being the representatives of various state agencies in their relations with certain innovative groups and the sections of the population these groups manage, or those who speak in their name. Hence, the stated policy and implementation of an ambitious public program creating coordinated home services and facilities were developed mainly through state initiative and were intended to maintain the social integration of the aged. They were therefore the result of an unstable compromise between, on the one hand, a group of innovators made up essentially of senior civil servants in association with a few university men, a number of members of private associations and representatives of supplementary pension funds, who, for various reasons, were in a position to receive and pass on any new feelings or aspirations that might come to light; and on the other hand, certain state agencies (the Bureau of the State Plan, the Ministry of Health) who wrote the innovations into their own implementation processes. This compromise elicited hostility or resistance from certain other segments of the state, such as the Social Security Office, or the Ministry of Construction, [4] and also from certain private as-sociations (for example, private nursing homes for the elderly), all of whom were intent upon preserving their own way of doing things and maintaining their special rapport with their respective clienteles. [5]

Three Periods

In recomposing the history of public action in the field of old age since 1945 in the light of the two issues we have isolated analytically and in the light of the system of social actors those issues bring into play, we are led to distinguish three main periods. Each is characterized by a specific dynamic of state action in the field of the aged; each is related to the nature of the dominant issue and to the social forces which that issue brings into play; each associates a process of reconstruction of the social reality of old age with its dominant mode of old age management.

In the *first period* (1945-1960) the only question being considered was that of the *standard of living of the aged*. This issue, and the main social actors it brought into play, were therefore at the center of the dynamics of caring for the elderly during that period.

Caring for the elderly was provided mainly through the development of retirement schemes[6] to which a few supplementary welfare measures were added, the effort being to fill in the gaps left by the old age protection scheme brought into being by the creation of the social security system. Hence, in the first period a number of social measures for the most impoverished of the aged were taken, the main ones being the *carte sociale* or 'social card' for what were called the 'economically weak' (1949), a noncontributory allowance from the Fonds National de Solidarité (1956), as well as several other measures providing in-kind and/or financial aid.

The system of social actors is represented by the different social classes brought into a complex conflict over the question of how much should be paid to take care of older generations. After the Liberation, the decline of the popular movement resulted in a renewal of opposition within the retirement system to the social security scheme by the traditional middle classes (artisans, storekeepers), by the new middle classes (upper-level white-collar workers) and by the ruling classes. At this time, retirement schemes developed in an anarchistic fashion according to the interests of each class and to the balance of power existing between trade unions and management in the different sectors of the economy, giving rise to contractual supplementary pension funds.

The same social class actors were to be found at the start of the welfare programs being put into practice outside the retirement system in order 'to improve the living conditions of the aged'. Here, these same actors acted in their political capacity, and the divisions revealed by an analysis of the debates and voting records in Parliament on the Fonds National de Solidarité (1956) perfectly represent the logic which set in opposition the parties of the Left who were 'seeking greater justice' and 'a quick, viable answer to the plight of the four million elderly people', on the one hand, and the 'independents' and Poujadists, on the other, who refused any increase in taxes, fearing the inflationary effects of the proposed programs, and opposed the mode of financing of the latter which, it may be noted, caused the MRP to abstain from the vote.

Around the 'standard of living of the aged' issue, a dynamic of old age policy formation came into being, and correspondingly, there appeared a kind of double representation, seemingly contradictory, of the elderly.

As we have already seen, the generalization of retirement schemes conferred on the elderly an identity of situation:[7] they were retired people. A whole new territory came into view. However, the economic and social conditions of the elderly being what they were, these welfare programs, though designed to alleviate their poverty, in fact made old age in this period into a separate form of indigence. Thus, what was new here was that for the first time old people were not mixed indiscriminately with the other categories of those receiving state welfare since in this case social aid was allotted specifically for the elderly. Old age was identified as a new social territory for social policy but was still associated for the most part with poverty.

The old age being talked about and written about in the newspapers at the time was that of the working class. This is obvious from all the outward features pointing to the working class: the old people were poor, with no income or wealth to speak of; they survived on coal bonds and on state-distributed sugar; they lived in the destitute conditions of poor houses.

The *second period* was characterized by a coming into focus of the way of life issue and of the social integration of the elderly. Along with this new issue, a new system of social actors, as we have already seen, also appeared in which various state agencies played a special role, the nature of which we will strive to delineate. Among the actors brought into play — besides certain upper-level civil servants from various state agencies — we find a number of institutions specializing in social work and certain supplementary pension funds.

Indeed, the development of supplementary retirement schemes

placed the latter institutions in a special position as social actors involved in the 'way of life' issue. On the one hand, these institutions were in direct contact with the feelings and aspirations of a new generation of elderly who received generous pensions and who on the whole were better off than their predecessors on all scores. On the other hand, given the intense competition among these institutions to increase their memberships, they were led to anticipate the demand they felt was growing in this new, captive market of their pensioners and hence developed original social programs likely to serve as effective enticement with respect to companies. It was in this fashion that some supplementary pension funds put new services into practice rather early — in particular an upper-level white-collar worker fund which was created as early as 1947 — including leisure and vacation activities for the retired.

Hence, the qualitative question of the way of life of the elderly, and no longer simply the quantitative question of their standard of living, became ground for public social action and state policy. The concurrent development, as we have seen, of specific welfare programs for the elderly had as a further consequence the awakening in some of those in charge of carrying out social work and in certain associations in which they worked (such as UNIOPSS[8] or UNABAS,[9] of a new sensitivity to the new needs of the aged, needs which took expression less directly in material terms than in the moral ones of solitude and marginality.

The state gave impetus and form to this new debate with its decision in 1960 to create a special commission to study the problems of old age (La Commission d'Etude des Problèmes de la Vieillesse), headed by Pierre Laroque (Advisor to the Government), which consulted closely with all of these organizations. The state organized into a coherent doctrine what before had been only a series of isolated actions and speeches. It continued to provide impetus to this movement. The major points of the debate continued to be linked to state-initiated action, such as creation of the Travaux de l'Intergroupe Personnes Agées, (Work Group on Old Age), created as preparation for the Sixth Plan, which resulted in the first state programs of community services for the elderly; the report by the Inspection Générale des Affaires Sociales (1968-69); and, more recently, the formation of a study group under the auspices of the plan on the theme 'Growing Old Tomorrow'.

Yet, the stated policy of this doctrine embodied the functional logic of the official commissions which had served as its crucible. It is common knowledge that the members of such commissions, however good their intentions may be, work from the existing state of things in order to rectify their functioning and do not attempt to call into question the principles underlying the situation. Consequently, while it is true that the debate was furthered by these study groups, it was also confined to a limited area. [10]

The emergence of the question of the way of life of the elderly brought with it a new approach to old age care, a new vision totally opposed to that which had prevailed up to that time. To underline the change, the new vision was given the name of 'old age policy'. [11] This policy may be defined as a comprehensive project aimed at re-integrating the elderly into society through community care as opposed to segregating them into homes for the aged, the aim being to prevent dependence and the institutionalization of the aged. A new, comprehensive and preventive strategy was hence substituted for the social action that had complemented retirement policy and that had been based on individual, partial and curative care.

As in medicine where the shift from curative prophylaxis to preventive prophylaxis led to the supervision not only of sick patients, but also of the whole population to ensure proper, effective health care, the new preventive approach towards old age resulted in the elderly as a whole becoming the target group of a new mode of public action. This new approach extended its aid to classes other than the most impoverished. The introduction of new, collective management principles to old age brought with it the concurrent development of a new vision of old age and of its needs, just as, to continue our analogy, new definitions of sickness and health were associated with preventive medicine.

As this new, alternative mode of dealing with the aged was being promoted, old age began to free itself from its world of poverty and inability to work. What could be called a new 'naturality of old age' came into being, visible in the French expression *troisième age* (literally 'third age' and usually translated by the expression 'senior citizens') which was coined at about the same time as the new principles of old age management were being defined. The elderly, who had been seen as immobile and dependent, became active, autonomous, and responsible citizens. Old age was seen as a new stage of life in which one was free to develop one's aptitudes and interests and no longer one in which only poverty and destitution were foreseeable.

In actual fact, behind the transformation of the cultural image of old age presented in this or that period, what we have is an evolution of the social class that is being referred to. We have already seen how strong affinities existed between the retirement behaviour of the new white-collar, middle-class people and the new way of life of the elderly, defined by the nascent old age ideology as active and participative. [12] In the first period everyone was told of the miserable lot of the working-class elderly; in the second period, the retired upper-level white-collar workers along with their life-style and cultural and financial assets became the focal point of the new mode of caring for the aged which was being implemented and which presented their way of life as exemplifying new norms for successful old age.

One of the hypotheses guiding our investigation is that promotion of the issue of the lifestyle of the aged might very well constitute for its most active protagonist — i.e. the state, or at least part of it — an attempt, given the rapid and relatively anarchistic development of retirement schemes and given repeated trade union offensives, to lower the retirement age. The state increasingly lost control over the expanding pension system, as happened in the setting up of supplementary pension funds.

From this standpoint, if we wish to recompose the formation process of the social policy towards the aged, it appears necessary to follow closely throughout this period the criss-crossing of the two issues of debate — 'standard of living' and 'way of life' — and the way in which their protagonists entered into the controversy using these issues as the basis for their argument. Hence the widespread, unified trade union offensive that grew out of the retirement question between May 1969 and December 1971 certainly did not win satisfaction for its claims in the passing of the Boulin law (December 1971) which dealt with the level of pensions and the age of retirement, for the concessions granted were indeed limited. On the other hand, this trade union offensive was strong enough to have consequences later that same year when, as part of the Sixth Plan, a program marking the first middle-range financial commitment by the state to alleviate the marginality and segregation of the elderly was adopted. It was as if the state was responding to demands concerning retirement schemes with a program dealing with the way of life of the elderly, attempting in so doing to shift the issue of debate from the standard of living to the way of life issue.

After the debate centering largely around the way of life of the aged, it appears to us that the present, and third period can be characterized by a vigorous revival of the 'standard of living and retirement age' issues. This has accompanied the unemployment crisis and the spread of pre-retirement schemes and guaranteed redundancy payments for aging workers. This new debate, in our view, has taken a decisive role in the dynamics of old age management, and the major actors involved — the trade unions and employers — have once again come to center stage. Of course, the question of integrating the elderly into society continues to be topical; but it is losing ground. On the contrary, what today marks the last stage in life is less and less a specific mode of social integration than a progressively earlier and more widespread rejection of work and of productive activity, bringing along in its wake certain consequences, namely marginalization of the aged and a tainting of the image of old age. A new definition of old age is coming into being in which one becomes 'elderly' earlier and earlier (at 50 for certain workers in the steel industry) and by virtue of which aging workers lose, to a certain extent, their 'right to work'. The image of the elderly, or, to use a euphemism, the 'picture of senior citizen life' which was painted during the previous period no doubt concealed the scope of this phenomenon to some extent by euphemizing through the expression 'voluntary pre-retirement' what was in fact the result of a number of subtle pressures closely related to the new image of workers over a certain age as having no right to work.[13] It is nonetheless true that between the moment one stops working and the beginning of retirement, there is, more and more often, a period of variable duration in which one is unemployed.

Let us add that the unemployment in question is of a rather special type as the unemployed person is guaranteed redundancy payments, even if he has not attempted to find another job. In fact, this new stage in life, i.e. that between working life and real retirement, is more closely akin to a precarious form of retirement due to three of its main characteristics:

— the reduction of rights (especially the constitutional right to a job) that comes with pre-retirement;[14]
— the temporary aspect of this legislation;[15]
— the extreme complexity, fragility and, depending upon the judgement of the unemployment office studying the case, variability of the transition from unemployment to pre-

retirement before the age of 60 to guaranteed, pensioned retirement after 60.

Available information points to the fact that precarious retirement is progressively becoming the predominant situation for private sector workers of the 60-64 age group in France. On the one hand, in December 1980, for the age group in question, 213,567 persons were receiving guaranteed redundancy payments, [16] of whom 142,429 were men. On the other hand, the results of a survey on employment carried out by INSEE (National Institute for Statistical Studies of France) in October 1980[17] make it possible to conclude that the number of active, private sector salaried workers in the 60-64 age group[18] reached 228,400, among whom there were 138,400 men.

Thus, for private sector salaried workers of the 60-64 age group, the pre-retirement phenomenon is as common as that of having a job, the former in fact being predominant in the case of male workers.

Thus, workers are entering in greater and greater numbers into a period of precarious retirement between working life and true retirement and this usually after the traumatizing experience of being made redundant.

In this attempt to draw a statistical picture of the pre-retirement phenomenon, we should not overlook all those who are between 55 and 59 years old and who, having lost their jobs and receiving unemployment benefits (there were 80,580 male workers in this situation in March 1980), will in most cases receive guaranteed redundancy payments at the age of 60. This group of workers does not take well to being excluded from the working world which more and more tends to see them as 'job-snatchers'. In a study which we carried out on a sample section of the working population in the 55-65 age group receiving redundancy payments, 25 percent wanted to find another job[19] and less than one-third considered themselves as being retired, identifying more with unemployed workers.

Do these facts in themselves not constitute a kind of backward step for the policy of social integration of the elderly, partially implemented by the state in the previous period? They certainly point to the advent of a new mode of handling the question of the elderly. The state as major social actor in the management of old age has made way for a confrontation between the trade unions and the employers over the main issue at hand, that of the retirement age.[20]

Faced with a situation in which employers are restructuring their activities because of the slumping economy, invoking the necessity to improve profitability and competitiveness, the trade union movement finds itself in a defensive position and appears relatively weak. In this position, it has to struggle against the most immediate and deleterious effects of this process of reorganization for workers: wholesale lay-offs, production unit closures. The trade unions have had a hard time drawing up a counter model of economic development to that of the ruling classes, and have attempted on the active level to preserve an industrial fabric which is in the process of decaying. [21]

Regarding the premature 'retirement' of aging workers, the trade union movement finds itself in the grip of its own contradictions, which dampens its capacity for action. These contradictions provide an explanation for the fact that this is the only field in which trade unions have, since 1972, signed a series of nationally-applied agreements — and without much controversy — with employers. (The 1972 agreement regarding guaranteed income for the aging unemployed; the 1977 agreement regarding voluntary pre-retirement at 60 years of age, renewed first in 1979 and then in March 1981.) These contradictions may be summarized by two general statements. On the one hand, the trade union movement, as part of its constant struggle to see that worker exploitation is reduced, has launched numerous offensives to get the retirement age lowered. It was therefore difficult not to respond to certain proposals made by employers which, though part of a general strategy — albeit based on a very different logic — of outbidding the unions at their own game, did make it possible for certain workers to retire at the age of 60. On the other hand, the trade unions have been the scene of internal generation conflicts which have grown in intensity since the advent of the economic crisis that has made the questions of job and income distribution controversial issues. Arbitration of disputes is made along the lines of what is in the interests of the dominant group: young people of working age. A number of problems will no doubt come up in some *départements* and regions (for example, the loss of elderly union activists, a loss that is in no way compensated by the activist sections of retired workers that trade unions have tried to develop since 1969).

The survey that we recently carried out on a dozen companies, in which the employers' and trade unions' strategies regarding employment and redundancy of aging workers were analyzed, clearly pointed out the contradictions of trade union action in this field. In particular, on the company level, the trade unions have been less sensitive to the erosion of the right of aging workers to work and to the perversion of retirement schemes implied by this new system" and more interested in the fact that the exclusion of aging workers from jobs has not had the beneficial effect on the unemployment of young people that had been expected.

The survey also shows how employers are able to make the system work to their advantage: they can modify the number of aging workers sent into pre-retirement to suit their manpower and reorganization needs by using various options and by making these options more or less attractive or coercive to workers. Employers, who have always sought to make the retirement system into a manpower policy, have in this system found at little cost a flexibility that suits their needs perfectly. This system is, however, likely to bring about an imbalance in the age groups of the labor pool and corresponding organizational problems, but few employers today have bothered to look into these points.

Recomposing, as we have done, the history of the recent two-tiered debate around which public action has been defined has made it possible to distinguish three separate periods, each characterized by a specific dynamic of policy production and old age care in relation to the nature of the dominant issue and the social forces that issue brings into play. In the first period the balance of power between the ruling class and the working classes was struck around the issue of the 'standard of living of the elderly', which gave rise to the implementation of a state retirement policy. This policy came to represent the dominant mode of old age management and at the same time produced a unified cultural image of this the last stage of life which remained characterized by working-class poverty. In the second period, old age management concentrated on the new question of the way of life of the aged and brought onto the scene, not conflicting social classes as before, but rather the state, along with its specific relations with certain innovative groups and with the sections of the population cared for by these groups. This new dynamic resulted in a social integration project for the aged which was given the title 'old age policy'. It was associated with a new cultural image of the aged, which became known as the 'third age' (*troisième âge*). Lastly, in the third period (the present one), initiative for action in the field of the elderly has moved back to a crude relationship of power between the social classes involved, bringing once again to the fore the question of the 'standard of living of the elderly and the retirement age'. The measures so far taken indicate a clear tilt of the scale in favor of the ruling classes. A new image of the elderly is coming into focus in which old age is seen as a time in life when work is illegitimate.

An examination of this pendulum swing of state action from one issue to another and from the domination of one system of social actors to another makes it possible to isolate alternating modes of old age management associated with the successive reconstructions of the image of old age. However, this pendulum-like movement itself requires explanations and this can be done by analyzing the transformations of the social structure at that time.

Hence, the shift from the first to the second period, when the state took the major responsibility for handling the way-of-life issue, is to be clarified through an analysis of the evolution not only of social relations but also of relations between the state and various social and economic actors. A study of the characteristics of the elite occupying the highest posts in the state apparatus should enable us to draw, as Pierre Birnbaum has done, the network of lines of fusion and separation between this elite and the ruling class. This study indicates the state's degree of freedom with respect to society at large and thus its autonomy to act as an agent of change.

By the same token, the passage into a third period when the dynamics of state action regarding the elderly are more directly determined by the ruling class reflects a loss of autonomy by the state with respect to society as a whole and a greater fusion of the political and administrative systems with the centers of economic power.

SOCIAL RELATIONS AND THE FUNCTIONING MODES OF OLD AGE MANAGEMENT

For clarification's sake, four major axes have been identified around which transformations in society are seen to take place. The transformations underlying the dynamics of state action with respect to the aged are as follows:

— the evolution of social and economic structures;
— the forms of social conflicts and their intensity;
— the prevailing cultural image of old age and its contradictions or discrepancies with respect to the other dimensions of society;
— the mode of state action.

The application of this analytical framework to an understanding of the shift from one dominating mode of old age management to another is the subject of a heretofore uncompleted study on the formation and evolution of state policy in France with respect to the aged. We will limit ourselves for the purpose of this paper to a limited analysis of one type of such a shift.

Using the proposed conceptual tools, and to provide an example, we will briefly analyze those transformations in society likely to elucidate the emergence of what we have defined as the second period in the recent history of state policy towards the aged. We will attempt to bring to light the social conditions preceding the implementation of a new dynamic of state action regarding the elderly which in fact took the name of 'old age policy'.

Class Conflicts, State Organization and the Emergence of an Old Age Policy Dealing with the Way of Life of the Elderly

The emergence in the field of old age of the question of the way of life of the elderly and of a system of social actors involved in the debate in which the state occupied the predominant position can be understood in the light of the converging changes in several factors:

1. the advent of a growth-oriented society and the increasing importance of consumer values in the economic system combined with the appearance of an 'elderly class' having more financial and cultural assets, which gave retired people a new social utility;

2. the emergence of new feelings and aspirations and of new social struggles in the field of old age;

3. an 'identity crisis' in the cultural image of old age;

4. the acquisition of greater autonomy for the state with respect to society at large.

Specific articulation of all these evolving factors makes it possible to explain the emergence of the 'way of life of the elderly' issue and also to explain the formation process of the whole of state action in this field. Nevertheless, for clarification's sake, we will evaluate, factor by factor, the effects of the above-mentioned transformations on the dynamics of care for the elderly.

Growth, Consumption and the New Retired Elderly

If one considers, firstly, the transformations that had taken place within the system of production and the after-effects these had on the social structure, it becomes clear that at this level, from 1958 onwards, conditions came into being that favored a focus of attention on the question of how the elderly lived.

The onset of rapid economic growth after 1958 made stimulation of consumption an important issue, even if the basis of that growth was the development of investment and exports. During this period, the state played a greater and greater role in the organization of the collective means of consumption and gave its attention more and more to the regulation of consumer demand. At the same time, various stimulants to consumer demand were being implemented in the marketplace, in particular through the expansion of credit and the growth of advertising.

In order to understand the impact of the new economic context — i.e. the advent of a growth-oriented economy and the key role consumption played in that economy — we must also take into consideration the transformations taking place within society. The major social transformation may be summarized as the birth of new middle classes of salaried, white-collar workers (engineers, lower and middle-level managers, teachers and technicians). When these people reached retirement, the social group of retired workers took on a new look, characterized by high intellectual aptitudes and financial resources, stronger aspirations and an extensive system of social protection that was in keeping with the position this new group had occupied in the production system and in accordance with the group's negotiating power. In the economic context we have described, it became an important social imperative to stimulate, supervise and make solvent the rising consumer demand. From that point onwards, an awareness of the new social utility of the elderly began gradually to come into being. The concomitance between, on the one hand, the sharp increase in the number of middle-class retired people and, on the other, the announcement of a new old age policy centered around the way of life of the aged appears to constitute an element towards the confirmation of the importance of this factor's role in the production of old age policy. Indeed, we have pointed out that it was in the 1959-1967 period that the highest rise in the percentage of middle-class retired people within the social structure of the total elderly population took place. It was during this same period that new programs were being drawn up and put into effect, policies that were to be tied together under the term 'old age policy'. It should be pointed out that the content of all these programs had the stamp of the socioeconomic situation of the period as they all put forward an image of the elderly as 'senior citizens', the reference framework for which was that same middle class.

Feelings, Aspirations and Social Struggles

While our analysis of the transformation of the social structure of the aged population attests to the development of a group of new retired people made visible by the group's specific characteristics, this analysis also points up the existence during the same period of large pockets of impoverished old people who have paid a considerable price for the intensive restructuring of the economy. Added to these contrasting situations were contradictory experiments which turned old age into an explosive social issue.

The transformations that affected French society between 1945 and 1960 brought into play in the working classes new aspirations with respect to old age.

The setting up of the social security system in 1945, followed by the creation of supplementary pension funds, developed a new sensitivity in society to welfare systems. Action to help the needy was no longer viewed as charity but rather as a right.

Secondly, the rise of household consumption, observable from 1959 onwards, encouraged new modes of life and new aspirations in the light of which — and in contrast to which — the lot of most elderly people became even less acceptable than before. In their daily life, the new retired population discovered the sharp differences existing between, on the one hand, the experience of retired life as, more often than not, one of inactivity and boredom and, on the other, what they had believed retired life would be: the hard-won right of the working man to rest and to a guaranteed pension.

Out of these contradictory experiences a certain awareness and a number of demands came into being. An opinion poll carried out by IFOP in 1961 and sponsored by the Commission d'Etude des Problèmes de la Vieillesse (Study Commission on the Problems of Old Age) revealed that the problem of old age occupied first place in the preoccupations of the public, along with the housing crisis. In the same poll, of those aged 60 and over who were interviewed, 45 percent said they were dissatisfied with their material situation and only 25% said they were satisfied. Public concern and the dissatisfaction of the elderly were directly linked to what from then on was to be called the *scandale de la vieillesse* (scandal of old age). The poverty of the elderly had become shocking since the right to guaranteed pensions in the name of participation in the production effort of the country had been won.

Throughout the 1945 to 1967 period the trade union movement and political groups focused their attention essentially on the struggle to alleviate this poverty and on the question of retirement schemes. Demands in the field of old age were characterized by the same traits as the other popular struggles of the period: they were mainly economic and defensive in nature.

The aspirations of the new elderly population coming from middle and upper-level white-collar occupations for better social integration and for a better old age — i.e. one based less on quantitative norms and more on qualitative ones — were not picked up by their professional or political organizations. These launched a comprehensive attack not on the marginal position in which society had placed retired people, but rather on the material consequences of this phenomenon.

Hence, the emergence of the 'way of life' issue cannot be understood in the logic of the dominated classes and their organizations. During this period there was no popular counter-model of old age management to call into question the position of retired people in society and to propose a new mode of management based on an equality of rights between generations.

The Identity Crisis of
the Cultural Model of Old Age

Any mode of old age management implies, on the one hand, action in the field of the elderly as the target population and thus, the elaboration of an ethic of old age care and, on the other hand, the production of a social image of that target population. It is in this sense that we use the expression 'cultural model of old age'.

The processes of evolution we have described have led the cultural model of old age to work in contradiction to the other dimensions of society.

The traditional mode of old age management relied mainly on the Bureau d'Aide Sociale (Welfare Office) and poorhouses to deal with the elderly. It was aimed essentially at helping the working-class aged, and operated on a charitable and assistance-based ethic, putting forward a dissuasive image of old age as poverty-ridden. This model was held up as an example and throughout the 19th century contributed to the moral training of adults and children of the poorer classes by encouraging foresight and thrift. It made possible the use of old people to moralize all generations of the working classes by molding their attitudes and behavior with regard to the future. The generalization of retirement schemes undermined the utility of such an image by substituting statistical solidarity for individual foresight. In addition, this generalization of retirement schemes drew an entire generation of old people into retirement without making any distinction between classes, thus fundamentally transforming the scale of the problem. The discourse on the future held by the traditional mode of old age management was in complete contradiction both to the new circumstances of old age being experienced by the different social classes (financial and cultural assets) and to the growth-oriented, programmed society that was coming into being. Such a society sought to set up a relationship with the future that would be based on estimation strategies and not on simple foresight.

The negative picture of old age put forward by the traditional system of management closed off any possibility for viewing the future. It burdened with debt each person's future in a society of hope and expansion which operated on the basis of middle or long range plans and was to set up tighter and tighter mechanisms demanding of each individual a personal strategy based on the same vision of the future (a more 'plannified', long range view of schooling and training for children, buying on credit, etc.) as well as confidence in that future.

While it is possible to consider that in some ways any state policy for the elderly tends to use them to moralize the whole spectrum of generations, it also becomes clear that the traditional mode of old age management brought about a mentality that was in complete contradiction to what was being demanded by the programmed society that was coming into being. It became apparent that a new mode of old age management was needed, one that would be capable, through its approach to the future, of adapting mentality to the new social system that was coming into being.

Furthermore, we have seen that the presence of a new, rising middle-class elderly became, in the context of stimulated consumption, an important issue and brought about a renewal of the social utility of the aged. At the same time the traditional practices of assistance to the aged became obsolete. These traditional practices had been designed to alleviate excessive poverty, whereas from that point onwards, it became important to consider what to do with the surplus of goods that were still useful to the system. The potential purchasing power of newly retired workers made it clear that the traditional mode of old age management constituted a wasteful approach to these new sources of consumer demand. In addition, the cultural image of the aged as marginals and as wards of the state was called into question, by the same token calling into question the traditional modes of assistance. The new class of retired workers, in short, upset the entire cultural model of the elderly, especially since the traditional practice of relegating the elderly into assistance channels was made more and more costly by a rise in the percentage of old people in the population. [23] For this reason, the traditional approach was viewed as extravagant, insofar as its social usefulness grew much less than the investments those practices required.

Transformation of the State and of Its Mode of Action

Examination of the first three analytical dimensions of society reveals that at the start of the 1980s, the old age question was an explosive one from the economic, social and cultural standpoints.

The evolution of the social and economic situation made stimulation and orientation of the demand of retired people an important social issue. While for the most part trade union claims focused on retirement schemes and the defence of a minimum income for the elderly, it is possible to discern a rise in new aspirations centered around the way of life of the aged, though there was no organized expression of these aspirations. Furthermore, public opinion was on the whole very sensitive to these questions. Lastly, the cultural model of old age was going through a kind of identity crisis. The cultural orientations promoted by the model were totally out of tune with the times, with the society of economic growth and programmation that was taking root. Its ethic of thrift and foresight was in contradiction to society at large which put a premium on hope for the future, communication and integration.

The transformations that took place within the state with, in particular, the formation of the Gaullist regime, conferred on that regime a new capability for taking the issue in hand and becoming the major force in the promulgation of the new aspect of the old age question, namely, that of the way of life of the aged. After the parliamentary-based government of the Fourth Republic, which gave most important powers to the legislature and left the executive with little scope for autonomous action with respect to the wider society, the Gaullist regime, with its strong executive, radically changed the possibilities for action. The Gaullist state was characterized in particular by a new and high level of collaboration between the executive and the upper-level civil service,[24] significantly widening the range for autonomous action. At this point the state acted as the instigator of a new economic and social logic. During this period, it intervened in all aspects of society — in particular in the economic sphere — in order to implement its policy of modernization and concentration of the means of production in an effort to prepare them for foreign competition. It set up a whole series of intervention structures and created new state agencies to enable it to act outside the usual hierarchical processes.

The creation of a study commission on the problems of old age can be understood in this context as can, by the same token, the prospective 'old age policy' which gave form to a new series of issues centered around the question of the life style of the elderly and their integration into society. This was an attempt to 'reform' old age so that old people would become active participants in the debate and in the process of modernization of the country. Indeed, as the authors of the report pointed out, there was a risk of the elderly becoming a burden on the living conditions of French society as a whole, while during the same period the prospect of economic growth for all of Europe, as a result of the Treaty of Rome, began to materialize. It was therefore imperative to propose a new social logic with respect to the elderly, a social logic that would constitute a viable answer to the contradictions brought about by the delayed influence of the cultural model on the other dimensions of society. The new principle of integration took into account the new social utility of certain parts of the elderly population while at the same time resolving the question of the rising cost of their institutionalization and conferring on old age a new image and a new profile. Beyond its effects on the elderly, the new approach to old age adapted public attitudes to the prospect of economic growth by granting each individual a secure future.

In a society in which old age is everyone's future — given the increase in life expectancy — old age policy has become an important tool for acting on public attitudes towards the future.

The implementation of a new mode of old age management based on the life style issue, i.e. the shift to what we have called the second period of old age management, seems to be the result of a series of changes which in turn made old age into a controversial question with strong economic, social and cultural overtones. These transformations were combined with the advent of a government desirous of modernizing the country and of dealing with the thorny questions facing it. This government, having more autonomy of action because of its freedom from the controlling influence of sectional interests, was able to promote a new logic for the mode of management of the old age question in collaboration with certain innovative groups.

This paper has described the successive functional modes of old age care and has proposed an analytical framework for the explanation of the shift from one dominating mode of old age management to another. Over and above the concrete analysis presented herein of a specific stage of old age policy in France, this analytical framework should make it possible, on the one hand, to isolate the social conditions in which old age policies are formed, and on the other, to identify the main factors influencing or determining their successive changes.

What we have tried to do in this brief study is to draw up a macrosociology of the making of old age policies, using as our starting point the French example. It would of course be useful to ask whether this analytical framework could be pertinent in the study of old age policy formation in other industrialized countries. At present, however, there is a dearth of comparative analyses of old age policies which would enable us to answer, even partially, that question. Nonetheless, we may say that advancing the understanding of this question constitutes an important political and scientific issue. At this time, while industrialized societies search anxiously for answers to the crisis in the field of welfare policies and solutions regarding the future of the welfare state, it has become apparent that reflection on the why and how of old age policy making and development must be intensified. Indeed, it is well known that in industrialized nations today the largest percentage of public expenditure goes to the elderly. The welfare state is, first and foremost, a 'welfare-state-for-the-aged'. From this standpoint, it may seem strange that the scientific community has up to now neglected for the most part the making and evolution of old age policy, focusing its efforts rather on the other aspects of welfare policies.

NOTES

1. In a recent work (A.M. Guillemard, *La Vieillesse et l'Etat*, Paris, PUF, 1980) we have drawn up a summary of research results on this topic, some of which will be used in the interpretation developed herein. In most cases, however, it will not be possible to re-present the studies and observations on which the research results are based.

2. While the various interpretations put forward on the formation of the social security system differ on many points, they do agree on this general description. The reader should see the work of Victor George (*Social Security and Society*, London, Routledge & Kegan Paul, 1973), Patrice Grevet (*Besoins populaires et financement public*, Paris, Ed. Sociales, 1976) or Henri Hatzfeld (*Du paupérisme à la Sécurité Sociale 1850-1940*, Paris, Armand Colin, 1971).

3. This example demonstrates that the dynamics of public action in the field of old age can only be understood from a study of the interaction of the debates

stemming from the two analytically identified issues. The opening of a debate on retirement schemes made possible the emergence of another debate, that on the way of life of the elderly.

4. Hence, an analysis of the social impact of the social security system between publication of the report entitled 'Politique de la Vieillesse' (1962) and 1970 reveals that the policy of that system followed, despite the new orientations of social integration laid out in the report, a program of nursing home construction, the effect of which was increased segregation. Furthermore, the first finalized home services program for the elderly was adopted as part of the Sixth Plan without any preliminary consultation whatsoever, either with the Sécurité Sociale, even though the latter agency was to bear the financial burden of a portion of the program, or with the Ministry of Construction, despite the fact that an improvement of public housing policy with respect to the aged was the cornerstone of the program.

5. The studies of Xavier Gaullier on certain local programs, such as those carried out in Grenoble or in the 13th *arrondissement* of Paris, clearly point out the characteristics of the local system of actors involved in the way-of-life of the elderly issue. Once this issue has been singled out, in a sense, by state initiative, certain local programs like those studied by the authors have played a key role in promoting and implementing a policy for the elderly focused on the way-of-life issue. See Xavier Gaullier's 'Une politique médico-sociale de la vieillesse: le 13ème arrondissement de Paris' and 'Une politique municipale de la vieillesse de la région grenobloise' (Paris, Fondations des Villes, 1975, mimeo).

6. Various indicators point to the development of retirement schemes during this period:

(a) The percentage of French people receiving pensions (from Sécurité Sociale and agricultural and special schemes) rose steadily. The percentage of the total elderly thus protected increased from 67 percent in 1955 to 76 percent in 1960, to 87 percent in 1964 and 95.6 percent in 1970 (INSEE social statistics, 1974).

(b) From 1959 to 1974, the number of pensioners receiving social security benefits doubled while the rise in the number of aged in the population was from base number 100 to 126.

(c) Supplementary pension funds grew in number. 1947: agreement signed on a supplementary retirement scheme for upper-level white-collar workers; 1957: creation of the Union Nationale des régimes complémentaires des salariés non-cadres (National Union of Supplementary Retirement Funds for Lower-level White-Collar and Blue-Collar Workers).

7. That the retirement situation conferred a common dimension on the elderly does not mean uniformization. On the contrary, this common dimension represents a backdrop against which differences were to become discernible.

8. Union Nationale Interfédérale des Oeuvres Privées, Sanitaires et Sociales (National Interfederal Union of Private, Sanitary and Social Work).

9. Union Nationale des Bureaux d'Aide Sociale (National Union of Welfare Agencies).

10. See in particular the analyses developed in *La Vieillesse et l'Etat,* op. cit., pp. 73-98.

11. The report of the Study Commission on Problems of Old Age was, in choosing the above name, the first to introduce this new concept which, it may be noted, corresponded to the general development of social policies: a policy regarding the young was drawn up in the 1950s, a policy of psychiatric community

care preceded that of gerontological community care.

12. See, in particular, *La Politique de la Vieillesse — Genèse et Usage Sociaux d'un retournement doctrinal,* a report by the DGRST, Centre d'Etude des Mouvements Sociaux, December 1976, and *La Vieillesse et l'Etat,* op. cit., pp. 87-97.

13. A recent poll by the French newspaper *Le Monde* on the various kinds of freedoms confirms this fact — if confirmation is in fact needed — by pointing out that nearly one in every two readers (48 percent) considers that pre-retirement should be imposed on aging workers in order to reduce unemployment. It is to be noted that *Le Monde*'s readership belongs mainly to social and professional groups (upper-level white-collar workers, intellectual professions) which are in general more in favor of extending working life than are working-class and lower-level white-collar workers.

14. The French social security old age fund clearly distinguishes between retirement pension rights and the right to a job: the ending of occupational activity is not a condition for entitlement to a pension. On the other hand, persons on 'pre-retirement' are entitled to a pension only if they no longer have an occupation (for voluntary or involuntary reasons). Accordingly, 'pre-retirees' have their rights reduced, since the right to a job (guaranteed under the French constitution) no longer applies.

15. The national interprofessional agreement of 1977 extending the right to redundancy compensation to workers over 60 choosing pre-retirement has to be renewed for successive periods of two years.

16. Source: *Bulletin de Liaison UNEDIC,* December 1980. The figure cited corresponds to the total number of persons receiving redundancy or resignation compensation.

17. This comparison can give only an approximate idea of this phenomenon, for two reasons:

(a) the INSEE survey in question is a poll and not a compilation of the exact number of workers in this situation. Consequently, these results are evaluations, unlike the figures given by UNEDIC;

(b) the definition of the private sector used for the employment survey does not completely fit with that used by UNEDIC.

18. These figures refer to the number of employed workers in the ILO sense of the term, i.e. workers having worked at least one hour in the reference week.

19. Even though, for all practical purposes, their efforts would be fruitless.

20. On this point, see Michel Wieviorka's article, 'Blues Syndical: la cote d'alerte', in *Autrement,* No. 29, February 1981, pp. 216-224.

21. It is possible that the electoral success of the Socialist party in France on 10 May 1981 will give a new vigor to the way the state deals with the question of the elderly. Attention may once again focus on the issue of 'how the elderly actually live', and we may see state policy change accordingly. It is at present too early to tell.

22. While the right to retirement pensions in our system is not subject to that condition. Hence, the right to financial resources is granted only on the loss of the right to work.

23. From 1954 to 1968, the institutionalization rate of the aged rose by 38 percent and the number of those housed doubled. At the same time, it should be noted, nearly all of the aid to the elderly came in the form of financing institutionalization.

24. We are here referring to the conclusions of Pierre Birnbaum in his work *Les Sommets de l'Etat* (Paris, Seuil, 1977).

5

THE STRUGGLES OF FRENCH MINERS FOR THE CREATION OF RETIREMENT FUNDS IN THE 19TH CENTURY

Rolande Trempé
Université de Toulouse

Any discussion of the 'prehistory' of social security must begin by recalling that insecurity has been an essential characteristic of industrial workers' lives. Jobs and wages have been threatened not only by conditions in the labor market and employers' arbitrariness but also by the risks of sickness, accidents and old age. Among these, only the latter is unavoidable. But what does it mean? This question is not without value, for the concept of old age has changed significantly during the last hundred years. In the middle of the 19th century, industrial workers took it to mean the period when they were no longer able to work and earn a living. Old age meant disability rather than a definite age. Disability and old age formed a fearsome and feared combination because giving up one's job led to poverty, the poorhouse, or dependency upon public charity or one's offspring.

Growing old happens faster or slower depending on the individual and his occupation. If his strength is quickly exhausted by his job, a man ages prematurely — before an age generally considered to be old. Workers with hard, dangerous or unhealthy jobs run the risk of premature disability. Miners have always belonged to this category, as the chairman of the Mines Commission acknowledged in 1887: 'We know that a worker is forced to retire earlier insofar as he has been subject to accidents, sickness or unhealthy conditions during his working life.' Though they were unable to provide scientific proof,

workers were quite conscious of this relationship. They expressed it
clearly and frequently along with the fear of ending their lives in
poverty.

In 1848 during a parliamentary investigation of working
conditions, a miner from the Loire coalfields testified on behalf of
his fellow workers. After describing the poor working conditions,
he concluded: 'These men are sometimes disabled at a tender age.
Begging is then their only means of existence. What a squalid
degradation for men whose hearts still feel alive enough to want to
work' (Archives Nationales [ANC] 956). During his testimony, he
was led to explain exactly what he meant by the unusual phrase
'tender age'. It referred to the shortness of a miner's life, at work
or in general. The miner then stated that if no remedy were found,
'in a very short time, you will see disabled miners not more than 35
or 40 years old' and, in his words, 'it is well-known that the miner's
average life expectancy is no more than 38 or 40' (ANC 956). How
could he have formulated more clearly the fact that miners died at
work because they did not have the means to stop working before
exhaustion?

Forty years later, the anguish provoked by the feeling of
premature aging was once again voiced by miners' delegates before
the Mines Commission of the House of Deputies. In 1883, Michel
Rondet, also from the Loire coalfields, stated, 'Contrary to what
bosses say, a 40 year old miner, even if he has more experience, is
already much weaker and unable to carry the same work load as at
35.' In 1886, he added, 'We want to earn our own bread and our
children's bread during our old age' (ANC 3383).

The 1880 statues of the Loire miners' trade union set as an
objective 'the creation of a legal institution like a friendly mutual
fund that will shelter old miners from the hard necessity of
dependency on public charity and will keep them from going to the
poorhouse to die' (Article 5).

There are many similar quotations. All express the same lurking
fear of ending life in the poorhouse and being unable to provide
support for wife (or widow). Miners therefore demanded a
retirement scheme that would offer a daily allowance sufficient for
leading a normal, family life after stopping work. First voiced in
1848, this demand came up again and again throughout the second
half of the 19th century and during the early part of the 20th. The
way it was formulated was significant.

In the 1882 *Cahiers de Doléances des Mineurs*, the Loire miners asked for a two franc per day pension after 25 years of work in the mines and *without any age limitation*. Calvignac from Carmaux supported this at the Federal Congress of Miners in 1883: 'Only those who have escaped throughout their lives from the deleterious effects of the atmosphere in the galleries, from explosions, from cave-ins, etc., are qualified to declare that 25 years of such living gives then an undeniable right to rest.' Since miners began going down the pits at an early age, retirement could be set at 45. In spite of the reserve and outright hostility of MPs in 1884, M. Rondet firmly maintained this age and refused retirement at 50 because, he said: 'Miners are worn out sooner than workers in other industries. Working from 15 to 50 — deducting time in the army — means 30 years in the mines. Under such conditions, the proposed law would be useless because most miners would not reach that age' (ANC 3383). The miners stuck to this position. In 1912 during debate about modifying the 1894 Mines Act, those MPs who were miners accepted delaying retirement until 50, given progress since the 1850s, but they insisted on maintaining 25 years of work because, they said, 'At 50, a miner is an exhausted man'.

Clearly, miners considered that the primary criterion for retirement was not age but the wear and tear, weariness, and premature exhaustion caused by the hard work in their industry. Thivrier, worker and MP from Commentry, said as much before the Mines Commission on 5 March 1912: 'The trend of present legislation is not to set a uniform retirement age for all occupations but to vary this age as a function of the wear and tear of each trade' (ANC 7476).

The need independently to protect security in old age before becoming disabled or worn out gave rise, during the 19th century, to the mutualist movement. It was also behind the employers' policy of 'paternalism'. Workers from all occupations founded friendly societies for mutual benefit in order to deal with the costs of sickness and old age. What happened in the mining industry was somewhat different because of the nature of the work and the behaviour of the big capitalistic coal companies.

The latter tried to profit from workers' need for security by participating in these friendly societies or else by setting up their own. The promise of a pension was a means that employers used in order to recruit workers, who were more frightened than attracted by the mines. It was also a means for stabilizing and controlling the work force. Keeping workers in the company for years ensured the 'stability and regularity of personnel, which are as necessary for the prosperity of the mines as to the improvement of miners' existences' (quoted by Trempé, 1971, p. 585). The promise of a pension upon retirement could help slow down the personnel turnover that was 'so detrimental to safety and output', in the words of a chief engineer from the Saint-Etienne coalfields in 1901. In this area, labour turnover was high. The ratio of the number of workers recently signed on and those leaving the mines to total workers was 56 percent at Saint-Etienne, 64 percent at Rive-de-Gier, 70 percent at Roche-Molière and Firminy and as much as 186 percent at Villeboeuf! These figures help us understand the companies' need to stabilize the work force. They also throw light on the conditions fixed for receiving a pension, namely, 25 to 30 consecutive years of work in the same company. Under company-run pension funds, miners lost their contributions and any hope of benefits if they were dismissed or quit voluntarily. They were thus bound for life to the same company. They could never take a break in their careers.

The companies also supported retirement funds as a means for getting rid of older, less productive workers who cost higher wages due to seniority (Trempé, 1971, p. 585). They could not throw them out onto the streets, for such an act would incense fellow workers and the local population. 'Wouldn't it be damaging to let a legend arise in which a man works long years for the company, has contributions deducted the whole time from his wages and still lacks bread in his old age?' (Trempé, 1971, p. 604). In contrast, miners declared in the 1883 *Cahiers de Doléances,* 'Men who perpetually live in contact with death have the right to demand compensation for accidents and a pension for old age.' A 1910 report by the Retirement Committee of the Federal Congress of Miners commented, 'How disgusting to see a worker, who has given his strength to serve his company and has amply contributed to the creation of national wealth, thrown away like a rag, an old tool or a useless object, and thus reduced to begging while others have taken the fruit of his labour and enjoy it to the full!' This is positive evidence of the growing awareness of miners. Their demand for a retirement fund had, ultimately, to be advanced in terms of the class struggle. Mine owners who developed retirement policies were trying to dampen the class struggle and ensure 'social peace' while protecting profits.

During the second half of the 19th century, a complex set of friendly societies and pension funds was set up for miners in response to both workers' need for security and owners' determination to obtain a stable, submissive work force. An evaluation of these institutions can be drawn from an investigation undertaken by the Mines Service in 1883 upon request by MPs in the lower house. On first reading, the Keller Report (*Annales des Mines*, 1884) seems quite satisfactory: a large majority of miners (98.1 percent) were members of such institutions. The miners, however, were far from satisfied. Since 1848, they had been severely critical of the operation of these funds and of their insufficient benefits.

The 146 friendly societies and pension funds that existed in 1883 were divided into three categories in terms of their financial sources: (1) from workers alone; (2) from workers and employers together; or (3) from companies alone. Out of 111,317 miners, 109,237 had both sickness and old age protection. Most of these institutions provided multiple coverage. None specialized only in retirement. This was the basis of one of the workers' major complaints. It was also the weakness of these institutions because they devoted most of their resources to covering sickness and were thus unable to pay out pensions. In the Loire coalfields for instance, only six out of 57 funds actually paid pensions. Even when retirement was covered, the benefits were too small and irregular. As Mazeron declared before the lower house of parliament on 7 July 1885: 'The double conditions of age and of seniority are so difficult that they can be fulfilled only by an insignificant number of workers because of work-related exhaustion and consequent illnesses' (*Journal Officiel*). Two years later, the Audiffred Report to the same body admitted: 'Strength starts to wear down at the age of 50. . . . Fixing retirement at the age of 60 is a steep requirement, but at the same time, requiring 30 years of continuous work in the same mining company often makes it impossible to open rights to a pension' (*Journal Officiel,* 21 March 1887). Most funds, moreover, demanded that applicants for pensions be recognized as 'absolutely unfit for any job':

Chances of a pension were further reduced by the fact that management of these funds — even of those exclusively financed by workers' contributions — was in the hands of the companies for which the miners worked. Employers had written the rules, had laid down the conditions, and were also exercising moral and financial control over the funds. Workers' delegates to the governing bodies of these funds were intimidated in the presence of the director or chief engineer, who generally presided over meetings. Calvignac, secretary of the trade union at Carmaux, declared as representative at the National Congress in 1883: 'The delegates on the boards of these funds — regardless of the coalfield — always feel involuntarily terrified when they voice their opinions. They are convinced that persisting in a discussion can bring unfortunate consequences, the least of which would be dismissal at the first opportunity.' The miners were unable to prevent these funds from being diverted from their real destination. Some companies used them to cover not only sickness but even work-related accidents, which should have been at the employer's charge according to an 1810 Act. Accordingly, compensation for such accidents came out of these funds. A chief engineer called this practice 'vicious' because it emptied the treasury and prevented the payment of expected retirement benefits. Some companies went so far as to use these funds to run, under religious orders, parochial schools that they had built!

Even more serious, these employers' funds had no assets to back up services. They were supplied with cash on a day-by-day basis. If the company went out of business or if management of the fund were bad, pensions were no longer paid. Workers' contributions could be swallowed up, as happened during the 1888 bankruptcy of Terrenoire Compagnie in Bessèges.

Finally, no one was protected from unfair dismissal just before retirement, in spite of many years of work. Workers had in mind the example of Aniche Company in 1872.

For all these reasons, dissatisfaction was widespread among workers. In his 1893 report, Cuvinot, who was both a senator and a member of the board of Anzin Mines, admitted the development of 'permanent uneasiness and insoluble difficulties' between companies and personnel. Discontent intensified. Strikes broke out in various coalfields: Loire in 1869, North and Pas de Calais in 1872, Carmaux in 1869 and 1883, etc. The institutions that should have been the source of labour peace were turning into causes of conflict because of flaws in their operations.

Miners were demanding:

(1) *control over these funds*. As early as 1848, Viaud, a delegate, asserted: 'Miners, after examining their position, see that they can no longer bear that those who exploit their wages also exploit their savings. For every cent contributed to these funds, a drop of blood

has to fall from the forehead of a sweating worker who refuses to
see his mates die from starvation' (ANC 956).
(2) *specialization and autonomy of these funds* in order to prevent
misappropriations.
(3) *the guarantee of an adequate pension at a reasonable age.* As
already seen, the miners thought that occupational exhaustion
ought to be taken into account when the age of retirement was
fixed. Years of service was therefore a better criterion than age
alone. They stuck to 25 years of work but, since they had to, agreed
to the age of 50 as the basis for a guaranteed pension. Two
conditions were indispensable for providing adequate pensions.
First, contributions had to be made equally by workers and by
companies (with the government putting up a share). Second,
insurance must be made compulsory.
(4) *the creation of an individual, inalienable pension certificate* in
order to protect retired miners from all contingencies resulting
from employers' arbitrariness (unfair dismissals or harsh
regulations) or from poor management. The certificate holder
would be safe from the unexpected and free in his occupational
activities.

This set of demands constituted the program that miners
gradually defined and elaborated between 1880 and 1890. They
doggedly called for its application until 1914. This conflict went
through several phases and took various forms, which will be
surveyed next.

The present period of social security has been related to the
'welfare state' or, as some say, the 'state of providence'. Labour
disputes in the mines partly explain why the liberal states of the
19th century were, little by little, forced to intervene in employer-
employee relations by laying down regulations in order to limit the
pernicious, socially dangerous effects of 'freely' contracted labour.
This intervention occurred under pressure from one of the parties:
wage-earners. The latter had become conscious of their lack of
control over employers' pension funds. Workers resented the
failure of the disputes in the Loire coalfields from 1860 to 1869.
They became aware of the impossibility of setting up a complete
system of protection, especially a reliable pension fund, financed
exclusively by themselves. There was the portentous example of La
Fraternelle. This institution, created by the Loire miners in 1866,
aimed to provide benefits complementary to the allowances paid by
the companies. Though grouping several thousand miners, it

collapsed during the 1869 strike. The fluctuations of the Sainte Barbe Fund at Carmaux were no less significant (Trempé, 1971, pp. 577-580). No private institution — whether funded by employer or employee — was able to guarantee adequate pensions for aged or crippled workers. The amount to be paid was too large.

Evidence for this came from the figures (in gold francs) that experts furnished to members of the lower house of parliament in 1883. The director of the Caisse des Dépôts et Consignations affirmed that twelve francs of irrecuperable contributions were necessary for one franc of pension. Miners were asking for two francs per day, hence 770 francs per year! Moreover, they were demanding that this amount be paid *immediately*, regardless of the funds to which potential retirees had previously contributed. The Mazeron Report (*Journal Officiel,* 7 July 1885) calculated that the following amount per person at the given age would have had to be paid *all at once* in order to satisfy miners (based on a rate of 4.5 percent):

Age	Alienated Capital (gold francs)	Reserve Capital (gold francs)
50	4,915.40	8,898.20
51	4,818.60	8,896.40
52	4,726.20	8,894.60
55	4,430.60	8,888.40

According to the parliamentary committee responsible for preparing these figures, only the Treasury could meet such expenses. No company, however big, could block such sums in a retirement fund, and none wanted to. As already mentioned, the few pensions that were paid came out of the daily cash flow. They were backed by the expectation that companies would remain prosperous. This was thought to be sufficient guarantee.

Miners thought that help from the government was necessary in order to put an end to this situation and safeguard the future. If the state alone were to be a safe place for money, the government would have to exert the necessary authority so that sufficient contributions be *regularly* made by workers and *all* companies to the pension funds. For that, contributions had to be made compulsory, and both parties had to submit to the authority of the law, which could fix benefit scales and stipulate the conditions for receiving pensions.

Both the determination to shelter their old age from poverty and arbitrariness, and the memory of the negative experiments tried out during the second half of the 19th century led miners to turn toward the government for its active support and protection.

STATE INTERVENTION:
AN ISSUE BETWEEN MINERS
AND COMPANIES

State intervention was not new. The Loire miners had already used it in 1848. After declaring that the concentration of operations in the hands of one company (Compagnie de la Loire) had worsened working conditions, their representatives had asked the government to intervene so as to stop abuses and break up this monopoly:

> It would be easy for the government to oppose the behavior of shareholders....
> The first way to improve workers' lives would be that the government help them.
> It should force the companies to stop unemployment, to stop organizing it as they have been doing since the birth of the Republic. It should regulate the length of working hours, fix daily wages, and support workers' efforts to organize and take control by allowing them to elect their governors (i.e., supervisors) (ANC 956).

In 1882, the Loire miners returned to this theme with a call for government intervention, as they were reorganizing after the failures of the 1869 strikes and the repression of the Commune in 1870. They sent a delegation to MPs to voice their grievances and demand a law that would guarantee safe working conditions and decent living standards.

Although the essential point of the *Cahiers de Doléances* concerned recognition of miners' delegates, their grievances also included a demand for the reorganization of relief and pension funds, as well as for the eight hour working day. For miners, the improvement of working conditions (including a minimum wage) had always been connected with their demand for retirement since, as seen, the latter was conditioned by wear and tear at work.

While the miners' local unions and the National Federation of Miners were mobilizing to bring pressure to bear on the government, the mining companies were grouping regionally (North and Pas de Calais) and nationally (Comité Central des

Houillères de France) in order to oppose state intervention. Several factors were behind this opposition. First, it had to do with the free enterprise theory of economic 'liberalism' as well as with the desire to let parties contract freely. Second, it arose out of fear of a growing role for the government in the mining industry. Company directors were even more wary inasmuch as their firms held concessions granted by the government. According to a law of 1810, the state reserved the right to control the conditions and methods used in mining concessions. A special mining engineering corps was responsible for inspecting operations and setting the rent to be paid for concessions. The companies argued against any new pretext for creeping state intervention. They fiercely defended the system of institutions that most of them had set up during the 19th century. As shown, the aim of this system was to entice, stabilize and discipline the work force, which was becoming harder to recruit as the century advanced. Retirement pensions were not the least important element in this strategy. The companies therefore rejected any proposal that would weaken their hold over personnel. Etienne Dupont, a retired general inspector of the mines who had become a member of the board of Mines de Brassac, expressed this view in 1883:

> The numerous bills proposed from November 1882 till March 1883 concerning the mines, in particular the obligation to subscribe to mutual help funds, the recognition of miners' delegates. . . and the guarantee of safe working conditions in the mines, these bills have scared operators in France. They feel that their freedom is threatened.

He recommended the rejection of all these bills.

Mine operators organized in order to block or at least water down parliamentary bills supported by miners. They undertook campaigns in the press and exerted pressure on various committees, particularly on the senate committee chaired by Cuvinot, a member and then chairman of the board of Mines d'Anzin, the most powerful French company. They also influenced parliamentary proceedings through deputies or senators who were board members of mining companies. They claimed that free enterprise, production costs and competitiveness with foreign products were at stake. Small companies would go bankrupt because of imposed costs. All means and arguments were used.

As for retirement funds, Jules Marmottan, president of the board of Mines de Bruay, had declared in 1870: 'The state cannot and must not intervene.' The mining companies strongly opposed measures that would keep retirement from being seen as a 'gracious gift' and 'act of generosity' or load down companies with extra labor charges and thus increase production costs. Accordingly, they opposed legal measures to make contributions compulsory, fix benefit scales, set the age of retirement or lay down conditions for receiving benefits. The big companies did, however, propose enforcing upon themselves the obligation to subscribe to pension funds. If such a law were passed, the expectation of retirement would no longer be a means for disciplining workers or for obtaining their gratitude and devotion. Retirement protected by law would make miners independent. This independence was what the companies dreaded most. The one side was defending profits and sovereignty; the other, pensions and dignity.

In response, the miners adopted a strategy that would deeply mark union activities. Their regional or federal congresses defined and discussed bills of law. They then sought out friendly MPs who would propose these bills and defend them before parliamentary committees and on the floors of the house or senate. In major coalfields, miners were even able to form a voting bloc and elect their own candidates to parliament. In this way, their interests could be defended directly. Miner MPs became the counterpart of board member MPs.

These tactics did not suffice, however, and miners went on strike. From the 1890s onwards, strikes controlled by the union became a means to put pressure not only on the companies but also on the government. The need to influence parliament and its decisions necessitated a display of force. The Miners' Federation was thus led to believe that a general strike would be one of the best means of bringing pressure to bear. The aim in 1902, 1912 and 1914 was not to propel a movement that would end in revolution but to oblige the government and parliament to take miners' bills into consideration. These three general strikes had modest, strictly professional objectives: in 1902, to win the eight-hour day, a minimum wage and the autonomy of the miners' pension funds, which had been created by law in 1894; and in 1912 and 1914, to overcome the senate's obstructive opposition to this autonomy. The force of these actions came from the power of the unions, their organizing abilities, and, more importantly, the major role of coal in economic activities. A drawn-out general strike in the mines meant, in 1910, that industry and transportation were rapidly paralysed.

In addition to socialist MPs, their natural supporters, the miners found allies among persons from the middle class and from the state corps, especially of mining engineers. Their bills were defended by those who thought that government policies of safety and security would help maintain social peace. The second Audiffred Report (*Journal Officiel*, 21 March 1887) had no doubts about this:

> The act about retirement and relief funds will be a law of appeasement. In short order, it will, in our committee's firm conviction, bring about a more thorough understanding between various parties: capital, operators, engineers and workers.

The senate report of 1893 adopted the same view and added: 'The creation of an individual retirement certificate will amply contribute toward the development of foresight, social progress and appeasement.' Companies' opposition came from a misunderstanding of their own interests, as stated in the Audiffred Report:

> We think that operators are also interested in the improvement of their equipment and the amelioration of the conditions of workers whom they employ . . . . Business men are just as interested in the progress of science in order to carry out desirable social improvements for workers. The value of human capital is higher than that of the capital invested in equipment. Unlike the latter, the former cannot be replaced at discretion. Leaving aside questions of humanity, those holding mining concessions have considerable interest in preventing accidents and sickness and also in attenuating their consequences by providing care and relief duly proportional to the need. It is also very important for operators to prevent or lower unemployment related to such sicknesses or accidents and to delay as long as possible premature deaths and exhaustion, which leads to early disability.

In summary, man is the most precious capital. To protect him against the short-sighted policies of private companies, MPs in the lower house gave the state the right to intervene in conformity with the 1810 law. The senate committee, chaired by Cuvinot, who sat on the board of Mines d'Anzin, opposed this decision.

In this conflict and under pressure from miners, the house and the senate voted a series of measures from 1891 to 1914, which led to the creation of an autonomous retirement fund in 1914. As early as 1894, employers' and employees' contributions to the Caisse Nationale pour la Vieillesse had been made compulsory. The same 1894 Act created the individual retirement certificate and separated relief from retirement funds.

That was only the first step. Assimilation of the retirement of ordinary workers with that of miners entailed retirement at the age of 55. Miners immediately asked that the 1894 law be modified so that their fund be autonomous. They could then freely lower the age of retirement to 50 (which they finally did in 1962). To obtain this and to raise pensions to 760 francs, miners went on the general strikes that have been described above. They won basic issues, but they obtained satisfaction neither about the age of retirement nor about the state's contribution to their fund, which some wanted.

Though relative, their victory nevertheless made a breach in the free enterprise theory of economic liberalism. Workers in the mines (and on the railroads) opened the way to a policy of state social security, which would finally be instituted in 1928 and fully developed after the Second World War. However, because of their attachment to the specific institutions that they had won in previous disputes, miners preserved their own system of social security, which they defend today as forcefully as did their forefathers.

REFERENCES

Annales des Mines, 1894.
Cahiers de Doléances des Mineurs, 1883.
Journal Officiel (Paris, Government Printing Office): the official publication of government proceedings and decisions.
Trempé, Rolande (1971), *Les Mineurs de Carmaux, 1894-1914* (Paris, Editions Ouvrières).

6

OLD AGE AS A RISK:
The Establishment of Retirement Pension Systems in France

François Ewald
Centre Nationale du Recherche Scientifique, Paris

The set of institutions created by laws in 1928 and 1930 is normally designated, in French, by the term *assurances sociales*. In fact, the idea, the term and the applications of social as opposed to private insurance date from the end of the 19th century.

Of course, the impressive example of Germany, which set up a system of worker insurance (sickness, accident, disability, old age) in less than ten years, from 1883 to 1889, does come to mind. This historically important system would be used as both a positive and negative reference mark for the institution of social security in other industrial countries at the end of the 19th century.

Although lagging considerably behind Germany, France also established a system of worker insurance in the late 19th and early 20th centuries. This system was composed of three elements. The 1 April 1898 law about friendly societies, the so-called mutuality charter, allowed the risks of sickness to be covered. The 9 April 1898 law about occupational hazards settled the risks of work-related accidents. Finally, the 5 April 1910 law about workers' and farmers' pensions completed the foregoing by insuring the risks of old age.

In the minds of members of parliament, these three laws formed a system, as Audiffred declared when he introduced the pension bill in

---

This article was translated from the French by Noal J. Mellott.

1896. Through the rational separation of risks, which was thought to be definitively acquired, these legal measures were to offer adequate provisions for contending effectively with the precarious and dangerous conditions of workers' lives. They proceeded from the same conception of security, they respected the principles of a common scheme of insurance; and they embodied the French version of worker insurance.

Notwithstanding the French legislature's affirmation of interpendence, these laws did not form a perfect whole. In particular, problems changed during the years between the first law in 1898 and the third in 1910.

For instance, the 5 April 1910 law laid down the principle of old-age insurance for wage-earners. Old age was thought to be a risk, a risk that had to be insured. So far, this law ensued from and directly continued the program that had been defined during debate about work-related accidents. It broke definitively with earlier programs like the 1850 law that instituted the Caisse Nationale des Retraites. Although old-age insurance did derive from compensation for work-related accidents, the 1910 law went beyond previous acts by adopting the principle of compulsory insurance, which had been rejected until then. The very essence of the 1898 law about friendly societies was freedom, a freedom to be encouraged, favored, subsidized and, above all, maintained. In fact, members of these societies saw, not without reason, a threat in the law on farmers' and workers' pensions. From another point of view, this law did considerably enlarge upon its antecedents: the notion of occupational hazard was more closely defined and came to overlap that of 'social risk'. As pointed out during parliamentary debates, the old-age risk insured by the 1910 law was definitely a social risk.

With respect to the conception of social insurance, study of the 1910 pension law can and should be undertaken from two complementary approaches. In the first place, how did insurance against old-age risks issue from a conception of worker insecurity that had formed elsewhere? What did it mean to objectify old age as a risk? What did old age thus become? What status was it accorded when made subject to compulsory insurance? In short, what conditioned the conception of old age as a risk? In the second place, what did old age itself bring to the notion of risk, as well as to pertinent institutions and programs? How did the specific problem of old age, at least in France, contribute to shaping the conception of social insurance, or social security?

The first set of questions leads to a study of the transition from individual foresight and private insurance in matters of protection and safety to social insurance for guaranteeing the security of workers' lives. The second set calls for study of the formative elements in the conception of social insurance.

FROM INDIVIDUAL PROVIDENT PROVISION FOR PROTECTION AND SAFETY....

The differences between schemes concerning old age at the beginning and end of the 19th century cannot be reduced to the nonexistence/existence of insurance. Old age, life, the life span and death had been, for a long time, subjects of insurance. In a way, they were the natural subjects for which policies were written up. Insurance served to justify government loans and entitlement to annuities. As long ago as the days of Mazarin, Tonti, his financier, invented the *tontine,* a financial formula based upon life expectancy. Johann de Witt, governor of the United Provinces, was the first to use mortality tables to calculate the reimbursement of government loans. Founded in 1787, the first French life insurance company, La Compagnie Royale, proposed, in its brochure, to be both a savings and a pension fund, and thus protect both rich and poor. With such examples in mind, Condorcet and the French revolutionaries were able to plan a vast system of state insurance.

Old age and its safeguards had been, since the 18th century, related to the idea of insurance. During the 19th century, however, changes occurred in programs as well as in the institutional forms that insurance assumed. New conceptions governed both practices with regard to old age and the rationality behind such practices.

La Caisse d'Epargne

This savings bank was the first institution created during the 19th century in order to insure workers against what were then called life 'crises' or 'accidents'. It opened in 1818 in Paris with headquarters in the offices of the Compagnie d'Assurances Générales. It corresponded to a purely liberalist plan. The underlying idea was that everybody was and must be made responsible for his fate. Accordingly, there was neither economic nor social responsibility for poverty, and the poor had no right to claim assistance. They had to help themselves by applying a fundamental social value, namely by being provident (Duchatel, 1836; Thiers, 1850). This did not mean that the rich, or those upon whom fortune had smiled, had no obligation toward the poor, but rather that this obligation should not be subject to legal measures. The duty of the rich consisted in 'moralizing' the poor and needy, in motivating and educating them to become provident, and in making available the means, such as savings funds, through which they could look after themselves.

The Caisse d'Epargne, which was but an elementary application of insurance principles, contained the idea that protection came from property, from capital accumulation, which would enable workers to rise above their condition. Labor mobility and savings mobility were essential to this institution (Thiers, 1850). To its credit, this system not only permitted families to accumulate savings that were not lost at the saver's death but also freed workers from being tied down to their company.

Conceived to be a universal means for being provident, this savings bank stood upon the idea that social differences resulted not from the division of society into classes but from fortuitous accidents and individuals' moral virtues. Thus was excluded the idea that individuals as wage-earners could and should be linked throughout their lives to their social status in the production process (Thiers, 1850).

The privilege granted this savings bank came under criticism as the important worker surveys of 1830-40 revealed the reality of 'pauperism'. Pauperism took workers in large-scale industry to be members of a class apart who were, in many ways, subject to their class environment and whose lives were conditioned by social and economic factors. As a consequence of these environmental determinants, workers could not themselves save or guarantee their own safety and protection.

This criticism of the Caisse d'Epargne, as well as the specific needs of industrialization, shifted the emphasis to friendly societies and to employers' funds. Grenado's *La Bienfaisance Publique* (1839) can be taken to mark this shift. A new program of provision for protection and safety would support a new scheme of insurance.

Les Sociétés de Secours Mutuels

These friendly societies — fraternal or mutual aid associations — were not all eliminated by the 1791 Le Chapelier Act, which, in order to prevent the formation not only of guilds but of any intermediary between citizens and the state, forbade master craftsmen and workers from joining an association, with each other as well as among themselves. These worker associations in friendly societies, more or less tolerated by the government, continued developing in the early 19th century (Laurent, 1862). The specifically working class friendly societies were what we can call fraternal orders with funds for various, undefined risks. They aimed to provide relief to members of their families in case of need. Much more was promised than could be supplied, but that had little importance insofar as these funds were destined not to settle the problem of pauperism but to provide mutual aid. As their names indicated, they offered assistance whenever workers were forced to stop work or take time off because of sickness, old age, accidents, injuries or unemployment.

The friendly societies became the center of attention for liberal philanthropists, who took them to be the necessary counterpart to the inadequate savings banks. Inasmuch as they were installed as the principal means of protection, the family mutuality of which they had given proof became a shortcoming. These societies would have to be developed since they were evidence of provident workers' foresight; but this development entailed rationalizing them so that they could keep their promises. The problem of pensions became a major means for this rationalization.

Until that time, old age had been among the 'accidents' of life that could deprive workers of their wages. It was but a type of disability. While still being so, it became, in addition, a specific cause of disability that had to be not only providently foreseen but also calculated in order to effectively apply foresight. The friendly societies could no longer be run like fraternities, but had to operate under legally binding contracts. This requirement entailed a rationalization in accordance with the laws of a science that could guarantee the execution of contracts, namely actuarial insurance. The key-note was that they had to adhere to the principles of insurance.

Employers' Pension Funds

Whereas friendly societies, even though they did welcome benefactors as members, were of working class origin, the employers' pension funds proceeded from a different principle (See Le Play, 1881 and *La Réforme Sociale*, a periodical publication by his followers). The second type of institution in this new scheme was directly related to the needs of industrialization — the employers' need to maintain a loyal and disciplined work force.

Employers, at least those in big industry, did not conceive of their relationship with workers in terms of common law or of a hiring contract; for such a contract was based upon an overly 'economistic' view of work and of business activities and, moreover, presupposed the freedom and equality of contracting parties. Employers' dealings with employees involved exchanging not wages for labor but rather one service for another. In return for the service offered by workers, an employer owed them protection and had to ensure that loyal workers' needs would be satisfied.

This conception, embodied in the principle of *permanence des engagements,* lay behind employers' pension funds. Accordingly, even if a worker contributed to such a fund, retirement was not a right but a privilege, a favor or a reward. He could not profit from the fund unless he remained loyal to the company; he lost all benefits if he freely quit his job or were dismissed.

This was another form of retirement, as a reward for good and loyal service. Conversely, the loss of the 'right' to retirement was a punishment. This way of protecting workers, though virtually exclusive to large-scale industry, would have major importance in a later period.

La Caisse Nationale des Retraites

During the 1848 uprising, problems of safety and protection were debated in the Constituent Assembly and the Legislative Assembly. Out of these debates came the two 1850 laws about, on the one hand, friendly societies and, on the other, the creation of a National Retirement Fund. These two laws innovated on the previous situation. Though reasserting the role of charity, they recognized the need to rationalize institutions through the 'science of insurance'. This rationalization entailed the clear-cut separation of risks. In particular, the risk of sickness, which was left up to the friendly societies, was separated from the risk of old age, which only a state institution could insure correctly. Among its effects, this rationalization through insurance methods brought about *state intervention* — the principal innovation in this legislation.

State intervention could not yet compel people to take out policies. Instead, it arose from the state's duty to encourage and stimulate people to be provident. The institution of the National Retirement Fund did not split with previous old-age programs. On the contrary, it was intended to reinforce them by providing more effective and pertinent means and by increasing the number and solidity of existing institutions.

This scheme for handling matters of protection and safety became the target of reformers at the end of the century. The 1910 law on workers' and farmers' retirement became the occasion for evaluating past programs. The National Retirement Fund, though based upon voluntary contributions and reformed in 1886, proved to be a failure. In 1903, only 2 percent of workers were contributors, and most payments were made collectively, usually by employers. The pensions paid out were ridiculous; 'the average did not reach the rate of 50 centimes per day' (Imbert, 1905, p. 37). The friendly societies also proved incapable of insuring retirement. As for the employers' funds, only a tiny number (3 percent) of workers benefited from them; 'the employers' personal effort is so weak that its general effects must be considered to be of no account' (Guieysse, 1900, p. 721).

To summarize, a century after their formulation, programs based upon individual foresight for provision of protection and safety turned out to lack the force and capacity of a program that could handle problems of workers' security. A new scheme had to be drawn up, namely, social insurance.

....TO SOCIAL INSURANCE
FOR SECURITY

This new insurance scheme gave rise to: labor legislation; the modern definition of 'salaried' employment; and the establishment of social security institutions. In France, this scheme developed out of the problem of work-related accidents. A combination of circumstances made it necessary to treat occupational hazards before retirement. In particular, work-related accidents directly raised the question of liability, a central question in any insurance policy. Social insurance implied changing the system of liability that had prevailed under liberalist programs. The new system that would preside over social insurance and, thus, over the risks of old age took shape around what is known as the occupational risk.

Occupational Risk

This complex notion, as developed by MPs from 1880 to 1898, was at the confluence of judicial, economic, social and political concerns.

The phrase expressed a new principle of liability. According to the Civil Code, a person was responsible only for his faults. Henceforth, a company head would be held responsible for accidents to his workers even though he had committed no fault and, moreoever, had taken measures to avoid such accidents. This conception of liability was entirely different from that which had informed past programs: it implied that an individual's safety could be made the responsibility of someone else. At the same time, accidents were 'normalized'; they were no longer exceptional events to be avoided through safety measures taken by employers. Accidents were regular occurrences, their regularity being a function of the type of company. Correlatively, imprudent or heedless acts by workers were not faults to be punished; they became risks that, like the explosion of a machine, entailed the employer's liability (unless the worker had committed an inexcusable fault, which, properly speaking, involved neither heedlessness nor lack of precaution).

This conception of accidents as a risk and the new principle of liability went along with a new definition of the contract binding employer and employee. This is the modern definition of the employment contract. In liberalist thought, the contractual relationship between employer and employee was limited to the exchange of wages for labor. Even though all their obligations did not reduce down to this exchange, it was the only aspect that could be legally sanctioned. Basing their jurisprudence upon articles 1382 ff. of the Civil Code, the courts added an obligation of safety at the employers' cost. The employee-employer relationship was thus subject to a double obligation under contract and as a tort.

The 1898 law introducing liability for occupational hazards made this double obligation into the source of the employment contract, which defined the employee's status as legal dependency. The employer became, in a way, a general debtor who owed safety to his employees as creditors, because of their dependency (Savatier, 1964).

The elaboration of the phrase 'occupational risk' gave rise to a general judicial interpretation, the theory of risk drawn out of article 1384 of the Civil Code about the responsibility for things in one's custody. The notion of risk as contained in this phrase would be applied broadly, beyond work-related accidents. It opened up the way toward a new system of liability, which would be more just, more equitable and more appropriate.

> More than ever, modern life is a question of risks...An accident happens. Someone has to bear the consequences, either the author of the accident or the victim...Who has to bear them? Necessarily, in accordance with reason and justice, this must be the person who, by acting, assumed responsibility for the consequences of his acts and of his activity (Saleilles, 1897, p. 5).

Old Age as a Social Risk

Occupational risk, once elaborated out of the debate about work-related accidents, remained ambiguous. MPs, or at least some of them, saw therein an exceptional notion that applied only to work-related accidents. Nonetheless, its elaboration led to the formulation of new — general, legal and political — principles. The 1898 law, though exceptional, had a universal dimension.

The question of workers' and farmers' retirement resolved this equivocation. The law about work-related accidents would not be an exception. It inaugurated a new program of security. Social risk superceded occupational risk.

The term 'social risk' was coined by Léon Say during parliamentary debate about work-related accidents:

> You have abolished the principle of occupational risk, and thereby, you have made visible what I called, but a short while ago, the principle of social risk. By extending the field upon which you have developed your law, you have managed to cover all industries and all farmers...(Say, 1893, p. 308).

For Say, occupational risk, if extended to a maximum, became a social risk. Extending the risk of accidents to other risks constituted the first definition of social risk.

Within the law on workers' and farmers' retirement, the idea of social risk was broadened in three ways. First of all, it was made correlative to the notion of social debt as formulated in the doctrine of *solidarité*.

> By producing more than what was strictly indispensable, the preceding generations have been able to more surely follow the road of progress. But new social strata, while acknowledging the debts contracted earlier, have the right to ask whether the distribution of this common legacy with its assets and liabilities has been made with justice and equity. The reply to this question is, unfortunately and only too obviously, negative. (Guieysse, 1900, p. 721)

Accordingly, a general social debt existed and had to be insured by the whole society. This conception of social risk was expressed in the opposition between bills proposed by the government and, for instance, by Mirman who wanted disability insurance for all, whether wage-earners or not. Parliament decided to separate assistance (the 1905 law) from old age (the 1910 law) so as to distinguish old age from disability. The latter was defined as the inability to work whereas the former was marked by age itself. Old-age as well as accident insurance necessarily involved a scheme of payments in advance. Why insure retirement at the age of 65 rather than 60 or 55? The answer partly depends upon the capacity to finance a given retirement age.

Secondly, the conception of social risk was influenced by the idea of prevention. In the foregoing, it designated a social debt. But if an individual had the right to have his security guaranteed by society, society had the right to obligate the improvident to have foresight in spite of themselves, whence the principle of compulsory insurance.

Thirdly, a sort of synthesis of the preceding two points further determined the conception of social risk whereby the insecurity of each became a social problem. Although poverty was an individual affair, its impact as well as the consequent social insecurity and danger were matters of general social concern. The causes of insecurity — sickness, accidents, old age — had a global social cost that society, once determined to insure them, had to control and, if possible, reduce. Social risk, social security or social insurance therefore had implications beyond mere compensation. They had to be placed as preventive measures at the center of modern programs of security. Vaillant developed this conception under the term 'social insurance'.

SOCIAL RISK AS A
GENERAL CONCEPTION

Just as occupational hazard gave rise to a general theory of risk, social risk — which, in fact, debate about workers' and farmers' retirement made 'social' — was discussed at the same time in a completely different context and field. It served as the basis for the 1895 law on compensation for judicial errors. Likewise, it was used by the Conseil d'Etat, the highest administrative tribunal, to hold the state responsible. Furthermore, it attained legislative recognition in the laws on compensation for war damages. These uses of social risk were a result neither of mere homonymy nor of lexical coincidence. The same conceptions of liability and security were at work in both the judicial notion of compensation for risks and the philosophical concept of solidarity.

This opens up an entire new field for research. This coincidence should help us look at social and worker history in a different way. Accordingly, we can no longer describe only the wretched conditions in which workers lived or merely relate the struggles to better these conditions. We have to show how these struggles were able to produce a truth. They thus take on a truly universal dimension.

REFERENCES

Condorcet, (1794), *Esquisse d'un tableau historique de l'esprit humain,* 10ème période.
Duchatel, (1836), *De La Charité* (Paris).
Gerando (1839), *La Bienfaisance publique* (Paris).
Guieysse (1900), 'Rapport au nom de la commission d'assurance et de prévoyance sociales de la Chambre des Députés', annex 1502 of the *Journal Officiel,* 3 September.
Imbert (1905), *Les Retraites des travailleurs* (Paris).
Laurent, E. (1862), *Le Paupérisme et les associations de prévoyances* (Paris).
Le Play, Frédéric (1881) and his followers in their periodical, *La Réforme Sociale.*
Saleilles, R. (1897), *Les Accidents du travail et la responsabilité civile* (Paris).
Savatier, R. (1964), *Métamorphoses du Droit Civil* (Paris).
Say, L. (1893), *Annales Parlementaires de la Chambre des Députés,* 18 May.
Thiers, *Rapport au nom de la commission d'assistance en 1850.*
Vaillant (1901), *Annales Parlementaires de la Chambre des Députés,* 10 June, pp. 309ff.

7

THE STATE, THE ECONOMY AND RETIREMENT

Chris Phillipson
University of Keele

INTRODUCTION

The main concern of this paper is to explore connections between the institutionalization of retirement and the political economy of Western capitalism (focusing, in particular, on the British experience). I shall examine how this political economy has influenced the way in which workers think about retirement, giving some attention to debates about retirement ages and the provision of state and occupational pensions.

THE POLITICAL ECONOMY OF RETIREMENT

In the case of Britain (as with many other capitalist economies) there has been a major change in the age distribution of labor, with a sharp decline in economic activity rates for men beyond pensionable age (the rate for men aged 65 plus fell from 31.1 percent in 1951 to 15.9 percent in 1976). The male economic activity rate has been in decline since 1890, the start of the so-called 'scientific revolution' in the capitalist economies. The decline has intensified over the postwar period, with the most rapidly growing sectors in the economy drawing upon married women as a key source of labor.

Changes in the composition of the labor force reflect a mixture of economic, sociological and political factors. First, Wedderburn (1975) suggests that there have been changes in the industrial and occupational structure which have reduced the number of semi-and unskilled jobs available for men with limited educational qualifications. It has also been argued that employers are unwilling to retain or hire older men, when stronger, better trained, and often less costly personnel are available. An additional factor in the depressed employment opportunities for older men would be the increased availability of middle-aged women for clerical, professional and service work (Clark and Spenger, 1980).

Secondly, the institutionalization of retirement may be seen as complementing the role of education in stimulating occupational and social mobility. Permanent retirement at 60 or 65 has — historically at least — helped to mask the reality of shrinking employment in capitalist economies, assisting the flow of personnel through work institutions.[1]

Thirdly, it could be argued that changes in the labor process in capitalist economies have produced a working environment unfavourable to the retention of older workers (in the American car industry, for example, the average age of retirement is 58 years, a phenomenon which reflects both the existence of occupational pensions and the rigorous nature of assembly-line work: Beynon, 1973; Friedmann and Orbach; 1974). Fixed retirement ages may also be seen by management to have the advantage of: (a) preventing people from growing old in their jobs; (b) avoiding lengthy decision-making by individuals about when to retire; (c) providing a means of promotion for lower-level personnel.

Fourthly, adherence to fixed retirement ages may also be regarded as providing a politically more 'neutral' solution to the crisis of unemployment, the fear of tension amongst young people and workers with families outweighing concern about the psychological effects of retirement.

A final reason for the decline in economic activity rates is the increasing number of workers who are choosing to retire (given financial safeguards). Important contradictions remain in the way retirement is experienced (see below), but there is impressive evidence to suggest that it is now more acceptable amongst workers. Françoise Cribier's (1981) conclusions from a survey of Parisian retirees, can be extended to Britain and many other Western countries:

The image of retirement has changed, retiring before the age of 65 is becoming more and more acceptable in the public eye. There is an increase both in the proportion of people content to retire and in those who would like to retire earlier. The new retirees are younger, healthier, better off. They have a more positive view of retirement, either as rest, relaxation, TV and family life, or as a new and active phase with more social, intellectual, and leisure activity — the latter being typically a middle-class pattern. Whatever the life style, retirement is seen as a positive gain corresponding to the workers' expectations; they want to retire earlier, to take better advantage of retirement and for a longer period. It is interesting to note that this aspiration for early retirement, always presented as a new phenomenon, was widely held by those petit and moyenne bourgeoisie in nineteenth-century France who lived on private income as soon as they had accumulated enough capital; it is Balzac's story of the shopkeeper who lives on 'beans at three pence a litre' in order to be able to retire at 50 (p. 68).

RETIREMENT TRENDS: THE POST-WAR EXPERIENCE

In the previous section we discussed the main reasons for the emergence of retirement. However, it might be argued that the precise role to be accorded to retired people, the degree to which they can expect financial support from the state, and the extent to which this period in the life-cycle can be welcomed unequivocally, is a matter of debate within capitalism. Concern about the elderly's 'lack of productivity' has been an important theme in postwar social policy. Writing in the late 1940s, for example, E.M. Hubback (1947) argued:

> From the point of view of the community it is indeed far more encouraging to spend money on children, since this expenditure can be regarded as a hopeful investment, than to spend it on old people — desirable as this may be from the point of view of individual happiness (p. 134).

And a PEP report (1948) commented:

> Clearly, as Lord Keynes suggested, there is a danger that an increasing ratio of retired dependent people to productive workers will reduce the buoyancy of state revenue while adding to the cost of social services (p. 84).

In its management of an ageing population, capitalism has tried to achieve two main objectives. First, whilst institutionalizing retirement around (in the case of Britain) the ages of 60 (female) and 65 (male), there have also been attempts, at different historical periods, to encourage earlier or later retirement. In the latter case where, for example, there has been a shortage of younger workers, the state has emphasized the burden of dependency arising from an aging population: a burden which may be lifted if older workers are prepared to remain at work. In the former case where, for example, there is a surplus of younger workers, older people are urged to accept redundancy and early retirement. For younger people, unemployment is described as a tragic waste; for older people, on the other hand, it is represented as a time to explore new opportunities for leisure (government propaganda for the job-release scheme is a good illustration of this). [2]

The state's second objective has been concerned with controlling demands that retired people may make for financial, welfare and cultural resources (Phillipson, 1982). Thus, while the broad political and economic framework surrounding retirement is fairly well-established, its sociological dimensions (the status of retired people, attitudes towards retirement, etc.) are difficult to unravel. Uncertainty and ambiguity still surround the period of retirement, aspects which continue to be exploited in the organization of social and economic resources for older people.

In the second section of this paper I want to examine the operation of these objectives and their influence on general beliefs about the experience of retirement. In the case of the first objective — flexibility over retirement age — we can identify two important periods in postwar British society. In the early 1950s considerable enthusiasm was expressed regarding the employment of older workers. From the late 1940s onwards the Ministry of Labour's annual reports started appeals to people to stay at work, appeals which became increasingly strident up to the mid-1950s. In his 1951 Budget speech, Hugh Gaitskell argued that the corollary of the reduction in hours of work, the increased holidays, and the later ages at which people now entered employment was that 'we should work longer and retire later' (Hansard, 1950-51, col. 849). He suggested an upward revision of the pension age. A few days later Fred Lee, Parliamentary Secretary to the Minister of Labour, made an impassioned appeal to older people thinking of retirement:

> I ask them to think again. Some of us may have become accustomed to the idea of retiring at a fixed age of 60-65, but a man of 65 can today look forward to a long period of useful life. I have no doubt that many people would have a happier and healthier old age if they continue in their work a little longer rather than give up their routine and sink into a premature old age. (Hansard, 1950-51, col. 1396)

Three factors underpin this enthusiasm for employing older workers. First, there was a considerable manpower shortage in the postwar period in many parts of the country, and as the Minister of Labour pointed out in 1952 'old people are one of our few reserves of labour' (NOPWC, 1952, p. 52). Secondly, there was a renewed sense of pessimism about the demographic balance between the productive and nonproductive sectors of the population (Royal Commission on Population, 1949). Thirdly, there were gloomy forecasts about the prospects for future economic growth. A combination of these factors increased pressure for people to delay their retirement.

This environment had two important consequences. First, there were a number of investigations into the work potential of the elderly. At a governmental level, there was the National Advisory Committee on the Employment of Older Men and Women (formed in 1952). At a more academic level, numerous projects emerged to look at questions such as retraining older workers, their accident rate in industry, their ability to learn new skills, and so on (Clay, 1960). In general terms, most of the projects were optimistic about the value of older workers to industry. Moreover, they contributed to a wider debate that work had therapeutic value to individuals and that to deny its availability — via compulsory retirement — was morally wrong. Optimistic findings from the work of researchers were convenient for those expressing concern about the economic effects of retirement. Of additional help was a range of medical and sociological studies suggesting that retirement was detrimental to the health of older men: anxiety, suicide, and premature death being listed among its consequences (Sheldon, 1948; Logan, 1953; Anderson and Cowan, 1956).

I would argue that what developed in this period of the 1950s was the manufacture of a myth concerning 'the trauma of retirement'. Trauma may well be an appropriate description for a situation where income falls by 50 percent or more. However, the perspective adopted in this period was that it was loss of work *itself* which was central, financial loss being of secondary importance. Evidence to support 'the trauma of retirement' was (and remains) remarkably limited (Minkler, 1981). Many of the studies quoted in evidence worked from small and usually nonrandom samples. Methodological problems were, however, usually ignored in government propaganda, and the view that 'to work longer is to live longer' became the touchstone of wisdom in manpower policy.

RETIREMENT IN THE 1980s
AND 1990s

The position of the older worker in the labor market has changed dramatically from the period discussed above. The effects of a world economic recession, and a weakening in Britain's position vis-à-vis other capitalist economies, have produced high levels of unemployment. Moreover, long-term changes in technology are turning temporary slumps in employment into a permanent fixture. As a number of writers have recently argued, an important trend in the 1950s and 1960s in most capitalist countries was the increased pace of technological innovation and the adoption of advanced labor-saving techniques. Gamble and Walton (1975) suggest that this process intensified in the 1970s with a new range of innovation based on computers and electronics. They argue that:

> Increasingly large numbers of workers are [being]displaced from the productive process and have to find jobs in the burgeoning service section. As Marx foresaw in 'Grundrisse', the historical tendency of capitalist accumulation is to reduce necessary labour to the minimum so as to increase surplus labour to the maximum. The rate of exploitation is raised by employing ever fewer workers, ever more machines, and thus increasing productivity to its furthest extent (p. 161).

This economic and technological environment was to shift once more the position of the elderly in the labor market, as it was to change ideologies concerning retirement. The crude celebration of the work ethic, evident in much government propaganda in the early 1950s, was substantially altered. People had now to accept the need for redundancies, for 'shake-outs', and early retirement. Britain's economic position (and the condition of her industry) demanded a smaller and more efficient workforce. Given also that a high birth rate in the early 1960s was now resulting in a boom of young workers, it was the replacement of the old with the young which was to become a strong theme in government policy (e.g. the job release scheme).

Throughout the 1970s there was an accelerated withdrawal of older workers from the labor market. Economic activity rates among men aged 55-59 fell quite sharply from 93 percent to 88 percent; amongst men of 60-64 the decline was even greater — from 85 percent to 75 percent (OPCS, 1980). Older workers continued to be disproportionately affected by redundancies, although the use of early retirement options served to mask the numbers involved (Oliver, 1982).

In the space of thirty years we have thus seen a remarkable turn-around in labor policies towards the retired. In the present context, the turn towards permanent retirement is also leading towards attempts to deflate demands and expectations which may emerge from the retired population. The state is, in fact, expanding the retired population, whilst at the same time attempting to channel expectations into acceptable forms.

CONTROLLING DEMAND

At the present time we see the state and private capital involved in a number of policies designed to restrict claims which retired people can make on society. At a very general level, retired people experience contradictory feelings about propaganda which encourages a view of retirement as relaxation and opportunity for leisure, whilst finding that the state pension (for a married couple) is worth only 50 percent of the take home pay of an industrial worker. Such feelings are reinforced by the way in which state benefits and occupational pensions are organized. In the case of the former, a minimum of 600,000 are failing to claim supplementary benefit, even though they are entitled to it (Walker, 1980). Although emphasis has been placed on the extent to which individuals fail to claim because of the stigma attached to a means test, the obstacles which the state places in the way of claiming (poorly trained staff, badly-designed forms, etc.), are of equal importance.

The organization of occupational pensions is a good example of how the process of pensions and other benefits becomes mystified and removed from the daily experience of workers. Only half of British pension funds have any provision for workers participating in the management of the fund (Pelly and Wise, 1980). Beynon and Wainwright's (1978) description of events at Vickers when the company introduced a new pension scheme is probably not atypical:

> At Vickers this involved discussions with certain national officials of the unions, the setting up of the pension scheme (with agreed contributions and benefits) and the selection of trade union trustees for the pension fund. All this was carried out in London. There was no discussion with the workers in the plants and no member of the AUEW (the majority union representing manual workers in the company) was selected as a trustee. The matter was signed and sealed as a fait accompli (p. 148).

Individuals close to the point of retirement may also be ignorant about the amount of pension they are likely to receive, and the way it has been calculated. Pre-retirement education is only available to a minority of employees (around 6 percent in the UK) with women working part-time and all unskilled workers being under-represented amongst those attending courses (Phillipson, 1981).

The demands that older people may make on society are also controlled by social policies which emphasize the contribution they can make to caring and supportive roles. Thus, as women reach middle and early old age, they may experience a range of new restrictions. Many will, in fact, find themselves involved in supportive and caring roles almost as demanding as those experienced at earlier stages of the life-cyle. The key point, therefore, is that the caring role allocated to women may be moved to various points in the life-cycle. As a consequence, even if a woman wishes to break away from this role, institutional support (in the form of work opportunities, day-care facilities for elderly parents, etc.) may be very limited. Indeed social policies towards women are currently intensifying the pressure upon them to assume formal or informal caring roles wherever possible (Phillipson, 1981; Equal Opportunities Commission, 1982).

Finally, it is important to bear in mind that state and occupational pensions reflect rather less a desire to improve the living standards of pensioners, rather more a concern to increase social harmony within the workforce (Ward, 1981; O'Connor, 1973). At the level of the state, increases in benefits for older people must be seen — at least in part — as symbolic acts of political propaganda. This is particularly well-illustrated in the case of the United States where amendments to the 1935 Social Security Act have almost always come in election years (Pratt, 1976). The lack of sustained commitment to improve material standards is represented in Britain by the bizarre juggling over indexation of pensions. The Department of Health and Social Security's discussion paper 'A Happier Old Age' (1978) proclaimed that with the index-linking of the state pension to prices or earnings (whichever rose faster) pensioners were assured of a 'continuing real...increase...in the value of [their] pension' (p.21). The link to earnings was abandoned two years later by a new Conservative government and the real value of the state pension, contrary to the discussion paper's intent, has declined. More recently, there have been suggestions from the government that the link with prices may also have to be dropped. Thus, within the space of three years, the state appears to be moving towards a dramatic reversal in its policy on pensions; a change which will mean a steep decline in the living standards of pensioners.

THE STATE, RETIREMENT AND
SOCIAL GERONTOLOGY

What these various elements represent is an ideological climate which conveys the idea of retirement as a *concession* by capitalism, one which may be partially withdrawn (in times of labor shortage), extended (in times of mass unemployment), and be subjected to cuts or increases in expenditure, depending on political elections and/or the need for social harmony. Seen in this light, it is scarcely surprising that theoretical debates within social gerontology should have been so dominated by approaches which stress the limited penetration of retirement within the social structure. What is perhaps more surprising is that proponents of a more radical political economy approach should see the lifting of age barriers as prerequisite to ending poverty and alienation in old age. Carroll Estes (1979) in her otherwise admirable study of the Older Americans Act, suggests that virtually all elderly people are capable of working beyond retirement age. Alan Walker (1980) speaks of the 'danger' that a change in the industrial structure will create demands for a lowering of the age of retirement.

Although this more radical political economy identifies poverty in old age as a reflection of 'low economic and social status prior to retirement' (Walker, 1981, p. 88), it sides with mainstream gerontology in emphasizing the individual's attachment to work and his/her distress at leaving the work environment. I would suggest, however, that both radical and orthodox approaches within gerontology over-emphasize the problem caused by compulsory retirement and exaggerate the virtues of flexible retirement. The key problem remains not the age at which people retire but the political and economic environment within which the institutions of work and retirement are located. In particular, I would suggest that the capitalist mode of production not only leads to unequal incomes which contribute to poverty in retirement, but, by limiting the access of workers to education throughout their lives and institutionalising the division between manual and mental labour, creates tensions and contradictions in the way workers experience retirement. Marx observes that: 'The worker feels himself at home only during his leisure, whereas at work he feels homeless' (Bottomore and Rubel, 1974). I would argue that retirement is still affected by this alienation within the workplace. The capitalist mode of production allows workers to develop only a limited range of skills (for some, none at all); it encourages methods of work (extensive overtime, continental shift systems), which make it difficult for workers to develop as individuals. When they retire — quite suddenly — they have the chance to do (they are told) all those things which work allowed no time for. But the contradictions are these: an active retirement depends on financial security, yet over 60 percent of retired people in Britain live in households which are below, at or close to the official poverty line; it requires a certain degree of health, yet one-third of manual workers retire in a poor state of health; it requires a range of educational and cultural facilities, yet present cuts in public expenditure are severely reducing opportunities in Adult Education and the university system.

The solution to these problems is unlikely to come through the lifting of age-barriers to the employment of older workers. Of more relevance would be the establishment of rights in retirement to which people are entitled: in the areas of health, finance, welfare, leisure, etc.; rights which cannot be removed simply through less favorable supplies of manpower or because of problems with inflation. Those who argue for flexible retirement ignore the increasing rigidities within the labor markets of capitalist societies. They ignore, also, that flexibility will only be operated on the employer's terms (i.e. he will have the ultimate say in the conditions on which the older worker is retained). Under these circumstances, flexibility may increase, rather than reduce, feelings of insecurity.

So far it has been the middle classes who have shaped the activities and institutions popularly associated with retirement. They have organized courses, produced magazines, pioneered retirement migration, and staffed every conceivable form of voluntary organization (including those concerned with the elderly). They have, in addition, accepted the reality of compulsory retirement, successfully achieving — and this is the true mark of their strength — occupational pensions. The images through which we view retirement are, then, essentially middle class. Whether working class people should respond with equal enthusiasm to these images is an important issue. Is having an addiction to plan, willingness to migrate, joining voluntary organizations, etc. an index of good adjustment? Many researchers and counsellors often assume that it is, and shape their research and retirement programs accordingly. I would suggest, however, that a critical task for sociologists of retirement will be to account for new forms of behavior and attitudes amongst working class people who are now facing unemployment and early retirement on a very large scale. Over the next few years these experiences may transform the theories and concepts we have developed about the period of retirement.

NOTES

The arguments of this paper are developed at greater length in the author's book, *Capitalism and the Construction of Old Age* (London, Macmillan Press, 1982.)

1. For American and British studies on the emergence of retirement see Graebner (1980) and Phillipson (1982).

2. The job-release scheme allows men of 64 years of age, and women of 59, to apply to leave work a year before official retirement age. If the employer agrees to release the individual, he must also agree to take someone from the unemployed register. Under the present scheme, the individual going on job-release receives a weekly tax free allowance of £50.50 pence (1981 rate).

REFERENCES

Anderson, W. F. & N. Cowan (1956),'Work and Retirement: Influences on the Health of Older Men', *The Lancet,* 29 December, pp. 1344-1347.

Beynon, H. (1973), *Working for Ford* (London, Allen Lane).

Beynon, H. and H. Wainwright (1979), *The Workers' Report on Vickers* (London, Pluto Press).

Bottomore, T. B. and M. Rubel (1974), *Karl Marx: Selected Writings in Sociology and Social Philosophy* (London, Pelican Books).

Clark, R. J. and J. J. Spengler (1980),*The Economics of Individual and Population Aging* (Cambridge. Cambridge University Press).

Clay, H. M. (1960), *The Older Worker and his Job* (London, HMSO)

Cribier, F. (1981), 'Changing Retirement Patterns of the Seventies: The Example of a Generation of Parisian Salaried Workers', *Ageing and Society,* Vol. 1, Part 1, pp. 51-72.

Department of Health and Social Security (1978), *A Happier Old Age: A Discussion Document on Elderly People in our Society* (London, HMSO).

Equal Opportunities Commission (1982), *Caring for the Elderly: Community Care Policies and Women's Lives* (Manchester, Equal Opportunities Commission).

Esland, G. and G. Salaman (1980), *Politics of Work and Occupations* (Milton Keynes, Open University Press).

Estes, C.L. (1979), *The Aging Enterprise* (San Francisco, Jossey Bass).

Friedmann, E. A. and H. L. Orbach (1974), 'Adjustment to Retirement', pp. 609-645 in S. Ariety (ed.), *American Handbook of Psychiatry,* Vol. 1 (New York, Basic Books).

Gamble, A. and P. Walton (1976), *Capitalism in Crisis: Inflation and the State* (London, Macmillan Press).

Graebner, W. (1980), *A History of Retirement* (New Haven, Conn., Yale University Press).

Hubback, E. M. (1947), *The Population of Britain* (London, Penguin Books).

Logan, W. P. D. (1953), 'Work and Age: Statistical Considerations', *British Medical Journal,* 28 November, pp. 1190-1193.

Ministry of Labour and National Service, *Annual Reports for 1947, 1950 and 1952* (London, HMSO, Command Nos. 7559, 8338 and 8893, 1948, 1951 and 1953).

Minkler, M. (1981), 'Research on the Health Effects of Retirement: An Uncertain Legacy', *Journal of Health and Social Behaviour,* Vol. 22, June, pp. 117-130.

National Advisory Committee on the Employment of Older Men and Women (1953), *First Report* (London, HMSO, Command No. 8963). National Old People's Welfare Council (NOPWC) (1952), *Report of the Sixth National Conference* (London, National Council of Social Services).

O'Connor, J. (1973), *The Fiscal Crisis of the State* (New York, St. Martins). Office of Population and Censuses and Surveys, (OPCS) (1980), *Monitor* (London, OPCS).

Oliver, C. (1982), *Older Workers and Unemployment* (London, Unemployment Alliance).

Parliamentary Debates (Hansard), *House of Commons Official Report,* Vol. 486, Nos. 83 and 86, 1951.

Pelly, D. and V. Wise (1980), *Trade Unions and Pensions' Funds* (London, CAITS, May).

Phillipson, C. (1981), 'Women in Later Life', in B. Hutter and G. Williams, *Controlling Women: The Normal and the Deviant* (London, Croom Helm).

Phillipson, C. (1981), 'Pre-Retirement Education: The British and American Experience', *Aging and Society,* Vol. 1, Part 3, pp. 393-413.

Phillipson, C. (1982), *Capitalism and the Construction of Old Age* (London, Macmillan Books).

Political and Economic Planning (PEP) (1948), *Population Policy in Great Britain* (London, PEP).

Pratt, H. (1976), *The Grey Lobby* (Chicago, University of Chicago Press).

Royal Commission on Population (1949), (London, HMSO, Command No. 7695).

Sheldon, J. H. (1948), *The Social Medicine of Old Age* (London, Nuffield Foundation).

Walker, A. (1980), 'The Social Creation of Poverty and Dependency in Old Age', *Journal of Social Policy*, Vol. 9, Part 1, pp. 49-75.

Walker, A. (1981) 'Towards a Political Economy of Old Age', *Ageing and Society*, Vol. 1, Part 1, pp. 73-94.

Ward, S. (1981), *Pensions: What to Look for in Company Pension Schemes and How to Improve Them* (London, Pluto Press).

Wedderburn, D. (1975), 'Prospects for the Re-Organization of Work', *Gerontologist*, Vol. 15, No. 3, pp. 236-241.

II

THE SOCIAL IMPACT
OF OLD AGE POLICIES

8

SOCIAL POLICY AND ELDERLY PEOPLE IN GREAT BRITAIN:
The Construction of Dependent Social and Economic Status in Old Age

Alan Walker
University of Sheffield

INTRODUCTION

Elderly people in all industrial societies occupy a generally low social and economic status in relation to younger adults. This is characterized chiefly by financial dependency on the state and may be illustrated by reference to their low incomes and restricted command over a wide range of other resources (Walker, 1980). In Great Britain about two-thirds of elderly people live in or on the margins of poverty, as defined by the state, compared with around one-fifth of the nonelderly (Layard, Piachaud and Stewart, 1978, p. 14). In the United States about one in every five elderly people has an income below the federally established minimum (Hendricks and Hendricks, 1977, p. 236). In Japan, 90 percent of elderly people have incomes in the lower half of the income distribution (Maeda, 1978, p. 61). A considerable body of similar information could be adduced to demonstrate the generally low level of income and other resources commanded by the elderly.

This low social and economic status has been accepted by society, including many gerontologists, as an inevitable consequence of advanced age, and as a result has received very little critical attention. One important reason for this acceptance is the domination in social policy, gerontology and popular discussion, of the life-cycle approach to need. Following Rowntree's (1901) pioneering studies of poverty and the life-cycle of family need, typical patterns of family development are superimposed on a chronological age scale and it is then assumed that periods of need are the natural result of age itself (Wynn, 1972). This effectively obscures inequalities between the elderly and younger people and amongst the elderly, as well as other social factors which play a part in determining need. Secondly, consideration of the activities of the state in relation to elderly people has been largely confined to an assessment of the beneficial or potentially beneficial aspects of; pension provision, residential accommodation and other social services. Although these social policies may be criticized for being inadequate in scope and coverage, they are usually accepted as wholly positive increments to the welfare of elderly people. The role of the state and state 'social policies' themselves in creating and enhancing dependency, therefore, has been largely overlooked.

The purpose of this paper is to argue that the 'dependency' of many elderly people and its severity consist of a structurally enforced inferior social and economic status in relation to the working population, and secondly, that social policies sponsored, directly or indirectly, by the state, occupy a central role in the creation and management of that dependency. On this basis we can explain not only the increased dependency amongst the elderly in the 20th century, but also the attitude of the state towards this group in periods of economic crisis. I am concerned primarily with the experience of Great Britain, but similar conclusions may well be drawn concerning the relationship between social policy and elderly people in other capitalist societies. My starting point is the relationship between social policy and social welfare.

SOCIAL POLICY
AND SOCIAL WELFARE

All societies have social policies and all societies have policies on aging. These may be implicit or explicit in the social institutions and groups developed and managed by different societies to achieve social ends. Here I am concerned primarily with social policies which stem directly or indirectly from the state, although social policies may also be based on purely private institutions. Indeed the assumption that public policies are synonymous with social policies is wholly false (Walker, 1981a) and has resulted, in Titmuss' (1963, p. 53) words, in 'a stereotype of social welfare which represents only the more visible parts of the real world of welfare'. Analysis of state social policies has, in turn, been restricted by two misconceptions about the nature of the welfare state and the relationship between social and economic policies, both of which have a direct bearing on our subsequent analysis of policies towards the elderly.

The epithet 'welfare state' is applied in all advanced capitalist societies to characterize first the different forms of intervention by the state in the private market to modify or change social conditions and secondly, the state provision of social services in cash or kind, usually in the form of social security, housing, social welfare, education and housing. According to the traditions of social policy analysis, and political and popular discourse, the purpose of this form of state intervention is to enhance welfare. The following definition of the welfare state is not untypical:

> A 'welfare state' is a state in which organised power is deliberately used (through politics and administration) in an effort to modify the play of market foces in at least three directions — first, by guaranteeing individual and families a minimum income irrespective of the market value of their work or their property; second, by narrowing the extent of insecurity by enabling individuals and families to meet certain 'social contingencies'....and third, by ensuring that all citizens without distinction of status or class are offered the best standards available in relation to a certain agreed range of social services (Briggs, 1961, p. 28).

The social construction of the welfare state represented in this quotation depends, first, on a limited conception of the state as a value-neutral coalition of all interests in society and of similarly neutral welfare state institutions, which are distinct from the social relations and values of other dominant institutions. Secondly, it rests on the assumption that welfare state institutions and social policies have the single function of promoting welfare.

There is no doubt that the welfare state in all capitalist societies has improved the absolute welfare of some groups, particularly elderly people, over the postwar period. But it would be wholly misleading to assess the welfare state in this one-dimensional way. It fails, for example, to account for the repressive aspects of the operation of some parts of the welfare state and the ambivalence of many of its clients (Fox Piven and Cloward, 1972). The reluctance of elderly people to claim social security benefits and to enter residential institutions is well documented (Walker, 1980; Hendricks and Hendricks, 1977; Tobin and Lieberman, 1976). To explain these aspects of the welfare state it is necessary to recast the dominant social construction and examine welfare state services within the context of the society in which they have been developed. This necessarily means that we are concerned solely with capitalist societies, because the structure of social relations is relative to the prevailing relations of production. This is not to imply that inequalities between old and young and amongst old people, and the adverse consequences of state social policies under discussion here are not also characteristic of other forms of society, but that their analysis requires detailed information about the precise assumptions and values underlying the development of those societies. In Westergaard's (1977, p. 165) terms, 'Different modes of production involve different modes of inequality'.

In fact the welfare state in capitalist societies reflects the contradictions embedded in those societies, and particularly the primary contradiction between the forces of production, the increasing productive power of labor and the relations of production, the continued private appropriation of surplus value (Gough, 1979, p. 11). Thus the state will operate to ensure the continued accumulation of capital and therefore the continued existence of the dominant mode of production and its attendant social relations. This process may be secured through welfare state, as much as other institutions in the form of social policies which both promote welfare and exert control. In other words, the welfare state '...simultaneously embodies tendencies to enhance social welfare, to develop the powers of individuals, to exert social control over the blind play of market forces; and tendencies to repress and control people, to adapt them to the requirements of the capitalist economy' (Gough, 1979, p. 12). So rather than representing an antithesis of capitalist values and social relations, the welfare state reflects them. The welfare state, therefore, embodies the same contradictions as any other social institutions in capitalist societies (Ginsburg, 1979, p. 2).

The welfare state consists of a set of institutions in societies whose primary impulses are geared towards the maximization of profit and the accumulation of capital. A welfare state based on wholly different principles to those which dominate distribution in the market could not survive, since it would cut across and interfere with them. Moreoever, the assumption that the development of these distinct institutions is possible, ignores the fact that the state itself is not a neutral agent, but is the embodiment of the dominant forces of production it seeks to reproduce. The state in capitalist society acts to promote the maintenance and reproduction of capitalist social relations and especially the continued accumulation of capital, but this is not its sole sphere of action because the state must also contend with countervailing pressure from opposing class forces. Thus working-class groups and organized labor have successfully argued for enlarged welfare provision and the state has, at times willingly and at others unwillingly, complied. The result is a welfare state which may at the same time enhance welfare and perpetuate unequal social relations, which may establish nonmarket principles of distribution such as need and reinforce the prevailing system of distribution.

But the welfare state is not, as Bismarck implied, a concession to the working class, because it performs a dual role and, therefore, has conceded few fundamental principles. Nor can it be assumed that the positive aspects of the welfare state are the result of working-class pressure while the negative aspects result from capitalist domination. The interests of capital accumulation may in different historical contexts be served by measures which enhance the welfare of certain groups; the case of state pensions is one example pursued later. Although the precise balance of the different interests represented varies between and within welfare state programs, the resulting institutions conform with dominant social and economic values. Thus social security benefits are not distributed according to need since the state defines both need and the social response to it and therefore these benefits do not challenge market principles of distribution. Yet as Leonard (1979, p. viii) has pointed out, the social construction of welfare institutions as maximizing human welfare has proved attractive to the modern state:

> The concept of the welfare state as a human response to need has performed an invaluable ideological function in the control and discipline of working-class populations, for in the name of 'welfare' much can be achieved which would be impossible by more direct methods of repression.

The second misconception stems in part from this social construction of the welfare state and social services as necessarily beneficial to welfare, that is, that a simple distinction may be drawn between economic and social policies. In fact, as the current economic crises in several industrial societies indicate, the economic aims of government policies cannot be disassociated from their social effects (Walker, 1982). Economic policy and economic management embody assumptions about society and social relations and are therefore, in part, also social policies. This false division, sustained by similar divisions in academic inquiry, has enabled the modern capitalist state to maintain the belief that advances in social welfare for groups such as the elderly depend on economic growth. By setting clear national goals and order of priorities this belief both protects the prevailing distribution of resources between different groups in society, and helps to ensure the achievement of the necessary climate for capital accumulation.

It is clear then that a consideration of the relationship between aging and social policy must take as its starting point the dominant values of the society in which those policies are framed. The social policies and institutions within which the 'problems' of aging are defined and managed reflect rather than contradict dominant values in society. These 'social' policies cannot be disassociated from the organization of production and decisions about the management of the economy, because these are even more crucial in determining the social status and living standards of the elderly. Changes in the way in which production is organized, for example, have a direct bearing on the development of retirement and age restrictive practices. The goal of profit maximization has provided the economic rationale for the superannuation of large numbers of older workers at a fixed age and for the compulsory withdrawal of younger workers from the labour market at an earlier age due to ill-health (Walker, 1981). If, in turn, the economy is deflated and managed at a reduced level of production in order to further economic and social goals, as under the Thatcher and Reagan administrations in Britain and the United States, there are important implications for elderly people. Recent economic policies in Britain have increased unemployment and reduced public expenditure on the social services; both have had a direct impact on elderly people by reducing their economic activity, cutting their pensions and reducing the support they receive from the personal social services. When these implications of economic management are coupled with values in capitalist societies which, partly due to assumptions about relative productivity, favor youth over elderly people, and more importantly, with the necessity of maintaining the work ethic amongst young people in a period of high unemployment, the economic and social status of elderly people is clearly precarious.

Aging and Social Policy

The approach to social policy and aging discussed here differs from the more familiar tendency in the gerontological literature to discuss aging and elderly people as if they were a distinct social minority, in isolation from social values and processes, particularly the process of production. We are concerned primarily with the relationship between the way production is organized and the social and political institutions and processes of society, such as pensions and retirement, and therefore our starting point is the organization of production and the social relations which it fosters (Walker, 1981). In other words there is a structural relationship between elderly people and the rest of society and amongst different groups of the elderly based on the social relations of production. The social and economic status of elderly people is defined not by biological age but by the institutions organized wholly or partly on production. Social policies are, therefore, part of the process of defining old age in different societies. Policies in social security, education and retirement, determine the period of working life and since work is the main source of economic status in all industrial societies, those outside of the labor market occupy a relatively deprived status.

The stereotype of elderly people as a homogeneous group with special needs has tended to dominate public attitudes and social policies towards this group. Approaches to age and aging based on the implicit assumption that the elderly can be treated as a distinct social group, in isolation from the rest of the social structure, have not provided an adequate basis for an explanation of the reduced social status of elderly people and the subordinate status of some groups amongst them. Social policies have been related closely to age, particularly retirement age, rather than to the specific needs associated with, say, disability. Needs are assumed to arise at different stages of the life-cycle, one crucial stage of which is retirement. Little attention has been paid, therefore, to the *differential* impact of retirement and other social processes on elderly people, especially the class and sex divisions in retirement experience. Secondly, the life-cycle approach to need has tended to obscure inequalities between elderly people and younger adults. Thirdly, by creating or reinforcing negative stereotypes through the portrayal of elderly people as a group with unique needs, there is a danger that a 'dysfunctional tension' will be set up between the elderly and the rest of society (Etzioni, 1976, p. 21). Resentment towards the elderly has not been openly and consistently articulated in British society, but periodic expressions of alarm at the 'burden' of dependency may be seen as one result of socially divisive attitudes and policies. Although they reflect a crude agism these attitudes cannot be so lightly dismissed since to do so would ignore significant variations in status and experience between different groups of elderly people. Alternative explanations of both widespread dependent status and deep-seated deprivation amongst some groups are called for.

It is important for policy-makers and practitioners to recognize that the process of assigning dependent status on the basis of age is a social and not a biological construct. There is no necessary relationship between chronological age and need or dependency (Walker, 1980). Even at the extremes of age, physical dependency is associated with functional ability rather than with age as such. But even this relationship between disability and physical dependency is by no means clear cut, because financial resources, aids and adaptations may mitigate this need to some extent. Yet the social security systems of most countries do not recognize the financial need created by disablement in old age.

The combined effects of different policies in the spheres of industrial organization and income maintenance are to disengage many of the elderly from the working population and from participation in productive activity. On the one hand society defines work as the main device for establishing a normal family life and on the other it denies access to work to some groups, including the elderly. Yet in the face of this *social* creation of dependency our categorization of, and response to, the 'problems' of old age are individually based. So, for example, the official British government publication on the elderly speaks of the measures taken *to care for* the elderly (Central Office of Information, 1974, p. 1). Stress is placed on individual response to aging through different social service agencies, rather than on the structural relationship between the elderly and the rest of society and the link between dependency and the creation of need. As I have argued, this approach stems from the fact that social policies reflect ideological assumptions concerning industrial and social values and these are the same values which also underlie the growth of dependency.

Individually based responses to the disengagement of the elderly by society through social and other agencies, also serve important social functions, such as control and the neutralization of conflict. By defining the problem of dependency in old age in individual terms, in theory it becomes manageable and more easy to solve. Of course it is not, but by concentrating on individual problems, on techniques of intervention and on a definition of the problem, social service agencies perform the function of de-politicizing issues such as the social creation of dependency and social division of deprivation. Similarly, use of apparently neutral terms such as 'helping' and 'care' hides the fact that the social definitions are *imposed* on elderly people by social policies and the agencies which apply them (Edelman, 1977, p. 67). In fact state social policies in Britain have both failed to counteract the imposition of the social costs of change on the elderly and other groups, and have not compensated the elderly, at least sufficiently to eradicate poverty, for bearing these costs.

Social services provide conditional welfare or rights to minimum welfare and thereby maintain the primacy of wage-labor and the market as a source of welfare. Thus as well as ensuring the welfare of elderly people in advanced industrial societies state social policies are an important aspect of the social process which defines the boundaries of old age, its membership and social status. Social policies are one of the means by which such societies are made more rigidly age stratified. The definition of old age in Britain also effectively sets the limits to full working life and therefore there is a critical relationship between policies on aging and policies on employment; a relationship that is obscured by concentrating on a set age as the criterion for the allocation of resources to elderly people. This socially constructed relationship between age and the labor market is one crucial component of the creation of dependent status in old age.

CREATION OF DEPENDENT SOCIAL AND ECONOMIC STATUS

Having established the dual nature of social policies in increasing control or dependency as well as welfare, the remainder of this paper is concerned with an anlysis of the specific role of social policies in increasing age stratification in British society and in distinguishing the elderly as a dependent and deprived minority. Over the course of this century various social policies have combined to create, enhance or maintain this dependent status. Three main sets of policies may be distinguished (Walker, 1980; Townsend, 1981): those concerned with retirement, pensions and social security and social services. In addition, recent employment and public expenditure policies in Britain have increased the tendency for elderly people to become economically and socially dependent.

Retirement Policies

Fundamental to the increased significance of the age boundary between independent and dependent status this century have been retirement policies. The growth of retirement has ensured that an increasing proportion of elderly workers has been excluded from the labor force, at a fixed age, and therefore from access to earnings and the other economic, social and psychological aspects of the workplace. This major social change has progressed rapidly and is continuing to do so. Between 1931 and 1971 the proportion of men aged 65 and over who were retired increased from under one-half to 78 percent, and by 1980 the figure was 88 percent (Office of Population Censuses and Surveys, 1981). Thus, in a relatively short space of time 'old age' has come to be socially defined as beginning at retirement age and whether by institutional rule or customary practice, the age at which older workers have to leave the labor force (Parker, 1980, p. 13).

This major social development has not occurred independently of the polity, organization of production and industrial demand for labor. Accounts of the emergence and development of retirement suggest that elderly people have, in fact, been used as a reserve army of labor to be tapped when labor is in short supply, and to be shed when demand changes (Phillipson, 1978; Graebner, 1980). Retirement is largely a 20th century phenomenon, which has been managed to remove from employment older workers in order to reconstitute and re-skill the labor force. This is not to suggest a narrow functionalist theory linking the growth of retirement with industrialization or the process of production but attempts to link them instead with the particular form of its development and management in late capitalist societies. The fact that significant proportions of elderly males were economically active in such societies during the early part of this century supports this conclusion. In France labor force participation amongst elderly males (over 60) was as high as 73 percent in 1906 (Guillemard, 1980, p. 21). By the 1930s over 50 percent of elderly males in Britain and 60 percent in France were still economically active. Over the course of this century, however, changes in the relationship between age and the labor market have been associated with changes in industrial processes (Laslett, 1977).

Work processes have been reorganized, the division of labor has increased and the labor process has been rationalized (Braverman, 1976). Under the influence of the scientific management school of thought in the United States, efficiency of the labor process was from the early part of the century seen to depend on the removal of those whose marginal productivity fell below a certain level. This was crudely related to age because the process of retirement was already established and because the reconstitution of the labor force with younger adults resulted in lower labor costs (Myles, 1981, p. 16). In addition, the exclusion of older workers has often been carried out to make way for the advancement of younger employees, or to reduce their social status in the labor market and therefore make their exclusion more likely (Wedderburn, 1975, p. 238). Secondly, the historical tendency of capital is to reduce its necessary labor to the minimum in order to maintain profitability and to this end it is constantly attempting to displace workers, and technological innovation during this century has aided this tendency. Thirdly, the high birth rate of the early 1960s provided a further impetus for the replacement of older with younger workers. Fourthly, the advent of large-scale unemployment in the 1930s was crucial in the institutionalization of retirement, and its return in the early 1980s has resulted in considerable pressure to institutionalize early retirement.

These main factors in the 20th century development of British society have combined to reduce the demand for older workers. At the same time, on the supply side, as retirement has been encouraged by employers and the state it has been accepted as customary and has become part of trade union bargaining for improved labor conditions. Moreover, many of the changes in production processes, such as the spread of assembly line production, have reduced the attachment of workers to employment (Beynon, 1976) and together with the failure of employers and state to improve working conditions has encouraged the widespread desire to leave work. Thus the perceived needs of capitalist enterprise and older workers have increasingly coincided on the issue of retirement. This consensus rests on the belief on the part of older workers that retirement is a status to be earned and looked forward to, a belief that is socially constructed and fostered in order to encourage retirement. One facet of this social construction involves the restricted perception of retirement as a short-term status (Walker, 1982a) to be enjoyed by the 'young-old' (Neugarten, 1974). The paradox that this social construction of a desired status represents in a society in which the market is pre-eminent in the distribution of rewards is glaring. Poverty and deprivation in retirement are not likely to be eradicated until the relationship between age and labor market is altered in such societies. So, the structural dependency that superannuation creates rests on the predominance of wage-labor and distribution through the market. The existence of welfare state provision, for reasons outlined earlier, does not challenge the prevailing system of distribution but supports it and therefore institutionalizes economic dependency through pension rules and regulations.

The conclusion that social and economic factors on the demand side were paramount in the institutionalization of retirement is supported by the absence of any evidence of a detrimental change in the ability and productive capacity of successive age cohorts reaching retirement age over the course of this century. Since work is the main source of social status, esteem and therefore self-respect in industrial societies, this trend has formed the basis of a more general devaluation of the productive skills and capacities of people over retirement age. For example, in a recent study of retirement the main reason given by older workers for having difficulty in getting a suitable job was the fact that they were 'too old' (Parker, 1980, p. 51). For those men and women who attempt to work beyond retirement age, there is a significant downward shift in occupational status. Even when they are 'productive' elderly people are relatively deprived in relation to younger age groups (Townsend, 1979, p. 795).

Social Division of Retirement

Like the experience of work the experience of retirement is socially divided and so attitudes towards retirement are similarly divided.

There is evidence, for example, that in industries which have arduous working conditions or boring and repetitive work (Barfield and Morgan, 1969) workers are likely to welcome retirement at the earliest opportunity. There is also a sexual division, with a higher proportion of both married and nonmarried women than men remaining in work after the normal retirement age (Jolly, Creigh and Mingay, 1980, p. 114). There are also differences based on employment status, with the self-employed being more likely than other groups to defer retirement. According to the 1971 census, in the 65 to 69 age group 37.5 percent of the self-employed were still working, and in the 70 and over group 22.5 percent. The proportions for those employed by others were 26 percent and 11 percent.

More recent evidence of the social division of labor-market withdrawal has been provided by the Danish National Institute of Social Research (Olsen and Hansen, 1981). With a retirement age of 67, in the age group 67 to 69 only 11 percent of the unskilled were working compared with 40 percent of salaried employees and 74 percent of the self-employed. Beyond the age of 70, one-third of the self-employed were still in work compared with one percent of workers. Moreover, when the results of this survey were compared with those of a similar one conducted fifteen years earlier in 1962 large differences were revealed in economic activity between various occupational groups. The decrease in overall employment rate amongst males in this period was borne almost exclusively by wage-earners, especially unskilled workers (Olsen and Hansen, 1981, p. 137). The Danish survey also, not surprisingly, revealed differences in attitudes to retirement. Three-fifths of employed men did not like the idea of having to retire, and only just under one-fifth looked forward to it. Less than one-tenth of the self-employed regarded retirement as something to look forward to, whereas 35 percent of unskilled and 26 percent of salaried workers did so.

Clearly, the degree to which individuals can determine their own retirement is crucial in creating differences in attitudes to and acceptance of retirement. The existence of compulsory retirement age reflects the absence of self-determination for many employees. Thus in the Danish survey one-half of salaried employees and between one-quarter and one-fifth of skilled and unskilled workers faced a compulsory retirement age. On the basis of a review of the American literature, Palmore (1978, p. 87) concluded in 1972 that

'Compulsory retirement policies may affect about half of the male wage and salary workers retiring at age 65 and will affect more in the future if recent trends continue'. Pension age was also found to be important in causing retirement, especially amongst workers, with about two-thirds leaving the labor force around that age. Thirdly, poor health was closely related to retirement, with three times as many retired as employed persons who rated their health as poor. Furthermore, just over one-third of retired men stated that poor health was the most important reason for retirement. Fourthly, working conditions were clearly a significant factor influencing the decision whether or not to retire. Finally, as research in other countries also indicates, the availability of an attractive pension has an important bearing on retirement (Friedmann and Orbach, 1974, p. 633). According to Olsen and Hansen (1981, p. 139): 'Unskilled workers seemed to look forward to retirement particularly because of stressful working conditions, while salaried employees regarded retirement positively because they had something to look forward to'.

For large numbers of older workers dependency is created by ill-health, redundancy and unemployment *prior* to retirement. In fact sickness and unemployment account for nearly two-thirds of men and one-quarter of women who retire prematurely (Parker, 1980, p. 10). Furthermore, a recent study of early retirement found that even amongst 'voluntary' early retirers two important factors were health and dissatisfaction with work on the job (McGoldrick and Cooper, 1980, p. 860). The nature and organization of production is responsible for the exclusion of a significant proportion of elderly people due to poor working conditions, industrial illness and injuries, but social policies have failed both to ensure adequate safety standards and to secure the return to work of injured and disabled workers. So, for a significant proportion of older workers the retirement age is effectively lowered by unemployment, sickness or injury. As with unemployment itself, semi-skilled and unskilled workers are over-represented amongst early retirees (Parker, 1980, p. 16). This policy of disengaging older workers from the labor force was made explicit in January 1977 with the introduction of the Job Release Scheme, which was 'designed to create vacancies for unemployed people by encouraging older workers to leave their jobs' (Department of Employment, 1980). The scheme covers men aged 64 and women aged 59 who are in full-time paid employment and do not take another job paying more than £4 a week. In view of the close relationship between retirement and low incomes, the Job Release Scheme may be seen as an attempt to shift the social costs of dependency from younger to older workers.

Pension Policies

The corollary to this process of exclusion from the labor force is that elderly people are heavily dependent on the state for financial support — about 90 percent of them receive some form of social security benefit. The concomitant selective definition of different states of need by the social security system may also reinforce dependency (Etzioni, 1976). The process of retirement results in an average fall in income of about one-half. The implicit rationale, or policy, underlying this differential is the assumption that social benefits in capitalist societies are intended to maintain monetary incentives and the work ethic (this is not to suggest, of course, that this ethic is not equally strong or perhaps even stronger in state socialist societies). Thus paradoxically, even those groups which have worked for a full term are not entitled to nondependent status, nor, for a large proportion, freedom from reliance on minimum income support. We have seen that retirement has a differential impact on elderly people, depending primarily on prior socioeconomic status, but because of the policy concerning the relative incomes of those in and outside of the labor force it imposes a lowered social status on the vast majority of the elderly in relation to younger adults. For some 5.1 million, or two thirds of elderly people, this reduction means living in poverty or on its margins (Walker, 1980). The level of the state retirement pension is roughly two-fifths of average net male manual earnings, and reliance on the state for financial support also results in relative* deprivation in access to a wide range of other resources, such as consumer durables and assets, and a generally reduced standard of living.

The dependency relationship between elderly people, the state and the labor market was institutionalized by the 'retirement condition', introduced in 1948, whereby state financial assistance is conditional on retirement. Older workers must retire before the receipt of the national insurance retirement pension to which they have contributed throughout their working life. This has encouraged an end to labor-force participation and has established an arbitrary retirement age as customary. Ironically, Beveridge had hoped that the retirement condition would encourage workers to defer retirement, but it has resulted in the adoption of the pension age as the retirement age. Together with the high marginal rates of taxation levied on pensioners who take up employment, it militates against the continuation of work by the elderly. More recently the social security system has been used to further enforce disengagement from the labor force with the policy of awarding the higher long-term rate of supplementary benefit (the minimum subsistence income) to those over the age of 60 who are unemployed but who agree not to register as such.

The social security system is also used in Britain to enforce women's dependence on men both prior to and after retirement. Although the Social Security Act 1980 contains some improvements in the status of women these are only a tentative first step, delayed until 1983, towards 'similar treatment' for women and men rather than equal treatment. Elderly married women are less likely than men to receive a national insurance retirement pension in their own right and are overwhelmingly less likely to receive a pension from a former employer (Hunt, 1978, p. 28). Moreover, the dependent status of married women under the social security system in earlier adult life is one contributory factor behind the certainty that, on reaching retirement age, they are likely to be poorer than men. Thirty-nine percent of elderly women live in families with incomes on or below the poverty line, compared with 26 percent of men and 16 percent of couples. In other words, just as discrimination against women, and married women in particular, in working life disadvantages them relative to men, further discrimination against women in the social security system and in the control and allocation of financial resources, within families (Pahl, 1980), superimposes on them dependency and reduced social status. Finally, the failure of the state through the social security system to meet the needs created by disablement in old age, means that the increasing numbers of elderly and especially very elderly people who become disabled experience even deeper deprivation than their nondisabled counterparts (Walker and Townsend, 1981).

Personal Social Services

Related to the crucial role of retirement and pension policies in the creation of dependency has been the development of care in the health and personal social services. In fact, the existence of a poor, dependent minority resulting from exclusion from the labor force and the concomitant restriction of access to resources has an important part in shaping policies as well as attitudes in the personal social services. There is a wide range of groups in the health and personal social services — from consultant geriatricians to domestic staff in old people's homes — which exert a considerable degree of control over the lives of elderly people, and which may enhance or reduce their dependence. Policies in the personal social services have, like other social policies, been treated as distinct from the dominant social structure and social values. But the pattern of residential and community care cannot be explained without reference to this structure, particularly the sexual division of labor within the family, the distribution of resources between different classes and age groups and assumptions about the role of elderly people in society.

There is a wide literature about the exercise of professional power, particularly on the part of doctors, in pursuit of narrow group interests (Freidson, 1975). The dominant elements in the medical profession have favored institutional care as opposed to community care for a very long time, and they are one of the important pressure groups resisting the switch to the latter form of care for elderly people. Through membership of planning and resource allocation agencies, from the Department of Health and Social Security to the Area and Regional Health Authorities, as well as through the proselytization of institutional models of curative medicine, some sections of the medical profession represent a powerful countervailing force to community-based forms of care. Studies of the exercise of professional judgement suggest that their implicit values concerning hygiene, cleanliness and consumption may be at variance with the interests of individual elderly people (Townsend, 1962).

Other interests, such as architects, caterers, builders, local politicians, administrators and planners may also tend to favor institutional forms of care. Achievements can be registered permanently in the form of bricks and mortar. Also, as staff unions have increased their influence, they too have tended towards narrow interpretations of their members' interests. Consequently, despite the fact that an explicit policy of community care has been in operation for over twenty years and that only 5 percent of elderly

people live in residential accommodation, residential care
dominates resource allocations within social service departments
(Treasury, 1980, p. 197).

Residential institutions like other social organizations perform
different functions, providing as well as care, the control of
'difficult', 'confused' and 'forgetful' residents and a cheap
substitute for public housing and community services. Independent
evidence collected over the last 20 years indicates that a significant
proportion of residents are capable of living independently and are
not, as the relevant legislation requires, 'in need of care and
attention'. For example, Townsend (1962) found in 1958-59 that 74
percent of new residents of old people's homes had only slight or
no incapacity. Ten years later a survey in Scotland showed that 67
percent of residents were able to wash, dress and use toilets on their
own and 45 percent had full capacity for self-care (Carstairs and
Morrison, 1971). A series of similar studies in the 1970s has
provided further evidence that a substantial proportion of residents
do not need constant care and attention (Townsend, 1981, p. 16).
Moreoever, there are important social divisions between residents,
suggesting social determinants of institutionalization. For example,
there are differences based on marital status, with 37 percent of
bachelors and 44 percent of spinsters aged 90 or over living in
institutions, four times as many as married men and married
women respectively of the same age. Those with close relatives,
especially daughters, are less likely than others to enter institutions.
In addition, there is homelessness and lack of community support
underlying the entry to residential institutions by relatively fit
elderly people.

There is also a body of evidence showing that once in residential
institutions elderly people are likely to become increasingly
dependent. For example, some recent research suggests that the
interests of the staff of residential homes are likely to tend towards
the creation of dependency rather than independence amongst
elderly residents. Preliminary results from the research surprisingly
showed that 60 percent of the staff interviewed in the local
authority homes stated that the most lucid and physically able
residents were most difficult to care for, while 41 percent said that
the 'confused' elderly were easiest to care for. Of those staff
prepared to declare a preference for working with certain groups,
71 percent said that they particularly liked working with the
confused (Evans, 1980). These findings suggest, perhaps, that

physically able residents are unlikely to receive encouragement and support to sustain relative independence, while some staff are primarily interested in performing more rewarding 'nursing' tasks with less able residents. They are particularly disturbing because a large proportion of elderly people are admitted to residential accommodation for 'social' reasons rather than physical or mental incapacity (Townsend, 1965). Taken together with the results of previous research, these findings indicate that the desire of staff for increased status and rewards is an important contributory factor in the dependence of elderly people in residential accommodation. In other words, in the definition and practice of their role, residential staff may, unwittingly, enhance the dependence of *both* the less physically disabled and the more severely disabled. Of course staff are not free to define the content of their roles, they are circumscribed by management, professional and training authorities, but they do have considerable flexibility in how they choose to carry out their roles and in how they treat elderly people.

Other aspects of the social organization of residential care also contribute to the loss of liberty and independence on the part of elderly people. Administrative regulations such as fire and safety regulations impose constraints on elderly people living in 'homes' which go far beyond their experience of independent living in their own home. Moreoever, they have no influence over the formulation and application of these regulations. Ironically, however, research by the Tavistock Institute of Human Relations suggests that old people are not necessarily safer when they are in care. Out of 133 fatal accidents amongst those aged 65 and over, 35 percent were in institutional care, although only 5 percent of that age group live in institutions. The authors commented that even considering that residential institutions contain a higher proportion of the infirm, the difference in accidental deaths is high (Norman, 1980, p. 17).

Clearly, there are variations in good practice between residential institutions and therefore variations in the quality of life experienced by elderly people, but a long series of research studies has shown that they deny freedom, privacy and comfort and are very far from resembling the commonly understood concept of a home. Consultation with the residents is still rare and democratic organization unknown. Management is often strict and rigid, with hospital-like daily routines for meals, bed times and visiting, lacking privacy and possibilities for self-care. The loss of independence suffered by elderly people on admission to a hospital or residential institution has been forcefully summarized by Norman (1980, p. 7):

> Old people are taken from their homes when domiciliary support and physical treatment might enable them to stay there; they are subjected in long-stay hospitals and homes to regimes which deprive them of many basic human dignities; and they are often not properly consulted about the care or treatment to which they are subjected.

It is not wholly surprising, therefore, that elderly people themselves associate moving into institutions with loss of independence (Tobin and Lieberman, 1976, p. 18). In turn, the likelihood of admission to a residential institution is increased by public expenditure cuts and the failure of successive governments to develop community care services (Walker, 1981b). In the face of increasing need the failure of community care policies falls on those least able to bear them. Townsend and Wedderburn reported, in 1965, that of those elderly people in social classes one and two who were severely incapacitated, only one-half already had a paid or local authority home help and nearly one-half of the remainder said that they needed it. But only one-sixth of those in social class five who were severely incapacitated had a home help and only one-fifth of the remainder felt the need for it. A recent official survey of elderly people living at home suggests that, despite a doubling of the coverage of the home help service between the two surveys, it is still the case that those in the higher social classes are more likely to provide themselves with assistance when they are incapacitated (Bebbington, 1979, p. 119). In addition, an analysis of the two surveys shows that an expansion in the coverage of the home help service has been carried out at the expense of the amount of service received by each elderly person: the jam has been spread thinner. In the official survey carried out in 1976, 42 percent of the elderly had home help visits more than weekly compared with 64 percent found by Townsend and Wedderburn in 1962 (Bebbington, 1979, p. 121). It is therefore becoming increasingly difficult for community services to provide sufficient support to prevent institutionalization. Future policy changes are unlikely to reduce the dependence of those elderly people forced into residential care because, as the previous discussion indicates, it is much easier to institutionalize than de-institutionalize elderly people.

In combination, these policies in employment, pensions and

social services have played an important part in creating and legitimating dependency amongst elderly people. It is on this foundation, moreover, that the impact on the elderly of recent policies in public expenditure and employment can be understood. The exclusion of older workers from the labor market has formed the basis for a more general devaluation of the contribution and social status of the elderly in British society, a judgement which, incidentally, is denied by the contribution of elderly people to family relationships (Walker, 1981b). Since the mid-1970s governments of both Labour and Conservative parties have reduced the growth of expenditure on the social services, which because they are the main client group of these services, has affected elderly people more than others. Furthermore, with the massive rise in unemployment to more than 13 percent of the workforce in 1982, under the Conservative government, their employment policies have positively favored younger workers to the detriment of the employment prospects of older workers (Walker, 1982a).

CONCLUSION

The increasing dependency of elderly people in Britain has been socially engineered in order to facilitate the removal of older workers from the labor force. At the heart of this social change has been the narrow financial goals of capitalism, and particularly its constant need to increase profitability. In this interest mass superannuation has been managed through retirement, early retirement and unemployment amongst older workers. Age-restrictive social policies have been used by the state both to exclude older workers from the labor force and to legitimate that exclusion through retirement. Retirement pensions are one of the means by which capitalism is able to enforce changes aimed at reconstituting the workforce. This changing social relationship between age and the labor market has formed the basis for a more general spread of dependency amongst the elderly. Age-restrictive policies in health and personal social services have been reviewed, but also in housing, the failure to provide a sufficient stock of sheltered housing for older people has tended to increase the likelihood of institutionalization, and therefore increased dependency. Similarly in education and training, age-restrictive policies have relatively disadvantaged elderly people in relation to changing knowledge and technology. Research and inquiry in social gerontology and social policy may also contribute to assumptions about the abilities and status of elderly people.

Increasing economic and social dependence may also contribute to increasing physical and mental dependence outside as well as inside institutions. What is certain is that dependency imposes reduced social status on *carers* as well as elderly people. Community care policies in the allocation of home helps, meals-on-wheels and other assistance are based on assumptions about the division of care within the family, particularly the sexual division of labor, and the responsibility of the family in caring for their own members (Walker, 1981b). Thus social services substitute for rather than support families (Moroney, 1976). Carers are usually women, and social policies which allocate social services in preference to those without wives or daughters to care for them, effectively lead to isolation, low incomes and restricted opportunities for these, predominantly female, carers. It is not surprising, therefore, that loss of status is frequently expressed by women who care for elderly relatives (Nissel and Bonnerjea, 1982). Remoteness from social services agencies of both dependent elderly people being cared for by relatives and also those providing care has been summarized by a recent study by the Equal Opportunities Commission (1981, p. 32):

> The elderly — and three quarters of all dependents were elderly — were not usually provided for spontaneously and their problems were only likely to be alleviated if the carer had somehow managed to discover what aids and adaptations were available and how to go about applying for them.

Increasing dependency amongst the elderly in Britain has stemmed from conscious changes in the structure and organization of capitalist production. These changes have encouraged an unnecessarily narrow, age-restrictive approach to employment and, therefore, social policies in the field of pensions and social services. The key to the dependent relationship between the elderly and the state is the labor market, and policies such as the abolition of age-barrier retirement and the encouragement of flexible retirement would necessitate changes in pension and other policies. This change would mark an alternative interpretation of the role to be played by the elderly in modern British society, from an increasingly dependent one to an active and productive one. Such a change in the social status of elderly people would be accompanied by increased incomes, better and more appropriate housing and improved social services.

REFERENCES

Barfield, R.E. and J. Morgan (1969), *Early Retirement: The Decision and the Experience* (Michigan, Institute for Social Research).

Bebbington, A.C. (1979), 'Changes in the Provision of Social Services to the Elderly in the Community Over Four Years', *Social Policy and Administration,* Vol. 13, No. 2, pp. 111-123.

Beynon, H. (1976), *Working for Ford* (Harmondsworth, Penguin Books).

Braverman, H. (1976), *Labour and Monopoly Capital* (London, Monthly Review Press).

Briggs, A. (1961), 'The Welfare State in Historical Perspective', *British Journal of Sociology,* Vol. 2, No. 2, pp. 220-240.

Carstairs, V. and M. Morrison (1971), *The Elderly in Residential Care* (Edinburgh, Scottish Home and Health Department).

Central Office of Information (1974), *Care of the Elderly in Britain* (London, HMSO).

Department of Employment (1980), *Job Release Schemes* (London, Department of Employment).

Edelman, M. (1977), *Political Language* (New York, Academic Press).

Equal Opportunities Commission (EOC) (1980), *The Experience of Caring for Elderly and Handicapped Dependents: Survey Report* (Manchester, Equal Opportunities Commission).

Etzioni, A. (1976), 'Old People and Public Policy', *Social Policy,* Vol. 7, No. 3, pp. 21-29.

Evans, G. (1980), 'Attitudes of Residential Care Staff in Homes for the Elderly', paper given at the British Gerontological Society.

Fox Piven, F. and R. A. Cloward (1972), *Regulating the Poor* (London, Tavistock).

Freidson, E. (1975), *Profession of Medicine* (New York, Dodd, Mead and Co).

Friedmann, E.A. and H.L. Orbach (1974), 'Adjustment to Retirement', pp. 609-645 in S. Arieti (ed.), *American Handbook of Psychiatry*, Vol. 1 (New York, Basic Books).

Ginsburg, N. (1979), *Class, Capital and Social Policy* (London, Macmillan).

Gough, I. (1979), *The Political Economy of the Welfare State* (London, Macmillan).

Graebner, W. (1980), *A History of Retirement* (New Haven, Conn., Yale University Press).

Guillemard, A.-M. (1980), *La Vieillesse et L'État* (Paris, PUF).

Hendricks, J. and Hendricks C.D. (1977), *Ageing in Mass Society* (Cambridge,

Mass., Winthrop).

Hunt, A. (1978), *The Elderly at Home* (London, HMSO).

Jolly, J., S. Creigh and A. Mingay (1980), *Age as a Factor in Employment* (London, Department of Employment).

Laslett, P. (1977), 'In an Ageing World', *New Society,* 27 October, pp. 171-173.

Layard, R., D. Piachaud and M. Stewart (1978), *The Causes of Poverty* (Background Paper No. 5, Royal Commission on the Distribution of Income and Health, London, HMSO).

Leonard, P. (1979), 'Editor's Introduction' to Gough, 1979.

McGoldrick, A. and C.L. Cooper (1980), 'Voluntary Early Retirement — Taking the Decision', *Employment Gazette,* August, pp. 859-864.

Maeda, D. (1978), 'Ageing in Eastern Society', pp. 45-72 in D. Hobman (ed.), *The Social Challenge of Ageing* (London, Croom Helm).

Moroney, R.M. (1976), *The Family and the State* (London, Longmans).

Myles, J.F. (1981), 'The Aged and the Welfare State: An Essay in Political Demography', paper presented to Roundtable on Public Social Policies and Aging in Industrial Societies, Paris, 8-9 July.

Neugarten, B.L. (1974), 'Age Groups in American Society and the Rise of the Young-Old', *Annals of the American Academy of Political Science,* Vol. 4, No. 5, pp. 187-198.

Nissel, M. and J. Bonnerjea (1982), *Looking after the Handicapped Elderly at Home: Who Pays?* (London, PSI).

Norman, A.J. (1980), *Rights and Risk* (London, NCCOP).

Office of Population Censuses and Surveys (OPCS) (1981), *General Household Survey* (London, HMSO).

Olsen, H. and G. Hansen (1981), *Living Conditions of the Aged 1977* (Copenhagen, National Institute of Social Research).

Pahl, J. (1980), 'Patterns of Money Management Within Marriage', *Journal of Social Policy,* Vol. 9, No. 3, July, pp. 313-335.

Palmore, E.B. (1978), 'Compulsory Versus Flexible Retirement: Issues and Facts', pp. 87-93 in V. Carver and P. Liddiard (eds.), *An Ageing Population* (Sevenoaks, Hodder and Stoughton).

Parker, S. (1980), *Older Workers and Retirement* (London, HMSO).

Phillipson, C. (1978), *The Emergence of Retirement* (Durham, University of Durham).

Rowntree, B.S. (1901), *Poverty: A Study of Town Life* (London, Macmillan).

Titmuss, R.M. (1963), 'The Social Division of Welfare', pp. 34-55 in *Essays on The Welfare State* (London, Allen and Unwin).

Tobin, S.S. and M.A. Lieberman (1976), *Last Home for the Aged* (San Francisco, Jossey-Bass).

Townsend, P. (1962), *The Last Refuge* (London, Routledge and Kegan Paul).

Townsend, P. (1965), 'The Effects of Family Structure on the Likelihood of Admission to an Institution in Old Age', pp. 163-187 in E. Shanas (ed.), *Social Structure and the Family* (Englewood Cliffs, NJ, Prentice Hall).

Townsend, P. (1979), *Poverty in the United Kingdom* (London, Allen Lane).

Townsend, P. (1981), 'The Structured Dependency of the Elderly: A Creation of Social Policy in the Twentieth Century', *Ageing and Society,* Vol. 1, No. 1, pp. 5-28.

Townsend, P. (1981a), 'Elderly People with Disabilities', pp. 91-118 in A. Walker and P. Townsend (1981).

Treasury (1980), *The Government's Expenditure Plans 1980-81 to 1983-84* (Cmnd. No. 7841, London, HMSO).

Walker, A. (1980), 'The Social Creation of Poverty and Dependency in Old Age', *Journal of Social Policy,* Vol. 9, No. 1., pp. 49-75.

Walker, A. (1981), 'Towards a Political Economy of Old Age', *Ageing and Society,* Vol. 1, No. 1, pp. 73-94.

Walker, A. (1981a), 'Social Policy, Social Administration and the Social Construction of Welfare', *Sociology,* Vol. 15, No. 2, pp. 225-250.

Walker, A. (ed.) (1982), *Public Expenditure and Social Policy* (London, Heinemann).

Walker, A. (1981b), 'Community Care and the Elderly in Britain: Theory and Practice', *International Journal of Health Services,* Vol. 11, No. 4, pp. 541-557.

Walker, A. (1982a), 'The Social Consequences of Early Retirement', *Political Quarterly,* Vol. 53, No. 1, pp. 61-72.

Walker, A. and P. Townsend (eds.) (1981), *Disability in Britain* (Oxford, Martin Robertson).

Wedderburn, D. (1975), 'Prospects for the Reorganisation of Work', *The Gerontologist,* June, pp. 236-241.

Westergaard, J. (1977), 'Class, Inequality and Corporation', pp. 165-187 in A. Hunt (ed.), *Class and Class Structure* (London, Lawrence and Wishart).

Wynn, M. (1972), *Family Policy* (Harmondsworth, Penguin Books).

9

AUSTERITY AND AGING IN THE UNITED STATES: 1980 and Beyond

Carroll L. Estes
University of California, San Francisco

The major problems faced by the elderly in the United States are, in large measure, ones that are socially constructed as a result of the dominant societal conception of aging and the aged, but it is a conception that emerges within, reflects and bolsters the economic and political structure of society. What is done for and about the elderly, as well as our research-based knowledge about old age and aging, are products of these conceptions. The key determinants of the standard of living enjoyed or endured by the aged are national social and economic policies, political decisions at all levels of government, the power of structural interests, and the policies of business and industry (Estes, 1979).

The policies that social institutions produce reflect the dominance of certain values and normative conceptions of social problems and their remedies. The value choices and definitions of existing conditions do not derive from consensual agreement of the members of society; nor do they result from a benign accommodation among different interests as the pluralists posit (Connolly, 1969), nor from the definitions of older persons themselves (Estes, 1974). In a class society, some individuals and groups have much greater power than others to influence the definition of social problems and to specify

The author gratefully acknowledges the assistance of Lenore Gerard. A version of this paper was first published in the *International Journal of Health Services*.

the policy interventions that address these problems.

The politically organized elderly seek to influence socially determined priorities and public policies. They are, however, only one of a number of sectors of the society that have a vital interest in determining policy choices for the elderly. Growing in power are those economic and political interests that have the most to gain from the Reagan administration policies of reducing domestic social spending and increasing tax benefits for corporations and upper income Americans.

Definitions of the 'social problem' of old age and of the appropriate policy solutions for this problem have reflected the ups and downs of the US economy and the shifting bases of political power during the past thirty years. With the economic rebound after the recession of the late 1950s, there was a period of rapid economic growth and corresponding political optimism in dealing with two difficult domestic social problems — racial discrimination and poverty. In gerontology this optimism was reflected in the activity theory of aging which was predicated on the assumption that health, mobility, adjustment, and general well-being were realistic outcomes for most older Americans; and policies to foster socialization and recreation were to be commended. US optimism also was evident in the enactment of Medicare in 1965, which aimed to provide the elderly with access to needed medical services.

In the 1960s the initial policy of treating the aged as a homogeneous category was established under both Medicare and the Older Americans Act. Conceptually, all aged were lumped together as a general class with little specificity as to whether they were disadvantaged or as to how income, race, sex, or ethnic differences affected their status. The Older Americans Act of 1965 provided limited funding, initially and mainly for Senior Center activities, reflecting a view of the problems of the elderly as social isolation and the lack of social activity (consonant with the activity theory of aging). Differences in hardship among the aged were downplayed in favor of social and recreational programs for which all the aged were equally eligible. The approach of the Older Americans Act in 1965 obscured the visibility of the elderly who were poor, extremely disabled, or ill (Estes, 1979).

As economic growth and the Vietnam war fuelled inflation, the optimism of the 1960s was replaced by disillusionment. The ensuing economic recession of the early 1970s and continued inflation was accompanied by a move of the Nixon administration toward retrenchment of federal programs under the banner of 'new federalism' and decentralization. The consequence of this policy and the revenue sharing programs it generated was ultimately to shift political and fiscal responsibility for many domestic programs increasingly from the federal to state and local governments. President Nixon's intention was that the decentralization strategy would curtail the growth of federal programs, while shifting the political and economic pressure of social programs from the federal to state and substate arenas.

Consistent with this trend, Older Americans Act policies shifted from recreation to a major emphasis on state and local coordination, planning and comprehensive service development. The 1973 Older Americans Act amendments assigned existing state agencies on aging the responsibility for designating local planning and coordination agencies (area agencies on aging), which, in turn, were assigned responsibility for generating local resources.

The decentralized planning-coordination policy of the 1970s largely ignored the widespread poverty of the aged, providing no direct economic relief. The emphasis, instead, was on the aged as service recipients and consumers, supporting the development of an expanding service economy and confirming Miller's (1976) thesis that the treatment of social problems during the 1970s mirrored the task of the decade — to put the economy on its feet.

Embarking on the decade of the 1980s, there are three dominant perceptions of reality that appear to be shaping public policy for the elderly under the Reagan administration. First, there has been a political declaration of fiscal crisis at the federal level which has generated a climate of intense psychological uncertainty and vulnerability of the American public to radical proposals to dismantle major social programs. The crisis definition of the US economy, now incorporated into law through both the Omnibus Budget Reconciliation Act and the Economic Recovery Tax Act of 1981, has assured the objective condition of a fiscal crisis in many states.

Second, there is a growing perception that the problems of the elderly and other disadvantaged groups cannot and will not be solved by instituting *national* policies and programs — but rather that the solutions must come from the efforts of state and local government, initiatives of the private sector or of the individual. The rationale enunciated by many politicians (*New York Times,* 1981) is that the problems which social programs address are neither remediable by, nor the responsibility of, the federal government. In this context, the cost of government intervention in itself is characterized as harmful to business productivity and to the US economy. There is a resurgence of the ideology that individuals create their own conditions and opportunities and that they are to be held accountable for their predicament. There is also much rhetoric about the decentralization of federal programs as a means of getting government 'off the backs' of the people.

Third, in the US there is a popular perception that old age is a social problem and that it is a problem resulting largely from the biological and physiological decline of the aging individual (Estes, 1979). Further, the dependency of the elderly is seen by many as a consequence of individual default (e.g., not planning well, not saving enough). Each of these perceptions has strengthened the support for policy intervention strategies aimed at the individual level rather than collective social change efforts.

DOMINANT PERCEPTIONS WHICH SHAPE PUBLIC POLICY FOR THE ELDERLY

The Perception of Fiscal Crisis and the Necessity for Reduced Federal Expenditures

Fiscal crisis is a concept that has had a major impact on the policies of local and state governments. Initially in the US the term 'fiscal crisis' came into currency in the 1970s to describe the problems of a local government that could not service its debts (e.g., New York City, Cleveland) or of a state whose expenditures exceeded its revenues. The term fiscal crisis is now being widely applied to describe federal expenditures for social programs and the US economy.

Since 1975 there has been a decline in federal, state and local expenditures as a percent of the gross national product (GNP) and a decline in per capita expenditures in constant dollars (Advisory Commission on Intergovernmental Relations, 1980a). After intergovernmental transfers (i.e. federal and state to local, federal to local), the most significant declines are at the local level

(Advisory Commission on Intergovernmental Relations, 1980b). Since 1975 state and local expenditures have declined from 15.1 percent to 13.5 percent of GNP, while federal expenditures have decreased from 12.3 percent to 11.9 percent of GNP.

Fiscal crisis at the local level will be exacerbated because of the severe cutbacks in direct federal aid; the community development block grants and the comprehensive employment and training block grants that have been eliminated, and others that have been significantly reduced (Advisory Commission on Intergovernmental Relations, 1980a; *Business Week*, 1981).

From *above* there are (1) federal limits on Medicaid expenditures for health care for the poor and (2) major block grant initiatives with a 20 to 25 percent reduction in the funding level of the prior categorical programs that the block grants replace. Both of these conditions are shifting medical care costs to the states, to local governments, and to the elderly themselves (Estes and Lee, 1981).

From *below* there are fiscal crises and tax revolts at the state and local levels. Caught in the squeeze, health and social services are involved in a 'fiscal crisis' of their own. During the 1980s all levels of government will seek to cut costs and shift expenditures to other jurisdictions. For example, at least one-third of the states were planning Medicaid cuts prior to the enactment of the Omnibus Budget Reconciliation Act of 1981. Many more will follow suit as a result of federal reductions in social spending and the limits that the Act placed on the federal share of Medicaid costs.

These fiscal pressures at multiple governmental levels pose a particular problem for Medicaid-funded services because of the magnitude and rapid increases in these expenditures, now outrunning the capacity of states to raise the necessary revenue (Estes et al., 1981). In view of the Medicaid expenditure escalation, and the fact that 20 percent of the elderly receive Medicaid and 39 percent of Medicaid expenditures are for the elderly, the costs of containing policy changes at the state level are likely to affect the elderly poor and near-poor directly.

The Perception that National Policies Should Give Way to Decentralization and Block Grants

Budget cuts have been made in the block grants which represent the major element in President Reagan's domestic social program proposals. In the 1970s this policy concept emerged under the banner of 'new federalism', which converted a number of categorical programs to block grant type revenue sharing programs (e.g., Title XX of the Social Security Act). Designed to decentralize responsibility for domestic social programs to state and local governments through block grant type funding and to limit federal involvement in those programs, new federalism augmented the fiscal and political responsibility of state and local governments for multiple programs, including those affecting health care (Lee and Estes, 1979). Both the block grants of the 1970s and those created in the Omnibus Budget Reconciliation Act of 1981 ease the constraints of categorical (i.e. targeted) funding and of federal requirements, resulting in increased discretion for state government decision making in multiple programs that affect the elderly, including such health programs as community mental health centeres, home health services, emergency medical services, and hypertension control.

A significant consequence of the block grant decentralization is that the wide discretion it provides individual states will augment the inequities in the same program across the states (Estes, 1979). This, in turn, makes it impossible to assure uniform benefits for the same targeted population (e.g., the aged) across the jurisdictions or to maintain accountability with so many varying state approaches. Finally, because the most disadvantaged (e.g., the poor aged) are heavily dependent on state determined benefits, they are extremely vulnerable in this period of economic flux.

The net result of the large-scale shift to block grants in health and social services, combined with the across-the-board expenditure reductions for Fiscal Year (FY) 1982 for the block granted programs, is increased pressure on state and local governments to underwrite program costs at the same time that many states, cities, and counties also are under extreme pressure to curb rising expenditures. The result is likely to be serious for the elderly poor and for the poor of all ages.

The Perception of Old Age and Aging as an Individual Problem

Consistent with the liberal philosophical emphasis on individual responsibility, public policy for the aged in the US has treated the problem of old age largely as resolvable through the provision of services at the individual level. Medicare and Medicaid policies, Title XX Social Services and the Older Americans Act are all predicated on the notion that treating *individuals* is the way to treat the 'problem' of aging. Further, the provider of service receives reimbursement under all of these programs, while the elderly are defined as 'recipients', clients or patients of service. Thus, the helping professions share, and benefit from, the individualized conception of aging, which is implemented through policies in ways that contribute to the further dependency of the aged. The medical profession has been the provider group to benefit most from this conceptualization and the US health policies that flow from it.

In the US, not only has aging been defined as a social problem, but old people themselves have been specifically defined as 'the Problem'. One important influence of this dominant perception is the research emphasis that has been given to the biological aspects of aging and the concern with disease processes rather than the causes of disease, particularly with the social, economic and environmental factors that contribute to disease. Social and behavioral science research has been focused on studying the individual old person; it has been heavily concerned about the adjustment, life satisfaction and morale of old people and with human development and the life cycle processes of aging.

The societal treatment of the elderly (through policies of mandatory retirement and reduced income) tends to be taken as 'given' by most researchers. The research task has been to learn how the aging process works (implicitly taking for granted the existing policies and conditions) and how adult development and adjustment occur under given conditions.

Thus, while aging is typified as a social problem, it tends also to be seen as one that occurs largely as a result of apolitical processes (i.e. individual physiological and chronological decline). The biological models and biomedical problem definitions of aging support the notion that aging is an *individual* problem and that it is largley a *medical* problem. This 'medicalization' of aging at least partially explains the strong support for current US health policies that have benefited doctors, hospitals and insurance companies far more than they have the elderly, who are now paying more out-of-pocket medical care costs than their entire health bills prior to the enactment of Medicare.

An important consequence has been the expansion of the health services industry. Increasingly in the 1970s, the formulation of the problem of aging in America, as described, led to policies that are service strategies — with a highly medical character — and with power largely in the hands of service providers, through policies which provide them reimbursement. Medical care dollars outstrip social service dollars $30 to $1 (Brody, 1979), this prior to the FY 1982 and FY 1983 cutbacks that are expect to curtail social services far more than medical services (Salamon and Abramson, 1981). The problem formulation has done little to address the root economic inequality of the aged or to directly alter the dependency status of the aged through policies that provide continued employment or adequate retirement income.

The policies that emerged also have the core characteristic of being largely separatist in nature — that is, separating the aged from other groups in society on the basis of their special need. As a consequence of this problem formulation and policy prescription, an 'aging enterprise' has been created to serve the aged. The 'aging enterprise' includes the congeries of programs, organizations, bureaucracies, interest groups, trade associations, providers, industries, and professionals which serve the aged in one capacity or another (Estes, 1979). The concept of the aging enterprise is intended to call attention to how the aged and their needs are processed and treated as a commodity in our society, and to the fact that the age-segregated policies which fuel the enterprise are socially divisive solutions, in contrast to those policies which do not single out, stigmatize, and isolate the aged from the rest of society (e.g., national health insurance, full employment). The policies and political processes that surround the aging enterprise have engendered competition between disadvantaged groups and between the generations; and in so doing, they encourage dangerous dichotomies.

Among many advocates and politicians, there is a firm belief that no equity is possible; there are just trade-offs. Such policies and politics do little to advance the cause of social justice; they perpetuate acceptance of the inevitability of scarcity, inequity and inter-group rivalries.

DIFFERENTIAL IMPACT OF
PUBLIC POLICIES

These definitions and policy prescriptions obscure an understanding of aging as a socially generated problem and status, diverting attention from the social and political institutions that, in effect, produce many of the problems confronting the elderly today. Political economy analyses, emphasizing the interaction between the policy and economy, have begun to re-examine and challenge these dominant conceptions (Estes, Swan and Gerard, 1982; Walker, 1980; 1981; Townsend, 1979; 1981; Myles, 1980; 1981; Guillemard, 1974; forthcoming; Dowd, 1980; Estes, 1979; Evans and Williamson, 1981).

The issue of the role and power of the state, constraints on state intervention and its legitimating function in the distribution of benefits has not been examined extensively with respect to public policy for the aged, although Ginsberg (Ginsberg, 1979), O'Connor (1973), Gough (1979), and others have addressed these issues indirectly in their analyses of the role and function of the welfare state. In the health field, major contributions to a political economy framework have been made (Kelman, 1975; Renaud, 1975; Navarro, 1973; 1976; Alford, 1976). Drawing upon the approach by Walton (Walton, 1979) the political economy of aging focuses on the nature of and intersections between aging status and class politics, which can be understood only in terms of their structural bases and how they are conditioned by the socioeconomic and political environment.

The political economy approach is distinguished from the dominant gerontological perspective by viewing the problem of aging as a structural one. The individualistic view assumes the overriding importance of the market in distributing rewards and in determining socioeconomic status. The dependency status of the elderly is explained by the individual and his or her lifetime (and work) behavior patterns. The theory, simply stated, is that 'you get what you earned'. Numerous US studies on status and income maintenance adopt this approach (Henretta and Campbell, 1976; Samuelson, 1978; 1981; Baum and Baum, 1980). Most policy interventions in the US reflect this perspective and, in the case of the aged, promote age-segregated policies and services for a detached and dependent minority.

In contrast, the structural view of aging starts with the

proposition that the status and resources of the elderly, and even the trajectory of the aging process itself, are conditioned by one's location in the social structure and the economic and political factors that affect it. The dependency of the elderly is to be understood in the labor market and in the social relations that it produces — and these as they change with age. Policy interventions from this perspective would be directed towards various institutionalized structures of society, in particular the labor market.

Current old age policy in the US reflects a two-class system of welfare where benefits are distributed on the basis of legitimacy (Tussing, 1971) rather than on the basis of need. Old people may have more legitimacy relative to other disadvantaged groups in society competing for scarce public funds (Cook, 1979), but old age neither levels nor diminishes social class distinctions. Social class, status, and economic resources in old age are largely determined by lifetime conditions and labor force participation established prior to retirement age (Walker, 1981). As Nelson (Nelson, 1982) indicates, both income and services policies in the US reflect different classes of 'deserving-ness' in old age.

Public policies in the US are very different for the aged who are considered 'deserving' compared to those who are considered 'undeserving' (see Figure 1). Three classes of the aged are entitled to some type of government program: (1) the middle- and upper-class (the deserving nonpoor) aged; (2) the newly poor in old age (the deserving poor); and (3) the aged who have always been poor (the undeserving poor). The nonpoor aged have the resources to permit access to public and private services without the necessity of government intervention. They also receive a disproportionate share of the benefits of the largest federal programs for the aged (e.g., Social Security, Medicare, and retirement tax credits). Most services policies tend to favor the newly poor in old age, largely because they are thought of as both deserving and deprived. Services have been designed largely to assist the recently deprived aged to maintain their lifestyles, rather than to provide the more crucial life-support services (e.g., income) needed by the poor aged. The aged who have been life-long poor are assisted largely through inadequate income-maintenance policies, such as Supplemental Security Income (SSI), the Social Security minimum benefit (now available only to current, not future beneficiaries), and through Medicaid which is high variable from state to state.

FIGURE 1
Class Basis of Aging Policies

Deserving Elderly **(1 Federal Policy)**	**Undeserving Elderly** **(50 State Variable Policies)**

SOCIAL SECURITY (SS)

Income	Regressive Taxation — No SS Tax After $35,700 Salary Level	Minimum Social Security Benefit Eliminated For All Future Eligibles

	PRIVATE PENSIONS TAX POLICY Individual Retirement Accounts (IRA) Tax Credits — Economic Economic Recovery Tax Act of 1981	Unlikely to Supplement with Private Pensions SUPPLEMENTAL SECURITY INCOME (SSI)* Payment Levels Below Poverty Means-Tested for the Poor Only

MEDICARE PROGRAM

Health	Expenditures are Highest for this Group Greater Capacity to Pay Deductibles and copayments	Lower Access to Physicians and Hospitals For Blacks and Other Minorities and Poor MEDICAID PROGRAM* Means-tested for the Poor Only — Approx. 50% of Persons Below Poverty not Covered

PRIVATE INSURANCE

More Capacity to Afford Coverage	Little or No Capacity to Purchase Coverage

SOCIAL SERVICES BLOCK GRANT*
(Formerly Title XX of the Social Security Act)

Social **Services**		No Federally Mandated Priority To Low-Income Eligibles

OLDER AMERICANS ACT*

	Provides Services Most Needed By Middle Class, e.g. Information and Referral; Transportation	No Federally Mandated Priority To Low-Income Eligibles

---

* State variable policies emerge primarily from state-federal programs in which states have much discretion over eligibility and scope of available services. State discretionary programs are fiscally vulnerable, uncertain, unstable, and highly vulnerable to swings in state level political and economic factors.

Deservingness in old age income policies is very much based on the principle of differential rewards for differential achievements during a lifetime. The Social Security system reflects the notion that there is no entitlement as a matter of right to those who have not earned it. For those individuals who have been casually employed or for those who had very low lifetime earnings covered by Social Security, mainly women and minorities, the minimum benefit has in the past guaranteed a basic monthly payment of $122. Since some estimated three million beneficiaries receive a higher monthly payment than would be payable under regular benefit formula, critics have pointed to the alleged welfare character of the minimum social security benefit. Successful Reagan administration and congressional cutback efforts targeted at eliminating the Social Security minimum benefit for all future beneficiaries (US PL 97-35, 1981) are illustrative of the efforts to eliminate the 'undeserving' aged from the Social Security trust funds. Proponents of this policy change argued that those who require income support beyond what they have actually earned in the labor market, ought to go looking to the Supplementary Security Income (SSI) program or other state discretionary welfare programs for relief (US Congress, 1981a).

The important point is that most, if not all, of the policies that deal with the 'undeserving' aged are 'state discretionary policy' — that is, they are in the hands of the states. As such, the eligibility and benefits under these policies depend upon the variable willingness and fiscal capacity of states to fund programs at the state level. Not only are these state discretionary programs different from state to state, they tend to be easily politicized and certainly they are more economically vulnerable and variable than uniform federal policies. Thus, the most economically disadvantaged aged (the undeserving aged) do not have the security of stable, uniformly administered federal policies (like Social Security and Medicare) that apply to those considered more deserving aged.

Health policy exemplifies the class basis of US policies. While most aged are eligible for Medicare, research has shown that more Medicare benefits are provided to the upper and middle classes and to whites than to lower classes and blacks (Davis, 1975). Inequities in Medicare benefits appear on the basis of income, race and region. In the southern region of the United States, where 56 percent of the nation's aged nonwhites reside, the disparities between white and non-white Medicare beneficiaries persist

(Ruther and Dobson, 1981). Further, upper and middle-class aged can afford to supplement these benefits with private health insurance, and they are better able to meet the increasing cost of co-payments and deductibles under Medicare than are the lower class (undeserving) aged. The Reagan administration and Congress have adopted policies in the 1981 Omnibus Budget Reconciliation Act and are proposing further Medicare reductions for FY 1983 that will increase the hardship of medical expenses for the poor elderly. In 1982 the cost of both physician and hospital services has been increased under Medicare. Such increases are particularly significant in the context of the already-high out-of-pocket costs borne directly by the elderly for their medical care — estimated to be in excess of $1000 per capita in 1979 — and the increasing rate of poverty among the elderly (US Congress, 1981b).

For the poorest aged, Medicaid is available as a state program. Medicaid is a highly variable program whose state-determined eligibility standards are so stringent that it has been estimated (prior to the 1982 cut-backs) that at least 50 percent of the people below poverty are not eligible because of the widely varying eligibility requirements across the states (Davis and Schoen, 1978). The effect of the most recent policy shifts in the US toward capping the growth in federal Medicaid costs, block grants, and reduced social spending will be to increase existing inequities in programs for the poor across the states.

The lesson is clear. The states which are 'generous' in terms of Medicaid eligibility standards and benefits must pay for it in large part themselves. It is not federal policy to formally address the needs of the most disadvantaged with a national policy that is uniform for all low income aged across the country. Both medical and income supplementation (i.e. Supplemental Security Income) for the poor aged are left up to the states and their varying willingness and declining economic capacity to support these programs.

As economic problems have mounted at the federal level, more and more human service programs have been delegated to the states. These pressures are occurring simultaneously with other growing fiscal pressures on the states — the loss of general revenue sharing at the state level, taxpayer revolts (real or threatened), and huge inflationary increases in state health expenditures.

The class-based policy treatment of the elderly just described may be affected by the new emerging strategy that would emphasize the adoption of 'non-service approaches' to problems of the poor and aged. Consistent with the declaration of fiscal crisis, the aim of the approach is to redirect expectations from the national policy level to the local level where individuals can help themselves without public funding by such means as advocacy, self-help, administration, and tax policy changes (SRI International, 1981). However, these policies are not likely to seriously challenge the predominantly medical services strategy. How this is played out and how it affects the services strategy now in place remains to be demonstrated.

SUMMARY

Programs and policies for the aged will be affected by the major policy shifts emerging with the Reagan administration in 1981. These comprise: (1) a reduction in federal spending for social programs, reflecting a major shift in priorities from nondefense to defense spending and from public to increased private allocation of resources (US Congressional Budget Office, 1981); (2) increased decentralization and block granting of program authority, fiscal and political responsibility to the states for social programs; (3) deregulation and the promotion of procompetition approaches, particularly in the health sector (Estes and Lee, 1981); and (4) a sharp reduction in federal revenues with the Economic Recovery Tax Act of 1981.

There will be increased competition and heightened tensions between the health and social services sectors as the cutback pressures mount on non-defense spending. States will be required to invoke stricter state-determined measures to limit their expenditures for health and social programs as a consequence of increased state and local responsibility and fiscal constraint.

Further, even the prospects for the most popular entitlement program for the elderly, Social Security, are under assault, to the extent that the aged are blamed for the fiscal crisis (Samuelson, 1978; 1981). The attribution of such culpability to the elderly is at least partly a result of the same separatist thinking that has fostered the aging enterprise. The consequence of such thinking appears to be dangerous in a period of economic retrenchment, for it is just such 'special' and 'different' groups (e.g., the aged) who may be used to explain the origin of the fiscal crisis — this in spite of the world politics and broad economic conditions and policies of which the aged are but a small part and which their policies only reflect.

REFERENCES

Advisory Commission on Intergovernmental Relations (1980a), *Recent Trends in Federal and State Aid to Local Governments* (Washington, DC, ACIR).

Advisory Commission on Intergovernmental Relations (1980b), *Significant Features of Fiscal Federalism, 1979-80* (Washington, DC, ACIR).

Alford, R. (1976), *Health Care Politics* (Chicago, IL, University of Chicago Press).

Baum, M. and R.C. Baum (1980), *Growing Old* (New York, NY, Prentice-Hall).

Brody, S. (1979), 'The Thirty-to-one Paradox: Health Needs and Medical Solutions', *National Journal,* Vol. 11(44), pp. 1869-1873.

Business Week (1981), 'State and Local Government in Trouble', (2711), pp. 135-181, 26 October.

Connolly, W.E. (1969), *The Bias of Pluralism* (New York, NY, Atherton).

Cook, F.L. (1979), *Who Should Be Helped? Support for Social Services* (Beverly Hills, CA, Sage Publications).

Davis, K. (1975), 'Equal Treatment and Unequal Benefits: The Medicare Program', *Milbank Memorial Fund Quarterly/Health and Society,* Vol. 53(4), pp. 449-488.

Davis, K. and C. Schoen (1978), *Health and the War on Poverty: A Ten-Year Appraisal* (Washington, DC, Brookings Institution).

Dowd, J.J. (1980), *Stratification Among the Aged* (Monterey, CA, Wadsworth, Brooks/Cole).

Estes, C.L. (1974), 'Community Planning for the Elderly: A Study of Goal Displacement', *Journal of Gerontology,* Vol. 29(6) pp. 684-691.

Estes, C.L. (1979), *The Aging Enterprise* (San Francisco, CA, Jossey-Bass).

Estes, C.L. and P.R. Lee (1981), 'Policy Shifts and Their Impact on Health Care for Elderly Persons', *Western Journal of Medicine,* Vol. 135(6), pp. 511-517.

Estes, C.L., P.R. Lee, C. Harrington, R. Newcomer, L. Gerard, M. Kreger, A.E. Benjamin and J. Swan (1981), *Long-Term Care for California's Elderly: Policies to Deal with a Costly Dilemma.* California Policy Seminar Monograph No. 10 (Berkeley, CA, Institute of Governmental Studies, University of California).

Estes, C.L., J.H. Swan and L.W. Gerard (1982), 'Dominant and Competing Paradigms in Gerontology: Toward a Political Economy of Aging', *Ageing and Society,* Vol. 2(2), pp. 151-164.

Evans, L. and J. Williamson (1981), 'Social Security and Social Control', *Generations: Journal of the Western Gerontological Society,* Vol. 6(2), pp. 18-20.

Ginsberg, N. (1979), *Class, Capital and Social Policy* (London, Macmillan).

Gough, I. (1979), *The Political Economy of the Welfare State* (London, Macmillan).

Guillemard, A.M. (1983), 'The Making of Old Age Policy in France', in this volume.

Henretta, J. and R. Campbell (1976), 'Status Attainment and Status Maintenance: A Case Study of Stratification in Old Age', *American Sociological Review,* Vol. 41(6), pp. 981-982.

Kelman, S. (ed.) (1975), 'Special Section on Political Economy of Health', *International Journal of Health Services,* Vol. 5(4), pp. 535-642.

Lee, P.R. and C.L. Estes (1979), 'Eighty Federal Programs for the Elderly', pp. 76-117 in C.L. Estes, *The Aging Enterprise* (San Francisco, CA, Jossey-Bass).

Miller, S.M. (1976), 'The Political Economy of Social Problems: From the Sixties to the Seventies', *Social Problems,* Vol. 24(1), pp. 131-141.

Myles, J.F. (1980), 'The Aged, the State, and the Structure of Inequality', pp. 317-342 in J. Harp and J. Hofley (eds.), *Structural Inequality in Canada* (Toronto, Prentice-Hall).

Myles, J.F. (1981), 'The Aged and the Welfare State: An Essay in Political Demography'. Paper presented at the International Sociological Association, Research Committee on Aging, Paris, 8-9 July.

Navarro, V. (1973), *Health and Medical Care in the U.S.: A Critical Analysis* (New York, NY, Baywood).

Navarro, V. (1976), *Medicine Under Capitalism* (New York, NY, Prodist).

Nelson, G. (1982), 'Social Class and Public Policy for the Elderly', *Social Science Review,* Vol. 56(1), pp. 85-107.

New York Times (1981), 'Reagan Reaffirms Determination to Cut Federal Aid Even Further', pp. 1, 32, 22 November.

O'Connor, J. (1973), *The Fiscal Crisis of the State* (New York, NY, St. Martin's).

Renaud, M. (1975), 'On the Structural Constraints to State Intervention in Health', *International Journal of Health Services,* Vol. 5(4), pp. 559-571.

Ruther, M. and A. Dobson (1981), 'Equal Treatment and Unequal Benefits: A Re-examination of the Use of Medicare Services by Race, 1967-1976', *Health Care Financing Review,* Vol. 2(3), pp. 55-83.

SRI International (1981), *Nonservices Approaches to Problems of the Aged* (Menlo Park, CA, Center for Urban and Regional Policy, SRI).

Salamon, L.M. and A.J. Abramson (1981), *The Federal Government and the Nonprofit Sector: Implications of the Reagan Budget Proposals* (Washington, DC, Urban Institute).

Samuelson, R.J. (1978), 'Busting the U.S. Budget: The Costs of an Aging America', *National Journal,* Vol. 10(7), pp. 256-260.

Samuelson, R.J. (1981), 'Benefit Programs for the Elderly Off Limits to Federal Budget Cutters?', *National Journal,* Vol. 13(40), pp. 1757-1762, 3 October.

Townsend, P. (1979), *Poverty in the United Kingdom* (Harmondsworth, Middlesex, Penguin Books).

Townsend, P. (1981), 'The Structured Dependency of the Elderly: A Creation of Social Policy in the Twentieth Century', *Ageing and Society,* Vol. 1(1) pp. 5-28.

Tussing, A. (1971), 'The Dual Welfare System', in L. Horowitz and C. Levy (eds.), *Social Realities* (New York, NY, Harper and Row).

US Congress, House Committee on Ways and Means, Subcommittee on Social Security (1981a), *Elimination of Minimum Social Security Benefit Under Public Law 97-35* (Washington, DC, US Government Printing Office).

US Congress, House Select Committee on Aging (1981b), *Analysis of the Impact of the Proposed Fiscal Year 1982 Budget Cuts on the Elderly: Briefing Paper Presented by the Chair* (Washington, DC, US Government Printing Office).

US Congressional Budget Office (1981), *Economic Policy and the Outlook for the Economy* (Washington, DC, US Government Printing Office).

US Public Law 97-35 (1981), 'The Omnibus Reconciliation Act of 1981' (Washington, DC, US Government Printing Office).

Walker, A. (1980), 'The Social Creation of Poverty and Dependency in Old Age', *Journal of Social Policy,* Vol. 9(1), pp. 49-75.

Walker, A. (1981), 'Towards a Political Economy of Old Age', *Ageing and Society,*

1(1), pp. 73-94.

Walton, J. (1979), 'Urban Political Economy', *Comparative Urban Research,* Vol. 7(1), pp. 5-17.

10

OLD PEOPLE, PUBLIC EXPENDITURE AND THE SYSTEM OF SOCIAL SERVICES: The Italian Case

Danilo Giori
Universities of Milan and Cagliari

Although old age is now a problem common to the vast majority of the populations of the industrialized countries, it remains confined to a particular sector about which one is little or ill-informed as the information available tends to deny or to belie the phenomenon.

The advent of industrial society and the improvement of the sanitary conditions first of the urban and then of the rural populations led to the elimination of many recurrent epidemics and other causes of mortality and to a consequent increase of the average life-span. In this way a new phenomenon developed in the industrialized societies: the populations got progressively older. At first, recourse was made to marginal social and sanitary measures founded on certain gerontological postulates, such as: (1) old people or most of them are poor; (2) their health is precarious; and (3) most of them live alone in physical and social isolation. It was sought in this way to legitimize 'charity' and assistance (private and therefore to be paid for) for old people who are poor because they are ill (the fact that they had worked for 30-40 years in unhealthy conditions being disregarded). And because they are poor and ill, they do not encourage visits or favor social relationships (the fact that often they have had to emigrate in search of employment being likewise disregarded).

This stereotyped view no longer makes any sense if one considers the real situation of the old in its economic, physiological and social aspects. The fact that these same old people can organize themselves and take action, e.g. in the formation of pensioners' unions, and can demand for themselves a new role in a new society, based on relationships different from the marginalizing relationships of capitalism, shows us that they are a very much alive social reality.

These new developments in the underworld to which the guilty conscience of our society (or at least of its rulers) has confined the old have made it clearer to us that old age is not something that is well defined or easily definable. A biological phenomenon, it has psychological and cultural aspects which give rise to characteristics and attitudes of an existential nature: in effect it modifies the individual's relationship with his time and, in consequence, with his history, even though he knows that his condition has been imposed on him by the society to which he belongs. The interrelationships and variability of its aspects are such that the problem cannot be considered simply in terms of analysis of its component parts. Since these interrelationships and variability are due mainly to causes of a social nature, it is necessary to take the social context into consideration. And in fact the primary cause of the 'alienation' of old people in a capitalistic society is their irrelevance to the fundamental relationships between capital and labor of such a society.[1]

It cannot be denied, however, that an analytical examination serves to bring to light the shortcomings and limitations of the partial solutions of the old-age problem, and also their ideological hypocrisy, for the problem has its roots in the social structure and its motivating principles, and the solution to the problem therefore calls for the modification of these principles.

The purpose of this paper is not only to describe the social condition of old people in Italy,[2] but also to give a summary description of the general institutional mechanisms concerned with the problems of old people and the place they occupy in the wider context of public expenditure for social purposes.

THE PROBLEM IN QUANTITATIVE TERMS

The problem of the aging of the Italian population became

significant in the 1970s as a result of the fall in the birth-rate, which in
its turn was the result of the spread of models of 'urban' life to all
regions from the mid-1960s onwards. The sharp fall in the birth-rate,
internal migration, emigration, urbanization and demographic
imbalance served to lay emphasis on the phenomenon of the aging of
the population to the point where its specific aspects had to be taken
into account in analyses and programs relating to national and
regional policies.

If we consider the development of this phenomenon from 1861 (the
year of the unification of Italy), we find that, while the total
population has more than doubled (from an index of 100 to 208), the
number of old people has increased more than fivefold (from an
index of 100 to 537). At the beginning of the century persöns aged
over 65 represented 4-5 percent of the population, today 13.1
percent. Another indication of the relative age of a population is
provided by the ratio between persons over 60 years old and children
under 14: in Italy in 1941 there were 27.8 persons over 60 for every 100
children, in 1951 46.4 and in 1979 74.8. This process, as we have
already said, is not uniform since there are differences between
regions (134.8 persons over 60 to 100 children in Liguria, 80 to 100 in
Apulia) and between town and country.

In effect the rapid process of industrialization in Italy has led to the
development of large towns in the North which today are faced by
problems relating to the aging of their populations. These problems
are less marked in the 'administrative' towns of the South (in Genoa
the over-60s represent 22.57 percent of the population, in Bologna
22.37 percent, in Calabria only 15.54 percent).

The phenomenon of the aging of the population has been
accompanied by that process of decomposition of the family typical
of strongly industrialized situations of urban character. The various
censuses have revealed the following average numbers of family
members:

1881	1901	1911	1921	1931	1951	1961	1971
4.47	4.52	4.46	4.38	4.21	3.97	3.63	3.35

Thus for fifty years changes were slight but in the following forty
years they were more marked, conforming to the model of the
European industrialized countries. The changes in the average life-
span have also affected family structure: the classic large family of
patriarchal type has increasingly been replaced by a family of
'vertical' nature in the sense that a couple with a single child is

linked to two other generations often in need of assistance.

Another serious problem derives from the fact that an old person consumes but rarely produces. This means that, whatever the system of production, it is the work of the active population that maintains the old people, hence the importance of the active/retired ratio, which in Italy has changed considerably.

In 1861 the ratios of active members of the population to over-60s and to over-65s were 9.28/1 and 14.56/1 respectively, which in 1971 had become 2.08/1 and 3.06/1. Thus, even though old people have a certain amount of economic and financial means, people who are economically 'active' have to contribute to the production of the goods required for the subsistence of old people. The increase of the total number of old people creates considerable economic problems for the collectivity. The old part of the population has to be helped financially by means of a suitable distribution of public expenditure made possible by taxes imposed on the 'active' members of the population. It is understandable that in Italy too the question of the lengthening of working life (by leaving the choice of the age of retirement to the individual) is of great current importance since retirement is a sort of social death in that it leads to a reduction of income and interrupts social relationships associated with work and the work-place.

Without wishing to contribute to a work 'mystique', it seems to us only right to acknowledge that work has played an important role in the processes of socialization and balancing of the personality. It is therefore necessary to avoid the need to make a momentous choice simply in order to escape from a burden or strain which is too great or for fear of marginalization or isolation. Hence the urgency of reconsidering the problem of retirement, of making it a free choice rather than an obligation, even though this means reversing in part what has hitherto been the policy of the workers' movement.

CONSTRUCTION OF A SYSTEM
OF SOCIAL ASSISTANCE

In Italy help for the aged was first provided by the Church and its charity organizations. They made use of both 'public charity' and private charity, administered above all by the Compagnia di Misericordia.

The social transformations caused by the French revolution made themselves felt in Italy, and in 1819, in the Kingdom of Lombardy and Venice (dominated by the Austrians), all the Charity Congregations were replaced by a 'Central Beneficence Commission' which established a charity organization in each commune. In 1840 Carlo Cattaneo, a Lombard economist, invited the population to form mutual help associations and in the 1850s fear of European socialism induced even the middle classes to form such associations. In Piedmont in 1859 (two years before the unification of Italy) beneficence was secularized, but the Piedmontese ruling class, not wishing to shoulder the full burden of caring for the poor, left ample legal space for private charity. Thus old charity institutions with strong popular traditions continued to exist without contributing to the public debt. Also in 1859 the Life-Annuity Fund for Old Age, optional for all citizens, was instituted but, since the ministerial decree establishing the date of its coming into effect was not issued, it never became operative. It was only in 1888, after the unification of Italy, that a law was passed providing for free sanitary, medical and surgical assistance to the poor at the expense of the communes. These free services were reserved, however, for poor people included in a special list drawn up by the commune and renewed each year.

Ten years later, in 1898, the National Social Assistance Fund for Invalidity and Old Age was instituted. The scheme was optional and open to all Italian citizens with regular or occasional manual jobs.

It was this particular characteristic that drew criticisms from the socialists, who were beginning to concern themselves with the question of social assistance in favour of the workers.

The next stage was to render sickness and old age insurance obligatory instead of optional. But while the socialist workers were favorable (to the point of including this objective in their electoral program of 1904), the trade unions (instituted in 1906) were divided on this point.

The war, however, had considerable social repercussions and these, together with the need to preserve internal 'peace', led to the development of conditions favorable to the institution of an obligatory system of social assistance.

In 1917, during the First World War, the various royal decrees established the obligation to insure all workers aged under seventy years, of either sex, employed in any way in the auxiliary establishments requisitioned by the government for the production of war materials. The insurance contributions were paid equally by the employer and the employee, the employer being responsible for their collection.

In 1920, after the end of the war, the Social Insurances Fund was instituted. This provided for the systematization of the various situations that had come into being in the preceding years.

In the years of fascism (from 1922), apart from some improvements and the addition of some complementary structures, e.g. the Sickness Fund, the situation remained practically unchanged.

The Second World War saw the financial collapse of the social insurance institutions for the workers in consequence of the fact that the Italian government took over the funds reserved for payment of pensions.

In and after 1945 the miserable conditions of the workers deteriorated to the point where certain trade-union leaders were reduced to begging in the streets and villages in order to obtain funds to distribute to old or sick workers.

The present social assistance structure has been developed gradually, by means of independent organisms, since the Second World War.

In thirty years (1951 to 1980) pensions paid by the state have increased from two million to over thirteen million, [3] with an expenditure of over 15,000 billion liras. An uninterrupted, though fragmentary legislative activity, first lowered the retirement age (1952), then extended the pension system to independent workers (farmers 1957, craftsmen 1962, shop-keepers 1966), made invalidity pensions easier to obtain, instituted social pensions (1969) and tied pensions to industrial salaries (1975).

In considering these modifications of the system of social security and their dates of application, it is noticeable that only one of these measures (the lowering of the retirement age in 1952, dictated by reasons contingent to the Italian economic revival) favored dependent workers in industry, and that these modifications were introduced in the years immediately preceding political elections.

Any doubt that the increase of public expenditure was an expedient employed by the government (always Christian Democrat though 'diluted' by the socialists), was shown to be groundless by the facts.

Of about thirteen million pensions paid by the Istituto Nazionale di Previdenza Sociale (INPS — National Institute of Social Security), approximately one million are for former independent workers (more than two million of whom enjoy a disability pension), 800,000 are social pensions, and five million are for former dependent workers (three million of whom enjoy disability pensions). It can be said that, whereas the number of old-age pensions paid by INPS to former dependent workers has registered a moderate increase and those paid to former independent workers even a slight decrease, there has been a considerable increase, particularly after 1970, in the number of disability pensions for both dependent and independent workers.

It is thus immediately clear that disability pensions[4] have played an important role in the redistribution of revenue in favor of particular social categories liable to support a certain 'power bloc'. A policy of this type was made possible by modifications with regard to qualification for such a pension. Provided that the conditions with regard to salary and insurance are satisfied, this right is obtained 'in the event that the capacity of a person of working age to earn a salary appropriate to his aptitudes and professional qualifications is reduced to less than one-third [recently two-thirds] of the salary considered normal'.

In the acquisition of this right it is clear that social and economic as well as pathological factors — 'if one wants to work it does not mean that one will automatically find a job' — play a part. The application of this criterion has practically converted disability pensions into unemployment indemnity.

But that is not all: the progressive reduction of the so-called 'weak' sectors of the labor force in the 1970s was made possible by a parallel distribution of disability pensions. In this way the state carried out a considerable redistribution of revenue, notably in favor of the less developed zones. This served to sustain the expansion of demand in these zones and to maintain a situation of 'controlled' underdevelopment.[5]

Intended by the public authorities as a measure of social 'justice' to counterbalance the disastrous effects on the populations of central and southern Italy of the chaotic industrial development in the postwar period, this policy had unfavorable repercussions which affected the national economy from 1965 onwards. Workers who, in the late 1960s and early 1970s, 'spontaneously' left the labor market in consequence of the opportunities offered by the state (anticipated pensions, disability pensions), were induced to return by the increase in inflation from 1972 onwards, constituting a supply of labor which was very attractive to enterprises affected by the general 'conflict situation' that followed the workers' demonstrations of 1969. The existence of a labor supply free from social security costs considerably widened the field of so-called 'irregular activities', favoring their concentration in little developed zones with populations including large numbers of 'assisted' persons. This tendency represented an opportunity for private industry, which immediately extended and developed the sector of irregular activities, but it was disastrous for the state.

The original hypothesis was to rid both the private and the public sector of 'obsolete' labor by favoring its 'voluntary' withdrawal in various ways. With the departure of these workers, private industry increased its degree of mechanization and, in consequence, the state had to supply money both for the retired workers and for the creation of new jobs that the stagnation of employment rendered necessary. Furthermore, now that pensions have recently (1975) been tied to industrial salaries, in order to adapt them to changes in the cost of living and to render the conditions of pensioners in an inflationary situation more tolerable, they are accused of ruining the Italian economy and corrective measures are being called for. It is certainly true that the automatic application of adaptive formulas to sums as large as the 15,000 billion liras of the pensions funds leads to considerable increases of public expenditure, further inflation and so on, in a vicious circle without end. But this certainly does not justify the attribution of responsibility for the 'widespread causes' of inflation to the weaker sectors of the community, retired people and pensioners.

FROM ASSISTANCE TO SOCIAL SERVICES

A discussion of what is normally referred to as assistance calls for some comments on the present system of production. In particular, it should be noted that in modern capitalism there is a considerable increase of public expenditure for purposes of supporting the increase in demand and employment. These 'assistance' measures, if one considers assistance proper and the sanitary aspect under the same heading, are one of the main components of this expenditure. Even if one considers only the assistance sector (which in Italy at present absorbs over 3000 billion liras, not to mention the 15,000 billions for pensions), one can see that the increasing expenditure of the sector is tied to the progressive increase in that part of the population which is without a working income (old people, handicapped persons). It becomes necessary, in consequence, to make special financial provisions to support or at any rate to help the families which cannot sustain the expenses involved in the care and rehabilitation of a handicapped person.

It is calculated that in Italy there are about 21 million persons in a needy condition, that is, persons who qualify for special contributions and services. Despite the far from small sum dedicated to the sector, only about 50 percent of these persons receive a (small) contribution, with the result that the real costs of assistance fall on the individual family which, in its turn, tries to obtain the funds required from private charity (organizations and parishes).

A similar situation of negligence on the part of the public sector, or at any rate of inadequate intervention, of fragmentation of the private sector and of precariousness of the family, calls for a sort of collective responsibility and effort for the purpose of constructing, by means of suitable campaigns and initiatives, a system of efficient, decentralized and democratically organized social services.

The Antecedents of
Social Service Policy

The type and the quality, that is, the efficiency, of the services offered and utilized by the community can be taken as the index of a country's industrial maturity. Furthermore, these services reflect the cultural and ideological roots of a population in the measure to which they are of religious origin. This is clearly revealed by a summary analysis of the different systems of social security of the industrial countries.

In northern Europe the birth and development of a capitalistic ideology imbued with the protestant spirit has confined the activities of charity and assistance to cases of real need, considered the field of collective (public) responsibility.

In the predominantly Catholic Mediterranean, assistance has

always been one of the pillars of the ideology and structure of the Church as a means of control which has also served increasingly as an ideological support.

In North America the pulverization of the religious sects and the emergence of individualism, together with the historical vicissitudes of this very rich country, have favored private enterprise and efficiency of social services (generally private). But this efficiency has been accompanied by considerable discrimination as to the possibilities of benefiting from it.

It is clear that Italy falls into the Mediterranean category and that an examination of the Italian situation can throw useful light on the interaction of economic, political and ideological factors involved in a system of social services.

This plurality of concomitant factors renders intervention in the sector, and the reactions to which it gives rise, of interest on account of a series of social mechanisms involving changes in a more general sense. Until recently, as we said above, the Church was the center of the assistance mechanism, whether for ideological purposes based on charity and inter-class collaboration or because its real estate made it possible to guarantee a capillary diffusion of the main form of social assistance: internment.

From medieval times the Church specialized in the organization of places of internment reserved for specific categories of people (lepers, vagabonds, beggars, orphans, wayward young ladies). It also developed a relative ideology which, on the one hand, served to justify the internment (reclusion) of 'misfits' and, on the other, encouraged 'normal' people to finance the system.

Mention should also be made of the numerous non-internees or ex-internees who maintained personal relationships with the assistance structures in order to be admitted to internment (which provided them with their daily bread) or to be helped financially after emerging from internment. In short, the Church governed a social system which extended from the lowest population strata (potential beneficiaries of assistance) to the highest (donors, benefactors), thus comprising the whole social pyramid. With the development of industrial society and workers' organizations, the role of the Church has diminished in importance.

Nevertheless, in Italy today, 50 percent of hospital personnel are religious and 40 percent of hospital beds are private (nearly always belonging to religious orders). In fact the charity aspect is accompanied by an 'insurance' aspect deriving from workers' assistance and insurance funds, which claim, on the one hand, a modern system of social assistance and security based only on nationality and, on the other, a non-religious character and public (state) participation in structures previously dominated by religious and private interests.

From a social point of view, the activities of the workers' fund organizations introduced a democratic principle of collective responsibility with regard to the functioning of structures for the protection of workers and their families.

It is therefore, and above all, industrialization and a modern organization of the economic system which led to an increase in the expenditure of the state and of local organizations (rarely controlled) in this sector, rendering necessary a complete revision of its internal structure and of intervention criteria. Even today the expenditure is made through more than 60,000 organizations of different natures and purpose.

This diversity makes it difficult, if not impossible, to intervene in any way with regard to rationalization programs and plans and, in consequence, practically impossible to measure the efficacy of the social assistance system and its appropriateness to real needs.

The pulverization of organizations and expenditure favors a policy of preference, costly and calling for a discrimination among beneficiaries (hence the plethora of institutes of public assistance). In effect, each sub-division, to protect itself and increase its share of public expenditure, has need of a patron, a protector, if possible involved in the mechanisms of distribution of this expenditure and, in particular, with influence in the ruling body (central or local).

The success of the trade unions as keystones of workers' organization and the progressive extension of their interest to aspects of social life outside the work-place have led to an increasing mobilization of public opinion with regard to themes closely related to the interests of the workers. This is because an efficient system of social services is determinant with regard to 'indirect' salary which concerns both the active life of the workers as a whole and also their retirement. The intervention of this new factor has made possible the process of reconstruction and renewal of a social services policy appropriate to a modern economic system.

Marginalization and Categorization

Fully occupied in the work of postwar reconstruction, the workers and the organizations that represented them were slow to intervene in the assistance sector, even though they were (and are) its main beneficiaries.

Social assistance for the old, minors, handicapped persons, was called for always and only in the case of persons belonging to the proletariat or sub-proletariat, on account of the inadequacy of pensions, the disastrous situation of the family in consequence of migration, bad hygienic conditions, the privations and hardships of the pregnant wives of these classes.

Until recently the traditional religious organizations could do more or less as they liked in this sector, cooperating with a public or para-public administration which allocated the needy to the various private institutes run by the religious orders without exercising any control over the treatment of inmates. This can be described as the period of uncontrolled internment of old people, minors, orphans, physically or mentally handicapped persons, problem children and wayward young ladies.

Police and judges in the case of minors, offspring and close relatives in the case of old people, had no difficulty in interning the persons they found on their hands. The social mechanism concerned in compulsory internment is relatively simple: the large family of peasant type obliged to emigrate in order to survive nearly always finds itself in a disastrous situation (in an unknown urban fabric, lacking services, sometimes openly hostile), especially if it includes a person, old or a minor, who requires constant care and attention. Such a situation is accentuated by the dispersion of the old family structures. And in such situations the internment mechanism begins to operate.

Some of the reasons for which 'socially useless' persons are interned may be surprising:

(1)   physicians and psycho-pedagogic personnel readily certify as deviants or abnormal minors or adults who find themselves in a difficult social situation and lack adequate means of subsistence, generally finding themselves in a social environment different from the one they are used to. It should be remembered, furthermore, that the scanty attention accorded to women in childbirth by medical and para-medical personnel tends to aggravate the physical or mental situation

of the offspring.

(2)   the organizations that manage the various internment institutions do not control and ensure the quality of their performance but 'sell' their service at a high price, the cost being borne by municipal and provincial organisms, the income levels of the families of the internees generally being extremely low.

(3)   the families of the internees, feeling guilty because of their internment initiative, refrain from interference with regard to the conditions or techniques of treatment of the internees.

(4)   public institutions, even though they accept very high prices for internment in private institutions, rarely check the standards of performance of these with regard to the inmates.

In this situation of general evasion of responsibility with regard to the future of the internees, it is not surprising that Italy is described as the land of the 'Celestines', with reference to the famous case of 'sister' Diletta Pagliuca and her maltreatment of the children interned in her charge.

Until the 1960s internment was practically the only solution offered by society to those who for various reasons were in need of care and assistance. Whatever the reasons for internment (senescence, handicap, lack of relatives), the effects are the same as imprisonment and the consequences, where the 'guests' are concerned, are evident.

Since controls are practically nonexistent, these institutions spring up like mushrooms and, in order to obtain the generous pensions distributed by public organizations, accentuate their 'mixed' character (i.e. they cater for several different categories), which is possible because their main function is simply that of keeping people under guard. This explains why assistance acquires the character of internment (necessary to receive assistance) and why the recipients of assistance are divided into categories permitting a single specialized intervention. Fundamentally, this categorization is linked to the general sociopolitical aspects of assistance. It gives the public authorities room to maneuver and to play off one category against another (cripples against invalids, handicapped persons against abandoned minors). Furthermore, categorization offers the assistance organizations possibilities of political support (politicians of the various parties are always present at congresses of war invalids, pensioners, cripples, handicapped persons, etc.), with a view to the promotion of special measures in favor of one category or another.

The plurality of funding mechanisms favors categorization and at the same time serves to imbue the recipients of assistance with what can be described as the assistance ideology, which amounts to a gradual acceptance of the fact that one is 'different' and useless to the society in which one lives. The assistance received in consequence comes to be seen as a favor rather than as a right. The precarious economic and social conditions of tens of thousands of families ensures a permanent demand for the creation of new institutions and for the expansion of this assistance industry closely associated with the religious orders, physicians and local political personalities. The categorization of the recipients of assistance permits the specialization of the service provided (and gives it the necessary technical alibi), and their inability to take part in the dominant system of production, whether for objective reasons (physically or psychologically handicapped persons, old people, invalids, etc.) or for subjective reasons, is the ideological pretext for their marginalization and exclusion from the life of the community. That assistance is a pretext serving to justify the processes of marginalization and internment of persons who, paradoxically, have a greater need of contact with the community, is also shown by the fact that the inmates of these institutions are not cared for but simply guarded or even subjected to exploitation.

CONCLUSIONS

According to some modern sociological theories, the bearing structure of capitalistic society (i.e. that structure that supports the capitalistic relationships and is linked to the class structure through the labor market) is to be seen in the structure of the professions and their hierarchy. According to this view of the internal functioning of the capitalistic social system and its reproduction, a person who is not part of this structure and hierarchy is not part of the social structure (his social position being without function or status). Thus school children, like housewives and old people, are parts of the population which are marginal by definition, that is, absent from the pyramid of the professions, and therefore 'parasites'. This view is now commonly accepted, so much so that these groups have acquired a special definition[6] in relation to the labor market, which is the nucleus of the social structure in so far as it is the place of formation of the pyramid of the professions: they are referred to as 'weak' sectors of the population because of their marginal position (partial or total) with regard to the productive process. Such marginality tends to become an important feature in the functioning of capitalistic production in the measure to which it serves to regulate the labor supply and consequently salary levels, especially industrial. Furthermore, it depends on the degree of development and the country's position on the industrial ladder.

Where development has been great (e.g. in the United States) the marginality of the 'weak' sectors will be subjet to wide fluctuations depending on the expansion of production and relationships with subordinate economies. On the other hand, where the level of development is average or low, there will tend to come into being a situation of structural exclusion from the labor market (as in Italy, for example). In this case the 'weak' sectors become the basis for the expansion of precarious labor and the development of a double productive circuit: large-scale industry with its stable labor force and small and medium-scale industry using precarious labor.

In accepting this theory, it has to be pointed out that there are variations of marginality even within the 'weak' sectors, and that old people in particular, in all countries whether developed or not, are subject to a marginalization which is irreversible. This phenomenon of exclusion of large sectors of the population from production points clearly to the inability of present social relationships to cope with the problems of a balanced economic growth of capitalistic society, this because the tendency of the classic age of expansion of capitalism has been reversed: capitalism then extended over increasingly large sectors of activity and of the population.

The possibility of giving old people a central role in present-day society is contrary to this segregational logic. It follows that this possibility cannot be realized in the context of capitalistic social relationships. Not only has capitalism created a commonplace image of old people as weak and useless, in order to justify their exclusion from production and their marginalization, but it has also and above all determined the general lines of their behavior in daily life. The lengthening of the average life-span and the simplification of working procedures have been accompanied by an increase in the expulsion of old people from productive roles. Technical progress (and we emphasize the word progress), which should reduce the effort of the producer, has been used to condemn old people and to anticipate their retirement from the productive scene. On the whole, therefore, the development of productive forces, instead of increasing collective participation in the production of wealth while at the same time reducing individual effort, has reduced the productive population by condemning large sectors of the population to private dependence (the wife dependent on the husband, or children on their parents) or public dependence (social assistance). The increase of dependence has generated ideological subcultures of irrational type which theorize the marginalization by confusing the cause and effect and sub-divide the area in a fictitious manner: age, lack of commitment, improvised fashions. In this way one comes unwittingly to accept a reversal of reality, deliberately disseminated by the social system, according to which it is not the capitalistic productive system that deprives young people of work but the young people who 'do not want' to work. It is in this context, in which the capacity of social relationships for adaptation to new economic and technological conditions and to the new structure of needs is diminishing, that the problem of old people should be considered. In a society of this type the reappropriation of roles by old people is clearly impossible, for it is society that accentuates their neuroses and exploits their segregative characteristics.

It is therefore clear that one can trace the problem of old age and of the role of old people in our society to their removal from production, [7] a process which plays a central role in producing marginalization, whether economic (drop in income) or social (restriction of relationships). The dividing line is represented by retirement in the measure to which it accelerates the processes of senescence, above all in the case of males. Economic marginality leads to political and social marginality and the result is to accelerate physical aging. The contradictions in development of the capitalistic social system call for reflection on the relationships between old people and their families (which can also be extended to other 'different' types).

The delicate equilibrium of family relationships is disturbed by the fact that the care and protection of those who are 'different' is confined to the private sphere. In this way, in addition to exploiting each family member before arriving at the final solution of internment, the process of dependence within the family is encouraged. The shortage of public services or their inefficiency is not casual but is instead linked to the dominant mode of production and its contradictions in that it obliges the nuclear family to adapt itself to the existing situation.[8] From this point of view, old people become a reservoir, a reserve labor force serving to solve the increasing difficulties of urban life, to make up for the shortcomings of the system of services, and to enable marginal enterprises to make large profits. This is why old people not only continue to carry out what can be described as 'service' activities (domestic activities in dwellings of offspring, care of young children, administrative formalities) but also become an important reservoir of under-employment which favors the accumulation of capital.

According to Sviluppo Economico Territoriale (ISVET) estimates, in 1975 in Italy there were 1,450,000 under-employed persons aged over 55 years (one woman to every two men). If this is added to the number regularly employed, one arrives at a labor supply of old people of the order of 3,950,000 (1,230,000 more than the figure supplied by the Istituto di Statistica [ISTAT]). Carrying the analysis rather further, one can say that the increase in fragmentary and precarious activities and the ideology of the care and custody of 'dependents' are two sides of the same coin. The shortage of hospital services and the blame attached to persons who intern their relatives lead to the extension of private charity, linked to the social crystallization of female roles.

Even though the problem of old people cannot be solved within the framework of capitalistic social relationships as a whole, something can be done with regard to some of its more serious aspects. We say this, even though we know that in Italy today the most common solution is to leave care to the family without specialized help, or, in the absence of a family, to resort to internment in an institution. There are no intermediate forms of intervention between these two extremes, which means that nothing is done to encourage the independence of old people or to maintain it when it already exists.

The possible remedies depend on the recovery of a social space favorable to old people and on the development of forms of support able to counteract the marginalization pressures deriving from the functional mechanisms of society. The limits of these possibilities are due to the fact that they refer to different phases of aging and depend on public resources which are now increasingly dedicated to the problems of young people rather than to the support of the old (it can even be said that there is 'competition' between the social groups affected by the process of exclusion, in an economic universe suffering from a chronic shortage of resources).

NOTES

1. See S. De Beauvoir, *La terza età* (Turin, Einaudi, 1970), P. Guidicini (ed.), *La condizione anziana* (Milan, Franco Angeli, 1977) and S. Burgalassi, *L'età inutila* (Pisa, Pacini, 1975).

2. D. Giori, *Essere vecchi* (Venice, Marsilio editore, 1978), and D. Giori, *Vivere la vecchiaia* (Rome, Savelli, 1981), which contains research findings on the Italian situation, with particular reference to Lombardy.

3.

TABLE 1
Pensions Administered by INPS (in thousands) in 1980

Fund	Old Age	Invalidity	Widows
Dependent Workers	3,800	3,200	2,100
Agriculturalists	540	1,600	80
Craftsmen	130	335	110
Shopkeepers	210	220	75
Transport Workers	30	10	25
Telephone Employees	9	2	4
Seamen	13	6	5
Electricians	31	3	14
Clergy	6	4	-
Others [1]	15	2	11
Social [2]	780	-	-

[1] Including tax officials, gas employees (integrative) and flight personnel.
[2] For citizens over 65 years without income.

A recent estimate by Guido Carli, ex-Governor of the Bank of Italy, of the growing difference between pensions paid and contributions received, published in the daily newspaper *La Repubblica* of 3 June 1981, gave the following figures for that year: payment of 29,660 billion liras in pensions, social security contributions of 17,000 billion liras.

TABLE 2
Ratio between Active Population and Senior Citizens

	61 Years and Over	65 Years and Over
1861	9.28	14.56
1951	3.58	5.31
1961	2.83	4.72
1971	2.08	3.06

4. Disability pensions, either for pathological and traumatic reasons or for social and economic causes, are given only if the prerequisite contributions have been made (i.e. insurance and old age contributions). They are available to workers irrespective of age: (1) when dismissed before reaching the minimum age necessary to receive an old age pension; (2) once the period during which they have enjoyed the unemployment benefit is over. The same pensions may be received by craftsmen and small-holders who, owing to new forms of industrial or agricultural production, are experiencing dramatic reductions in their incomes and have no other possibility of employment (depressed areas).

5. With regard to the 'economic' problems of the present social assistance system, see: A. Collida (ed.), *Sussidi, Mezzogiorno e disoccupazione* (Milan, Franco Angeli, 1978); D. Fausto, *Il sistema italiano di sicurezza sociale* (Bologna, Il Mulino, 1978); F. Terranova, *Il potere assistenziale* (Rome, Editori Riuniti, 1975); G. Castellino, *Il labirinto delle pensioni* (Bologna, Il Mulino, 1976).

6. On the structure of the labor market and 'marginalization', see: M. Paci (ed.), *Capitalismo e classi sociali in Italia* (Bologna, Il Mulino, 1978); F. Ferrarotti (ed.), *Marginalità, mercato del lavoro e classi sociali* (Milan, Franco Angeli, 1978).

7. Once again, see: De Beauvoir or Giori, op. cit., and above all: OECD, *Politiques Sociales de la Vieillesse* (Paris, 1979).

8. There is the same problem with regard to the situation of women in industrial societies. For Italy, see: L. Balbo, *Stato di famiglia* (Milan, Etas Libri, 1978).

TABLE 3
The Italian Population in Terms of Major Age Groups in the Years 1861, 1971, 1979 (Base 1861 = 100)

	1861	1971	1979
Men			
All Ages	100.0	202.6	215.2
Under 60 Years	100.0	184.4	196.2
Under 65 Years	100.0	190.7	199.6
61 Years and Over	100.0	457.1	479.9
65 Years and Over	100.0	473.5	569.9

TABLE 3 (contd.)

	1861	1971	1979
Women			
All ages	100.0	214.8	226.1
Under 60 Years	100.0	186.9	195.3
Under 65 Years	100.0	195.0	200.6
61 Years and Over	100.0	621.5	675.8
65 Years and Over	100.0	672.4	816.2
Total			
All Ages	100.0	208.7	220.6
Under 60 Years	100.0	185.6	195.7
Under 65 Years	100.0	192.8	200.1
61 Years and Over	100.0	537.4	575.5
65 Years and Over	100.0	571.8	691.6
Percentages of Old People			
Men			
61 Years and Over	6.70	15.10	14.93
65 Years and Over	4.22	9.85	11.16
Women			
61 Years and Over	6.41	18.55	19.16
65 Years and Over	4.14	12.96	14.94
Total			
61 Years and Over	6.55	16.88	17.10
65 Years and Over	4.18	11.45	13.10

Base: resident population.
Source: S. Somogyi: paper read at CGIL-CISL-UIL National Congress, 1980.

TABLE 4
European Social Assistance Expenditure (1973)

	% of National Income
Germany	28.9
Low Countries	28.0
Belgium	24.1
Italy	27.3
Luxembourg	26.6
France	24.4
Great Britain	22.1

TABLE 5
Distribution of Cost (%)

	Worker	Employer	State	Others
Germany	24	50	23	3
Low Countries	36	43	13	8
Belgium	20	46	30	4
Italy	15	54	24	7
Luxembourg	24	36	31	9
France	20	62	16	2
Great Britain	18	34	40	8

Source: EEC Commission, *Report of Social Developments in the Community.*

TABLE 6
Disability Pensions as Percentage of Labor Force (1975)

Molise	46.51	Toscana	23.67
Umbria	39.62	Emilia	22.33
Basilicata	35.62	Campania	21.44
Abruzzi	32.27	Trentino	20.85
Sardinia	31.52	Piedmont	19.52
Marche	30.42	Lazio	19.27
Calabria	27.55	Liguria	19.22
Sicily	27.28	Apulia	18.71
Valle d'Aosta	25.80	Venetia	14.23
Friuli V.G.	24.64	Lombardy	12.55

Source: Libro bianco sull'assistenza in Italia (edited by Censis) (Rome, November 1976).

Table 7 shows some findings of Italian and foreign research concerning the distribution of the most common disorders of old people and other indicators such as last hospitalization, its duration, percentage of bed-ridden persons and of those who are not self-sufficient.

TABLE 7

Disorders and Diseases (% of Respondents)

	Bresso (1.012)	Cassano (570)	Vimercate (2.486)	Melzo (181) G	Melzo (181) L	Valchiavenna (215)	Milano (200)
Circulation	47.6	29.3	26.9	14.0	27.0	35.8	53.0
Digestion	33.0	12.0	10.5	2.8	17.0	22.3	22.0
Respiration	20.1	12.6	13.8	7.7	15.0	20.1	18.5
Motor	n.r.	16.1	5.71	6.1	7.2	13.5	21.0
Sight	11.0	12.6	4.18	4.4	21.0	14.0	31.0
Hearing	9.5	6.8	3.4	3.9	12.0	7.4	12.5
Urogenital	6.5	5.9	4.7	n.r.	n.r.	3.7	1.5
Hemopoiesis	4.3	n.r.	n.r.	n.r.	n.r.	14.0	9.0
Rheumatism	55.6	29.0	23.0	5.0	15.0	21.4	40.0
Arthrosis			n.r.	14.0	22.0	52.6	49.5
Diabetes	9.5	6.8	5.3	6.6	5.5	7.9	7.0
Vertigo	n.r.	n.r.	1.6	n.r.		9.3	14.0
Fainting	n.r.	n.r.	n.r.	n.r.		3.3	4.0
Mastication	n.r.	n.r.	n.r.	n.r.		n.r.	18.0

(Rheumatism and Arthrosis are bracketed together.)

n.r. = not recorded; in the data relating to Melzo a distinction was made between slight (L) and serious (G).

This distribution of disorders corresponded to the hospitalization data shown in Tables 8 and 9.

TABLE 8
Last Hospitalization (% of Respondents)

	Bresso	Cassano	Liguria	Valchiav	Melzo	Milano	Denmark	GB	US
Less than One Year Ago			15.8			18.5	11	8	13
Less than Two Years Ago	17.3	25.6		39.0	34.0	29.5			
Less than Three Years Ago			37.0						

In some enquiries the 'less than two years ago' standard was used, in others, including the foreign surveys, the 'less than one year ago' standard. Data with regard to duration of hospitalization were obtained only with regard to Melzo and in two surveys from Great Britain and the United States. The data below show that the average period of hospitalization in Italy is greater than in other countries.

TABLE 9
Duration of Hospitalization (% of Persons with at least One Hospitalization)

	Melzo Over 60 Years	Melzo Over 75 Years		Great Britain	USA
Less than 15 Days	27.0	31.0		43.0	71.0
Between 15 and 30 Days	48.8	33.8		25.0	17.0
			½ Months	21.0	6.0
Between 1 and 3 Months	20.3	29.6			
More than 3 Months	4.7	5.6			
			More than ½ Months	11.0	6.0

The Melzo survey was carried out on a sample of 188 persons aged over 60 years, with a control group of 88 persons aged over 75 years.

The final comparative health data relate to frequency of medical examination of old people (here again the Italian data relate to the Melzo survey):

TABLE 10

Frequency of Medical Examination (% of Total Interviewees)

	Melzo	Denmark	GB	USA
Every 15 Days } Every Month }	8.9 24.0	22.0	34.0	30.0
Intervals of More than 3 Months	67.1			

We now pass to the distribution of incapacity based on the six questions of the Townsend incapacity index. We shall first give the percentage of bedridden persons revealed by various surveys from Italy and elsewhere.

TABLE 11

Percentage of Bedridden Persons (% of Total Interviewees)

Denmark	GB	USA	Melzo	Milano	Cassano	Vimercate	Liguria	Valchiavenna
2.0	3.0	2.0	1.7	2.0	2.8	1.0	5.5	1.4

TABLE 12

Townsend Incapacity Index (% of Total Interviewees)

	Valchiavenna			Melzo			Denmark			Great Britain			USA		
	Male	Female	Total	Male	Female	Total	Male	Female	Total	Male	Female	Total	Male	Female	Total
0	56	55	55	58	44	49	58	48	53	65	48	55	68	58	63
1-2	13	16	15	22	18	20	26	27	26	22	25	24	21	23	22
3-4	11	10	10	9	15	13	7	13	10	7	12	10	6	9	7
5-6	13	10	11	6	16	12	5	6	6	3	7	5	4	3	4
7 +	7	9	9	5	7	6	4	6	5	3	8	6	1	6	4
	100	100	100	100	100	100	100	100	100	100	100	100	100	100	100

It should be borne in mind that the Italian surveys relate to persons aged over 60 years old, the others to persons aged over 65.

11

ORIGINS AND TRENDS OF SOCIAL POLICY FOR THE AGED IN THE FEDERAL REPUBLIC OF GERMANY AND WEST BERLIN

Hilde von Balluseck
Fachhochschule für Sozialarbeit und Sozialpädagogik Berlin

INTRODUCTION

This paper will attempt to trace the historical development and make a theoretical interpretation of social policy for the aged over the last 130 years.

Social policy will be examined from two aspects:

— as a means of integrating the population into a situation of wage dependency and into the respective social and economic systems, and

— as a means of integrating women, in particular, into the institution of the family based on the concept of life-long sexual communion, sex-specific division of labor and a restriction of communal living to two parents and their children (nuclear family).

The institution of wage-based labor, i.e. the exchange of capital and labor in the context of a class-specific division of labor, and the

I am grateful to Angelika Trilling for many thoughts in this paper, especially concerning the functions of advice and education. Michaele Schreyer gave critical comments on the first version of the paper and helped me a lot in doing so. The translation is by Maggie Saunders.

institution of the family are seen to complement each other. Wage-based labor cannot continue to exist without female labor in the family or the institution of the family as an emotional refuge (however ideological and far from reality this often is). Neither would it be possible for the family to persist in its present form — if both sexes were given complete freedom of choice — without the pressure exerted by wage-based labor. Only this twin approach can help explain the economic and social problems that occur in old age. The risk of infirmity in old age is one that threatens to place every wage-earner in a situation of severe need, and was one of the first risks to be covered by an insurance scheme in the last century. Additionally, the economic and social connection to the family is often broken in old age through the departure or death of the breadwinner or the children leaving home. This break-up of the family affects those women who are economically dependent on their husbands — until recently the clear majority. Statistics continue to show that it is this dependence of women on their families which creates the problems experienced in old age.

The methods used by social policy to integrate wage-earners extend from manipulation of the labor market to social security and social control (Lenhardt and Offe, 1977; Narr and Offe, 1975). The same methods, which include political measures relating to the family and ideological campaigns, also serve to perpetuate the sex-specific division of labor.

The *manipulation of the labor market* is of relevance for the aged in that it is an attempt to influence labor requirements both quantitatively and qualitatively according to the state of the labor market. Further, it is, to some extent, a determining factor in establishing the number of insured years and hence the income of former wage-earners in old age. This paper will examine the manipulation of the labor market during each phase of the development of social policy with consideration of the general situation of all wage-earners and of female labor in particular. This variable will reveal the economic and social insufficiency of the institution of the family, into which social policy has continually forced women. The contradiction between ideology and reality is shown in the concentration of social policy on integrating women into the family and in the deficits which almost inevitably emerge for old women from such a policy.

Social security is one of the most effective instruments of integration. During the entire lifetime of a wage-earner it functions as a form of social control since withdrawal from wage-based labor would mean the loss of the advantages of social security. The concept of economic security in old age is a motivation for wage-earners and is therefore a stabilizing factor. As well as the economic 'bonus' for lifelong labor, there is economic security for surviving dependents which makes widows in old age dependent on the income of their late husbands. In the development of social security for surviving dependents, it is again possible to see the political aims of the state with regard to the family. Therefore, in addition to the economic security of all wage-earners, the question of widows' pensions will also be examined.

The second example of a special social policy for the aged has only become topical during the last twenty years. This is the extension of social policy measures to cover the areas of socialization and social control through planning, counselling and education. Until the middle of this century, social control of the aged was guaranteed by their own needs and by welfare for the poor (although, after a lifetime of social adjustment, resistance among the aged was rare). Today, however, the growth of groups not integrated into the labor process (e.g. the young and unemployed) has made certain measures necessary to give meaning to the lives of those who have no further function. Thus, educational measures have only a satisfaction function which conceals the uselessness of the aged and yet secures their continuing loyalty to the state (they all still have a vote). This reveals the limitations of special social policies for selected groups, which aim to improve the functioning of the process of exchange between capital and labor.

The third example is also taken from the social security sector and is related to *the risk of becoming in need of care*. This can be traced back throughout the history of social policy and remains an area where there is a lack of financial security. Increased life expectancy and the increasing frequency of chronic illness has resulted in a hitherto unheard of increase in the number of cases in need of care. This problem involves social factors which have still to be researched (the role of working and living conditions in the development of chronic illness), as well as the biological fact of death, the social and ethical problems of dealing with those in need of care, the question of the meaning of life in cases of incurable illness and the possibility of suicide. For the last 130 years, social policy has used by and large the same means in attempts to solve these problems: the exclusion of those affected, and, for reasons of cost, the encouragement of unpaid care by (female) relatives and the development of outpatient services. The weaknesses of a social policy which encourages wage-based labor and the unpaid or low-paid employment of women will be particularly clearly revealed. Not only has the problem of caring for those in need not been solved economically, it continues to be a fundamentally social and ethical problem.

The presentation of these problems will show that the problems of a growing and unproductive section of the population are the result of sex- and class-specific division of labor and are intensified by social policy for the aged. It will also be shown that the problems of those in need of care cannot even be adequately defined, because of the functions of social policy.

The aims of this paper can be only partially fulfilled because of the time and space available. Many points demand further research. The author sees this paper as a contribution to a discussion, not as a final statement on this topic.

INDUSTRIALIZATION AND WELFARE UP TO THE END OF THE 19TH CENTURY: THE BEGINNING OF THE OLD AGE PROBLEM

Wage-based labor and the family established themselves as the bases of existence during the 18th and 19th centuries. Wage-based labor, however, has its origins much earlier. By the end of the Middle Ages in Germany, a change in attitude to work became apparent which reached a high point during industrialization. As wage-based labor became the dominant source of income for the majority of the population during the 19th century, so the concept of labor with all its attendant virtues (acceptance of any paid work, acceptance of working times and conditions, no involvement in planning or production) became the rule. One of the means by which wage-based labor was able to assert itself was through welfare schemes for the poor which contained strong elements of control (Sachsse and Tennstedt, 1980).

At the same time as the population was freed from other commitments (and thus, other protective communities), human co-existence changed fundamentally. The idea of the house as the basis of a life-form which contained the processes of production and consumption and formed a center for the emotional and rational energies of its members, who were sometimes linked by family connections, but always through labor, was gradually replaced. This concept was not comparable with the idea of the extended family which was not widespread in Central Europe (Mitterauer, 1978). The new life-form was based on the 'family', a community in which a married couple lived with their children, but did not work together. This meant that all members of the family became dependent on work done outside the house, largely as the responsibility of the male head of the household. The word 'family' only enters common usage in German during the 18th century.

With the freeing of workers for purposes of wage-based labor and the mobility that this demanded, there was a gradual reduction in the barriers to marriage. These had previously prevented many dependents, in order to avoid poverty, from living together legally and having children. From the 17th to the 19th century, these barriers continued to apply to dependents, whereas they did not affect the new class of wage-earner (Heinsohn and Knieper, 1974).

As the gap widened between productive labor for a wage and unpaid work in the family, between public life and privacy, between rationality and emotion, elements were eliminated that constituted disturbing factors for wage-based labor, and so for the exploitation of the workforce. These different spheres were now distributed 'naturally', according to sex: wage-earning thus became the responsibility of the man, while the family was to be the woman's sphere of influence (Hausen, 1978). Marriage and the family became institutions that were the living and working area of the woman, but their form and structure continued to be dominated by the man. Compared with his former dependence on a master and/or the family, marriage semed to offer independence and the opportunity for the man to satisfy his sexual needs legally (feelings that were, in any case, denied women). The incidence of marriage increased dramatically. The ideological concept of the family as a refuge in a hard world of labor was another factor which contributed to this increase. While in 1871 20 percent of thirty year old women were still single, today this figure is only 10 percent (Bundesministerium des Innern, 1980, p. 37).

Old Age as an Economic Risk

The main risks to income facing a wage-earner were sickness, accident, infirmity and unemployment. Each of these could lead to a situation of absolute misery. For women who did not work continually, there was the added risk of the break-up of the family, since this formed the basis of her social status and economic security. For centuries, there had existed insurance schemes against these risks for certain groups of the population. The forerunners of the official sickness insurance schemes were the aid programs of the guilds and professional organizations, factory sickness insurance schemes set up by the owners, self-help schemes for workers and community sickness insurance for the poor. In 1880, about 5 percent of the German population was insured through such a scheme (Tennstedt, 1976, p. 396). The forerunners of accident insurance are to be found in aid schemes which also supported widows, and in the insurance liability law which was introduced nationwide in 1871. In this case, however, it was necessary to prove the liability of the employer in the case of an accident at work. Until there was general legislation on accident insurance, these measures covered only a small part of the population. Tennstedt (1976, p. 424) has estimated the level of insurance of factory workers to have been 10-17 percent in the case of all accidents and 35-40 percent for accidents for which the employer was liable.

Pension schemes existed as early as the Middle Ages for some farmers (*Ausgedinge*) and for certain groups such as members of guilds, miners and foundry workers. However, most wage-earners, especially the whole of the new industrial proletariat and their families, had no financial security in old age. There was therefore a restructuring of the poor population during industrialization. Before and at the onset of this period, food shortages, wars, rapid increases in population and liberation from feudal commitments created a large number of poor, to which came the self-employed, the unemployed, those employed on a daily basis, widows, orphans, the sick, the disabled and also soldiers in periods of crisis (Sachsse and Tennstedt, 1980, pp. 28ff., 181ff.). The aged did not appear as a special group because average life expectancy did not really increase until this century. Even at the end of the last century, a newly born child had a life expectancy of only 35 years. Before the Second World War, this had risen to 60 years, and today the average life expectancy for a man is 68.5 years and for a woman

72.25 years (Bundesministerium des Innern, 1980, p. 75f.)

As wage-based labor was extended to more and more sectors of the population and with the increased productivity of the last century, the risks encountered by a wage-earner became the main causes of poverty. Widows and orphans, the sick and the aged were now those who became poor, and consequently the new recipients of welfare for the poor. In Berlin in 1867, 67 percent of those receiving alms were over 60, 76 percent of them were women, and 64 percent were widows and deserted wives (Schwabe, 1969, p. 75f.). The problem of the poor became a problem of the aged and, in particular, a problem of women.

The Development of Welfare for the Poor

During the Middle Ages, welfare for the poor became increasingly the responsibility of the municipalities, whereas it had previously been almost entirely supported by the Church and private individuals. From the end of the Thirty Years' War (1618 to 1648) to the end of the 18th century, welfare for the poor was partially removed from the local communities and was organized centrally (Sachsse and Tennstedt, 1980, p. 85f.). Public welfare measures gradually took over from those of the Church. In 1794, the Preussisches Landrecht (Prussian law) placed responsibility for bearing the costs of caring for the poor on the communities. In 1842, the Unterstützungswohnsitzgesetz (residential maintenance law) was also passed in Prussia, according to which the poor no longer had to have their 'home', but only a place of residence in the community which was obliged to support them. This law, which Prussia was the first German state to pass, reflects the increasing mobility of wage-earners who no longer had a necessary economic function to fulfil in their home town. In 1870 it was extended to other German states. If it was not possible to ascertain which community was responsible for support the regional association for the poor was made to bear the costs. The increasing influence of the state on welfare for the poor shows its function in controlling negative social factors and thus ensuring the smooth functioning of the exchange of capital and labor. The forms of caring for the poor at this time reveal that wage-earners were integrated into their new lifestyle by repressive means (Sachsse and Tennstedt, 1980). One of the conditions of receiving financial aid was willingness to enter any wage-based employment, regardless of the conditions. Support for the poor was based on the lowest wage level, which in the last century was not even enough for physical reproduction, let alone for other needs related to possessions and health.

As well as the public schemes for the care of the poor, the churches and private organizations continued to concern themselves with the problem. However, they also began to examine 'the need and worthiness' of those who applied for aid. Spontaneous help and support for the poor without any form of selection thus became unacceptable.

The Risk of Becoming in Need of Care

Sickness welfare for the aged does not play a significant role in the history of welfare until the end of the 19th century, for the simple reason that few people reached old age. If an old person did become ill and in need of care, he received minimal care together with the poor in hospices which were, at the same time, poorhouses. It was only during the 18th century that there were the first moves to differentiate between institutions according to their function. Poor people who were willing to work were sent to the workhouse, the mentally sick were admitted to asylums, criminals were placed in prison, juvenile delinquents in homes and the aged who were in need of care ended up in homes for the incurable. The latter institutions expanded from the end of the 19th century.

Summary

In the early phase of the period examined here, various effects of the institutionalization of wage-based labor become apparent. The aged who for health reasons can no longer be integrated into the labor process are in need of particular measures which initially exist only in welfare schemes for the poor. This possibility is made use of by those wage-earners who are no longer able to work and particularly by women whose husbands have died or who have been deserted by their families. The aged form the lowest level of this hierarchy. They have neither economic security, nor do they receive adequate care in the homes for the incurable. Their fate is, however, not fundamentally different from that of poor wage-earners and their families, who can barely survive on what they earn.

FROM THE BEGINNING OF THE GERMAN EMPIRE TO THE FIRST WORLD WAR (1871-1918): THE AGED AS A SPECIAL GROUP

Wage-Based Labor and Female Labor

The decline in infant mortality led to an increase in the population of Germany from 22-24 million in 1800 to 56 million in 1900 (Sachsse and Tennstedt, 1980, p. 179). Urbanization and industrialization resulted in a shift of employment from the primary sector (agriculture, horticulture, forestry, fisheries) to the secondary sector (industry, crafts, publishing, mining) and the tertiary sector (services, trade, transport, banks, etc.) (Sachsse and Tennstedt, 1980, p. 180). While in 1882 the largest proportion of the employed was in agriculture, in 1907 the number employed in industry and crafts alone was larger than that of agricultural laborers (Kuczynski, 1963, p. 254).

Female employment increased faster than that of males. From 1882 to 1907, the number of women employed rose by almost 100 percent while that of men increased by 'only' 50 percent (Kuczynski, 1963, p. 254). However, for women, employment was usually only part-time or temporary. Dreher (1978, p. 73) has calculated, after removing sources of error, that in 1907 the percentage of workers' wives in employment was 25 percent. It is true to say that there was a considerable contradiction between the ideal of the woman as a wife and mother and the reality of female employment. Legislation and ideological campaigns, however, continued to be based on this maternal ideal. In 1896 the subordination of women to men, even in their 'own' area of influence, the family, was given legal sanction by the *Bürgerliches Gesetzbuch* (Book of Common Law), according to which it was no longer possible for a woman to take up employment without the consent of her husband. It was rare for a woman to undertake any kind of vocational training. Even the middle class women's movement based its arguments on the accepted female qualities when it demanded access to such professions as nursing, welfare work or teaching, claiming that women were by their very nature particularly well-qualified for these responsibilities. For middle class women, employment was seen as a necessary and/or temporary evil, while dependence on the employment of the husband remained the — desirable — rule.

Old Age as an Economic Risk

For the socially conformist wage-earner and his family, sickness, unemployment, and for the women the death of the breadwinner, were still the main causes of poverty. It was still possible for the employer to distance himself from all risks related to the lives of the workers (Sachsse and Tennstedt, 1980, p. 260). These factors now affected the aged above all. The 'alternative policy for the poor' (Sachsse and Tennstedt, 1980, p. 262) pursued by the state after the end of the 19th century was aimed at

> securing the existence of the wage-earners so that it would be generally impossible for the working population to decline into poverty, and thus protect society from the dangers of a proletarian revolution (Sachsse and Tennstedt, 1980, p. 262).

Without any direct action by the wage-earners themselves, and accompanied by the Socialist laws (1878-1890) which aimed to repress revolutionary tendencies, legislation was passed to secure sickness insurance (1884), accident insurance (1884, came into force 1885), and disability and old age insurance (1889, came into force 1891). These schemes initially applied only to workers, and then not to every group. Sickness insurance protected wage-earners by paying them a sickness allowance and by covering medical treatment. The aged wage-earner who no longer worked was not, however, covered by the scheme. Accident insurance protected those workers who had become invalids through accidents at work and paid pensions to widows whose husbands had died immediately after accidents at work. In contrast, disability and old age insurance schemes did not consider the widow at all. In order to benefit from this pension scheme, a worker had to reach the age of 70 (it was 1916 before the age limit was reduced to 65). In the period from 1891 to 1900, only 23,195 males out of 100,000 reached this age (mortality statistics, quoted from Tennstedt, 1976,

p. 449). A further condition for drawing this pension was the payment of contributions for thirty years, which meant that the effects of this legislation could not be seen until the 20th century. If a worker became an invalid before the age of 70, he only received a pension if his earnings dropped to below a third of his previous or usual earnings. This meant that his ability to work had to be severely reduced by illness.

It was mostly older workers who took advantage of this disability pension. At the end of the 19th century, 80.5 percent of disability pensions were drawn by the over fifties. Such pensions were very low since it was their stated aim merely to maintain a minimal standard of living (Tennstedt, 1976, pp. 448-451).

In contrast, the insurance scheme for white collar employees which was introduced in 1911 had the advantage that an old-age pension was paid from the age of 65 onwards and that inability to carry out a profession and not inability to work was sufficient to qualify for a pension. This meant that a white collar employee had been granted a lifelong connection to his profession (and his social status!), while the workers continued to be forced to take any work offered to them, to the point of complete poverty (Tennstedt, 1976, p. 452).

Widows of workers continued to be excluded from disability and old-age pension schemes. It was not until 1911 that their pensions were calculated on the basis of the earnings of their late husbands. Pension legislation for white collar employees included their widows. In the same way as there were differences in the treatment of male workers and male white collar employees, so their widows were treated differently according to their status. Widows of workers only received a pension if they were not able to work themselves. Theoretically then, they had to take up work at the age of 65 or over if they were unable to prove their inability to do so. In contrast, the widow of a white collar employee always received a pension, because it would have been unreasonable to expect her to go out to work after her husband's death. The widow of a worker also lost her right to a widow's pension if she had her own insurance policy. It is also important to remember that the daily allowance for the welfare of the poor, oriented as it was to the lowest income level, was still higher than the sum a worker's widow could expect to receive as a pension (Dreher, 1978, pp. 60, 62, 67).

Under these conditions — very slow integration of wage-earners into pension schemes, no sickness insurance for pensioners, no unemployment insurance (it was not introduced until 1927), insufficient security for women — it was logical that the services provided by the welfare organizations could not be reduced. The Deutsche Verein für Armenpflege und Wohltätigkeit (the German Association for Charity and Care of the Poor), founded in 1880 and known today as the Deutscher Verein für öffentliche and private Fürsorge (the German Association for Public and Private Welfare) included both public and private initiatives (i.e. the welfare organizations). The association had hoped that social legislation would ease some of the financial pressures on its member organizations and had even expressed the hope that social insurance schemes would eventually make welfare for the poor superfluous (Freund, 1891). A survey made at the beginning of the 1890s revealed no easing of the situation (Freund, 1895). Later, however, it could be seen that welfare schemes for the poor took on new responsibilities at this time, and were able to improve their services. This was partly the result of a general improvement in the standard of living. Unlike the social insurance schemes, for which certain conditions had to be fulfilled, the welfare organizations continued to be based on the principle of need, without setting any conditions. Since this principle of need remained linked to the lowest income groups, it was not possible for any critical potential to develop (Sachsse and Tennstedet, 1980, p. 264). The welfare of the poor therefore remained an instrument for integrating the wage-earners, with clear elements of social control.

The Risk of Becoming in Need of Care

Wage-earners who were old and sick were without any economic security. Their accommodation in institutions for the incurably ill, run mostly by the communities or welfare organizations, was paid for by public charity organizations. By the end of the 19th century these institutions were being extended and at the same time the beginnings of a differentiation could be seen in the functions of different institutions. The extension and development of the institutions for the incurable had, as documents of the Protestant Church of the time show, not only financial reasons:
— those who were visibly ill should be removed from public view,
— hospitals no longer wanted to care for incurables,
— the poorhouses were felt to be unsuitable for incurables,

— the Church wanted to assert itself in one area over the public welfare services (Büttner, 1884; Medem, 1888; Krippendorf, 1904).

The differentiation that occurred in hospital organization was, on the other hand, for reasons of cost. The old and sick should be accommodated elsewhere in order not to overload the expensive hospital system (Gottstein, 1913). The chronically sick were just one of the groups singled out as unproductive and therefore to be accommodated as cheaply as possible. The remarkable thing about the arguments presented then is that they have hardly changed over the last hundred years (cf. 6.5).

Summary

Maintenance in old age provides wage-earners with some economic security. At the same time, however, old wage-earners are isolated from the rest of the population by the very fact that they are treated as a special, and unproductive, group. It is almost impossible to document these two effects of social insurance. Widowed and, especially, divorced and deserted women are largely uninsured while sick old people are entirely without such economic security. The various causes of material and mental misery create the basis for further special social policies for the aged. The social insurance scheme which developed alongside the programs for the care of the poor brought a clear improvement to the living conditions of the old and sick. However, the intention of committing the workers to the existing economic system as wage-earners and supporting the complementary institution of the family also made its mark in the forms of insurance developed, and their consequences for the insured.

The extension of wage-based labor to more and more levels of the population tended to break up broad situations of co-existence, and thus edged to one side all problem cases, such as the aged, the sick, the handicapped. Any form of insurance that was not easy to comprehend in its organization, or was not based on mutual assistance and solidarity, was bound to add to this trend and weaken the potential for self-help that had already been reduced by the commitment of the workers to wage-based labor (Rodenstein, 1978). For women, the introduction of a scheme for the maintenance of surviving dependents was an initial form of security, but the form it took increased their dependence on their husbands. They continued to be bound to their marriages for reasons of financial security.

The state thus set the direction for future decisions on social policy. Firstly, it would be the state which would be consulted on future changes in social policy. Secondly, by reducing social insurance to the level of financial support and curative services, especially through the strict division of the areas of production and reproduction, it was possible for the state to ignore the causes of many problems of old age and sickness. Alienated wage-based labor and the structure of the family could therefore be excluded from the discussion.

THE WEIMAR REPUBLIC (1919-1933): THE AGED AS A GROUP WITH CLAIMS OF THEIR OWN

Wage-Based Labor and Female Labor

The Weimar Republic had decided against a revolutionary new social order. Thus the methods used to attempt to overcome the effects of the First World War were those of the existing system. However, social policy in the Weimar Republic was marked initially by efforts to increase worker co-determination in industry and social insurance, while at the same time guaranteeing the state a high degree of influence in these sectors. The severe needs among the population following the war, the political power relationships and the influence of the world economic crisis forced the state, however, to reduce its own influence and to again limit the rights granted to workers (Gladen, 1974, pp. 94ff.; Tennstedt, 1976, pp. 397ff.).

There were no fundamental changes in policy towards women apart from the introduction of female suffrage in 1919. The proportion of women among wage-earners had increased, and within female employment, there had been a structural shift towards the new professions in business and administration. In contrast to the social professions, these new jobs were based on the characteristics of women required by the development of production industry. Young and attractive women were employed to increase profits which meant that older women (those over 30!) had little chance of finding employment in this sector, or were even threatened with dismissal (Frevert, 1979, pp. 95, 101). From 1926 to 1930, the proportion of women in white collar jobs rose by 11 percent. By 1930, women made up 37.1 percent of those in white collar employment, while they comprised only 23.3 percent of the blue collar working population (Winkler, 1977, p. 20),

Working conditions for women were generally worse than those for men. As workers, they had to produce more in order to earn the same as men, and as white collar workers they were employed in the lower status positions which had developed from rationalization and bureaucratization or, in business, as salesgirls. They had few opportunities for promotion (Frevert, 1979; Winkler, 1977, p. 21).

The main workplace for women remained the family. Employment was either a temporary situation or was necessary for financial reasons. A survey in 1932 showed that 80 percent of married working women were only working for reasons of financial need (Winkler, 1977, p. 25).

Increasing unemployment after 1929 led to a revival of hostility to female employment. The trade unions supported this tendency with their demands for an end to double wage-earning — implying, of course, that women should return to the family. Further support came from Pope Pius XI who, in 1931, rejected the idea of any employment of wives and mothers (Winkler, 1977, p. 24). During this period, women found themselves being increasingly forced back into the family and thus into a situation of dependence on their husbands.

Old Age as an Economic Risk

Social insurance was overloaded because so many men had fallen while still relatively young, or were unable to work again after the war. In 1922, the situation was so bad that the state made 600 million marks available for those in need, mostly pensioners. The load on social insurance schemes was so great that there was talk of transferring from an insurance to a welfare scheme (Heimerich, 1924, p. 75). However, since the contributions of the younger participants in the pension insurance scheme were needed in order to finance the pensions, this idea was abandoned (Tennstedt, 1976, pp. 397, 461).

During the Weimar Republic, there were the first indications of a contradiction between the generally charitable attitude to the aged and the need of older members of the middle class to retain their former status and certain related rights. During this time, there was a first differentiation between two groups of pensioners with small incomes: *Sozialrentner* (social pensioners) and *Kleinrentner* (small pension receivers). The *Sozialrentner* were those who drew their pension through social insurance while *Kleinrentner* were those members of classes that had been well-off, but, because of the war debt and the devaluation of currency, were no longer able to survive on their savings and therefore were forced to apply for public aid. The *Kleinrentner* fought bitterly not to become dependent on the welfare services, but to achieve a special form of maintenance from the state. This dilemma between efforts to achieve equality of treatment for the poor in old age and recognition of earlier differences in social status is also revealed in the 'national guidelines on the conditions, form and degree of public welfare' of 1924, which accompanied a piece of legislation on the responsibility for welfare. Section 14 of the guidelines states that consideration should be paid to the previous standard of living of the aged, with specific mention of the *Kleinrentner*. This group should also be allowed to keep household and inherited objects, as well as a small freehold (Dünner, 1925). *Sozialrentner* should be treated in the same way, although this was an entirely unrealistic approach to the problem, since they had no such possessions. A special welfare scheme, aimed at supporting the *Kleinrentner*, was rejected by the Deutscher Verein which was for uniform treatment of *Sozial-* and *Kleinrentner* (Krug von Nidda, 1930, pp. 13ff.).

The degree and distribution of poverty among pensioners, many of whom were too ashamed of their situation to make use of their rights to public aid, is revealed by various statistics. In 1929, 23 percent of all *Sozialrentner* were receiving public support. More than two-thirds of widows over 65 were supported by welfare organizations (Niemeyer, 1930, p. 140). Of the *Kleinrentner* in Berlin receiving public support, over 70 percent were women (Wex, 1929, p. 31).

In the case of widows' pensions, there was also a gradual agreement on conditions. From 1923 onwards, the widow of a worker received three times the annual payment as a lump sum on remarriage. In 1924, this sum was reduced to one year's allowance for widows of both workers and white collar employees. In 1925, the figure was increased again to three times the annual sum for widows of white collar employees. In this case, the attempt to balance conditions for both social groups failed because of the bad financial situation and because the differences in status were too well-established. In 1927, the widow of a worker was automatically granted a widow's pension on reaching the age of 65. If she was widowed before then, she was still required to go out to work, in contrast to the widow of a white collar employee (Dreher, 1978, pp. 82, 88).

The Risk of Becoming in Need of Care

In the area of nursing welfare, there is a continued tendency to push the aged to one side. Institutions for the incurable are supposed to ease the burden on old people's homes and hospitals and reduce costs (Polligkeit, 1928, p. 18; Friedländer, 1926; ND, 1931, p. 145f.). Two-thirds of the places in homes for the aged or the incurable were financed by the *Freie Wohlfahrtspflege* (private welfare institutions) (Goldman, 1930, p. 245). Private initiative dominated in this area. However, care in institutions for the incurable was paid for by the public welfare system and these institutions were usually also poorhouses (ND, 1935, pp. 37ff.). Thus institutions for the incurable had very strict house rules which were aimed at disciplining the lower classes (Goldmann, 1930, p. 278). By this time the institutions for the incurable had become homes for the care of the old. The proportion of patients over 60 in the eleven homes for incurables in Berlin was 69 percent. The poverty among the middle classes after the First World War led to an increase in the number of patients from this social level (Goldmann, 1930, pp. 242, 267). This is the beginning of the lifting of class differences among the aged and sick, a trend which can still be seen today, and which contrasts to the principle of maintaining income differences in old age which was disturbed during the Weimar Republic by the effects of war and the breakdown of the private provision of the middle classes.

Summary

The aged finally become a special social group. However, there is a contradiction between their definition as poor and being in need of aid and the expectations that result from their earlier adult life and their private preparations for old age. This contradiction becomes particularly apparent and causes conflict at a time when it is not possible for the middle classes to maintain their standard of living in old age. The reaction of the state to this problem is defensive. While trying gradually to reduce such obvious injustices as the differences between the maintenance of a widow of a white collar employee and her working class counterpart, and rejecting special measures for needy middle class pensioners, the state tries, through additional measures, to reduce the problem of social decline in old age. This is, however, only true in the case of those old people who are still in good health. Those in need of care continue to be pushed to one side. This has less to do with the break-up of the extended family than with the fact that the problem of dealing with a growing number of chronically sick old people had not even been considered in the entire history of social policy, let alone had attempts been made to solve it.

NATIONAL SOCIALISM (1933-1945): DIFFERENTIATION BETWEEN THE AGED AND MOTHERS ABLE TO WORK, AND THE SICK WHO CANNOT

Wage-Based Labor and Female Labor

Under National Socialism, state social policy was an instrument 'that primarily served to extract a maximum amount of labour from the workforce in order to increase armaments production' (Gladen, 1974, p. 113). The restrictions on the freedom of movement and freedom of choice of workplace by the partial service legislation (Teildienstverpflichtung) of 1938 and the service legislation for all wage-earners (Dienstverpflichtung) in 1939, the freezing of wages and also the breaking-up of the trade unions in 1933 should be seen in this context (Gladen, 1974, p. 106f.). The seizure of power from the working class was possible because the National Socialist regime was quickly able to win the loyalty of the masses by reducing unemployment. National Socialist ideology confined women to the function of motherhood and so, at least theoretically, excluded them from the professional world. Economic support for this family policy was provided by marriage loans, which were introduced in 1933 provided the woman gave up her job on marriage. After the birth of several children, it was no longer necessary to repay the loan. Also in 1933, legislation was passed so that women were only allowed to make up 10 percent of the student population. While German women were being forced back into the institutions of family and motherhood, the regime introduced forced sterilization in cases of inherited illness in 1933, banned marriages between Jews and Germans in 1935, forced foreign laborers and Jewesses to have abortions (while making this almost impossible for German women!), and ultimately, murdered Jews, communists and those who were not defined as German (Bock, 1979). If one considers the minimal political resistance to these moves in Germany, it can be said that the division of the population into 'good, racially pure' elements, on the one hand, and 'bad' elements, to be got rid of, on the other, was an exceptionally successful strategy by the regime to establish itself as a dictatorship and to advance its imperialist aims.

The ideology of maternity during the 'Third Reich' was not wholly accepted among German women. From 1933 to 1939, the number of women employed rose from 11.6 million to 14.6 million. At the same time, however, women were forced out of the few qualified posts they had been able to attain. The numbers of female self-employed, civil servants and students dropped, while the numbers of women working in households, helping in family businesses or working in industry increased (Winkler, 1977, pp. 64ff.). During the war, when all female labor reserves were needed, middle class women who were financially secure were not sufficiently motivated to work for the people, the fatherland and the Führer (Winkler, 1977, p. 136f.). It has yet to be ascertained whether this was due to the success of National Socialist ideology or the women's lack of conviction that they would be taking on a meaningful activity. Whatever the case, National Socialist ideology contributed to the strengthening of the concept of women working only within the family.

Old Age as an Economic Risk

Under National Socialism, services in the area of social insurance were first reduced and then drastically cut. In 1933, pensions were cut by 10 percent and they were not increased in the years that followed. As a result, pensioners were often forced to seek additional sources of income (Gladen, 1974, pp. 108ff.). From 1936 onwards, pensions could be withdrawn if a doctor certified a pensioner fit for work (Tennstedt, 1976, p. 476).

These restrictive measures were followed by some improvements before and at the beginning of the war in order to secure the loyalty of the masses. While part of the capital of the social insurance schemes was invested in armaments production (Tennstedt, 1976, pp. 406, 476f.; Gladen, 1974, p. 113), in 1938 craftsmen were included in the old age insurance scheme. The most important development for the aged was the inclusion of pensioners in the sickness insurance scheme in 1941. A large proportion of pensioners were insured by then, either voluntarily (accounting for approximately one-third of all pensioners), or as members of a family, as war widow/ers or as working pensioners. The new legislation therefore meant a simplification of the administration (ND, 1941, pp. 275ff.). In addition, pensions for invalids and those unable to work were regranted if the applicant had worked during the war (Tennstedt, 1976, p. 477f.). These efforts to win additional labor are in stark contrast to the introduction during the war of the production-linked wage for the war-wounded, the frail and the old and infirm whose incomes were thus independent of the official agreements on earnings (ND, 1943, p. 56).

For German workers' widows, the National Socialist ideology of motherhood, restricted as it was to those of Aryan background, brought some improvements. In 1937, a worker's widow with more than three children who had a right to a pension (i.e. children of her dead husband), also received a pension. In 1942, she was entitled to a pension if she was bringing up two children under the age of six with a right to a pension, or if she had borne at least four living children and was 55 years old (Dreher, 1978, p. 81). Repayment in case of marriage was regulated according to the insurance scheme for white collar employees which, as early as 1911, had allowed for women to receive repayment of their entire pension contributions on marriage. This legislation, which assumed that, on marriage, a woman would have security for the rest of her life, was introduced for women workers in 1937 (Dreher, 1978, p. 97). The consequences can now be seen in the missing insurance years in the case of old women.

The Risk of Becoming in Need of Care

There were great changes in the organization of welfare. The Jewish Central Welfare Organization (Zentralwohlfahrtsstelle der Juden) and the social democratic workers' welfare organization (Arbeiterwohlfahrt) were disbanded and the other three major welfare organizations (Innere Mission, Caritasverband and the Deutscher Paritätischer Wohlfahrtsverband) were absorbed into the National Socialist welfare organization. The welfare system then concentrated its energy and resources entirely on the young and healthy (ND, 1934, p. 85). This absolute dedication to a concept based on health and achievement led to a feeling of contempt towards those who were no longer able to work. This feeling was so extreme as even to accept the idea of exterminating the old and sick, although there are similar feelings of contempt towards this group today. At the end of October 1939, Hitler signed a secret piece of legislation enabling mercy killings to be performed in the case of incurable illness (Landeszentrale, 1964, Sheet 2). Under pressure from the Church, Hitler ordered the mass murder of the sick to be halted on 24 August 1941. This program had led to concern among the 'healthy' aged population:

> among the aged, one frequently hears the fear expressed 'Never go into a state hospital! After the mentally sick, the aged will be the next unproductive consumers to go' (Hilfrich, 1941, in Landeszentrale, 1964, Sheet 5).

It was official National Socialist policy to collect and discipline in special institutions all those who apparently could not be socially integrated. Such collective institutions were to be created for the incurably sick and for the asocial who could not be resocialized. The cost of keeping them was to be reduced by the ability of some of the patients to work (ND, 1935, pp. 90ff.).

Summary

Under National Socialism, social policy for the aged revealed all the brutality of the regime, but also the ultimate consequences of dividing the population into 'productive' and 'unproductive' elements. Old, but able-bodied wage-earners were forced to continue to work, but this did mean that they did not feel socially superfluous simply because they had reached a certain age. It was not so much the old who were pushed to one side, but the sick. These received no humane consideration and would certainly have been the victims of mass murder if the Church had not protected at least them. These developments show the consequences of absolute norms, which continue to exist today.

RECONSTRUCTION AFTER THE WAR AND THE DEVELOPMENT OF THE WELFARE STATE: FROM THE ECONOMIC SECURITY OF THE AGED TO THE LIFELONG SUPERVISION OF THEIR NEEDS

Wage-Based Labor and Female Labor

For supporters of a free market economy, the most important step after the war was the creation of structures which would allow a rapid reconstruction of the economic and social order. The newly-founded federal state aimed, with the aid of the Allies, to integrate the wage-earners into an economic system in which the concept of ownership would be secure and in which the wage-earners would be prevented from practising effective co-determination (Gladen, 1974, p. 117f.). Parallel to the process whereby economic policy becomes dependent on the successful functioning of the world of labor in order to remain competitive and in which the demands of the wage-earners with respect to the improvement of their living conditions are directed at the state, social policy tends to develop a momentum of its own. It has as its function not only the removal of aberrations within the production process but should also 'establish and ensure a specific middle-class social status to guarantee the continuing existence of both people and state by maintaining social peace' (Gladen, 1974, p. 116). The development of situations of extreme and widespread need, which would call into question the legitimacy of the system, must be avoided in advance, and the area of influence of social policy must now extend far beyond guaranteeing subsistence level. However, a central function remains that of upholding class differences which continue to exist in old age. These factors form the basis of general social policy for wage-earners.

Under the government formed in 1949, women were returned to their traditional role. Policies relating to the family and the labor market were again based on the concept that women belong in the family. The Family Minister, Wuermeling (1953 to 1962) saw family policy as a vital factor in the fight against communism and the employment of wives and mothers a danger, because this would lead to trends comparable to those in the Eastern Bloc (quoted from Haensch, 1969, pp. 75, 108). Through payment of allowances for children and especially through tax relief, the government used tactics aimed at preventing women from working. Tax relief grew in proportion to income, so that middle class women who would be more likely to find greater professional satisfaction through working, had more incentive to stay at home than lower class women, who often had no alternative (Haensch, 1969, p. 110f.). Initially, and in contrast to their increased share of the labor market during the Second World War, women were edged out of employment. However, the numbers rose again as the need for labor increased, particularly in the case of married women. Of all married women, 32 percent worked in 1957 and 39 percent in 1977. Leaving women over 65 out of consideration, the percentage of married women integrated into the labor force was 44 percent (Schwarz, 1978).

The feminine image which had dominated during the reconstruction of the Federal Republic of Germany was changed by the increasing need for labor in the 1960s and the different views which the social-democratic-liberal coalition government brought with it in 1969. An additional factor in influencing change has been the women's movement which began in the 1970s and which intensified the critical discussion of the disadvantaging of women through limiting their activities to the household. However, the present situation shows that in times of unemployment and economic difficulties, it is always women who are edged back into the family — their 'proper' area of influence. Evidence for this is given by the fact that unemployment among women is greater than among men, and that girls have more difficulties in finding places for vocational education; and is illustrated again and again by appeals from politicians and welfare organizations for women to take up their responsibilities to their families, including the care of sick and disabled relatives (Balluseck, Rodenstein, Schreyer and Westphal-Georgi, 1981). This backward step is documented by, among others, the third family report of the federal government, which supports the idea of a 'freedom of choice' for women between work and the family, and advocates a revaluation of the status of the housewife (Deutscher Bundestag, 1979).

Outline of the Development of a Social Policy for the Aged

While in 1950 the proportion of the population over 65 years old was only 9.4 percent, this had risen to 15.4 percent by 1978. This was a continuation of a trend which had existed since the beginning of this century, and the figure had doubled in the previous 40 years (BMJFG, 1980, p. 14). At the beginning of the period of reconstruction the aged were a marginal group, whose economic situation was the subject of the pension reforms of 1957. During the 1960s, however, they became directly involved in some social policy measures which were supposed to remove, or at least reduce, this status as a marginal group. These measures include planning, advice, information and education for the aged. At the same time, the problems of those in need of care have increased enormously, and lead, because of the lack of economic security (such need is still not covered by sickness insurance), to increasing discontent. In this area, reactions are comparable to those of the past: development of special institutions and, as in the Weimar Republic, of out-patient services in order to reduce costs. The increasing number of old people who are no longer needed makes necessary special policies in order to keep them quiet, while the culmination of all problems of old age, the need for care, is dealt with by traditional solutions. The growth of counselling and education should be seen in the same light as similar strategies for other 'problem groups' (women, unemployed, youth, foreigners). The situation in which old age becomes a problem in itself and when the aged are really in need of aid is only discussed in terms of the economy and welfare, and this does not even make possible an adequate definition of the problems of those in need of care. The same could be said about the attempts to obscure the uselessness of an ever increasing group, a result of the increase in the constant in relation to variable capital, by means of the satisfaction techniques mentioned. The failure of social policy in this case is shown less by the despair and misery of those affected by it than by the continual increase in demand, which, in any case, tends to be unlimited. It will always be possible to demand more and better planning, therapy, advice and education. The problems of social policy in the welfare state result from the fact that social policy is based on the effects of alienated wage-based labor and family structures, but does not consider the institutions themselves.

The welfare organizations play a major role in supporting the relatively conservative social policy strategy, particularly with regard to the aged. They include the Diakonisches Werk (Protestant), the Caritasverband (Catholic), the Arbeiterwohlfahrt (originally social democrat) and the Paritätischer Wohlfahrts-verband. The Zentralwohlfahrtsstelle der Juden no longer has any great significance because of the extermination policy during the 'Third Reich'. During the years of reconstruction in the Federal Republic of Germany, welfare organizations were able to refer to the unification of welfare under the National Socialist dictatorship and were thus able to continue to dominate the welfare sector. Their union can be regarded as a monopoly (Heinze and Olk, 1981), since they influence every piece of legislation in the social sector, but are in no way as pluralistic as they pretend to be. They consult each other and then assume the role of a representative of their clients in their dealings with the state (Heinze and Olk, 1981). In the early 1960s, certain communities and Länder appealed to the Bundesverfassungsgericht (constitutional court) to reduce the influence of the associations. The court, however, again upheld the principle of subsidiary (i.e. that the state is obliged to subsidize associations providing social services prescribed by law) in 1967 and so strengthened the influence of these associations in the social sector. To give a concrete example of their power, if a social institution is under consideration and one of the welfare organizations is prepared to support it, then this organization has priority in the program over the state. The influence of the welfare organizations on policy for the aged includes the development of aid programs for the aged, the administration of the Bundessozial-hilfegesetz (the federal law on social aid) (with the exception of subsidies from the Sozialamt (the social aid office), decision-making on building accommodation for the aged and the construc-

tion of homes for the aged and infirm. They were also behind the
'new' policy for the aged, which includes planning, counselling and
education. The Kuratorium Deutsche Altershilfe (German
Curatorium for the Aid of the Aged) was founded in 1963 by the
wife of then German president Lübke to deal with the problems of
the aged. In 1970, the Institut für Altenwohnbau (Institute for
Accommodation for the Aged) was founded as part of the
curatorium which advises and plans for the associations that aid the
aged as well as for the aged themselves. Executive members of the
curatorium are representatives of the welfare organizations and the
Ministry for Youth, Family and Health. These bodies are also
represented in the Deutsches Zentrum für Altersfragen (German
Center for Questions of Old Age) which was founded in Berlin in
1974, is financed by the German government and the Berlin senate
and which aims to create contact between research and practical
work on the problems of old age. This illustrates particularly
clearly the common interests of politicians and welfare
organizations. The structures of social policy make sure that real
changes in aid for the aged — or in the rest of the welfare service —
cannot realistically be expected.

Old Age as an Economic Risk:
Economic Security

Since 1957, pensions have been linked to general trends in wages
and salaries, and have since actually risen faster than the net
incomes and salaries of the working population. From 1969 to
1978, pensions rose by 124 percent while net incomes increased by
only 98 percent (BMFJG, 1980, p. 25). This is one of the reasons
for the current discussion in Germany about linking pensions to
increases in net incomes. The reasons for creating index-linked
pensions were:
— pensions were now regarded as an official source of income in
   old age, whereas they had previously been seen as an additional
   source of income;
— adequate pensions were to enable a clear differentiation
   between welfare and insurance; class differences should thus be
   maintained in old age;
— by increasing economic security in old age, it should be
   easier to integrate workers into the working world (Deutscher

Bundestag, 1956, pp. 8334ff.; 1957, pp. 10181ff.).

In 1957, some improvements were made to the situation of widows. In 1949, the widows of workers and white collar employees had been given equal status. This meant that the widow of a worker had an automatic right to a pension on the death of her husband. From 1957, widows under the age of 45 who could not be expected to go out to work, but who had no children, received a 'small' widow's pension which amounted to two-thirds of the full widow's pension. If she had one or more children or had reached the age of 45 she received the full widow's pension which was 60 percent of her late husband's pension.

Following the results of an inquiry which showed that working women tended to become invalids earlier in life than men because of the double burden of family and job, the retirement age for women was reduced in 1957 so that they were able to draw a pension from the age of 60, providing they had paid insurance contributions for fifteen years (ten of them during the past twenty years). This improved the situation of widows and older working women. On the other hand, the side effects of this legislation were based on the concentration of female labor in the family. Early retirement for older female workers and the lack of necessity for a widow to go out to work mean that the basic structures which ensure a continual double workload for women, as well as unhealthy working conditions, bad training and little opportunity for promotion, will not change. Additionally, many older women wage-earners cannot take advantage of the lower retirement age because they do not fulfil the necessary insurance conditions.

Today this legislation offers an opportunity to remove older women and those with little work experience from the labor market. A similar function is fulfilled by another piece of legislation from 1957 which enables long-term unemployed to draw a pension at the age of 60.

In 1972, legislation brought further fundamental changes in pension insurance. The most important were the introduction of a flexible retirement level (the possibility of retiring on a pension at the age of 63 after a minimum of 35 years of pension contributions), and the introduction of a minimum pension. This meant that after 25 years of insurance contributions, the pension was calculated on the basis of 75 percent of the average earnings of all those insured, and had the effect of easing the burden on social aid and reducing the risk of the low-paid refusing to continue to work. Also important was the opening of pension insurance schemes to all members of the population, including the self-employed and housewives. The disadvantge of this last piece of legislation is that the necessary contributions lie above the limits possible for housewives of the lower classes.

In spite of improvements in the situation of women, legislation continues to be on the side of those who would confine them to the family, and, according to sex-specific division of labor, seek to make this the main female sphere of influence. One illustration of this is the planned new legislation on the maintenance of surviving dependents, which will be examined more closely.

As already mentioned, widows now receive 60 percent of their late husband's pension. It is significant that demands by the Bundesverfassungsgericht (the constitutional court) that the government should create a new legal basis for these pensions should result from the case of a widower. Arguing on the basis of the principle of equality of treatment, he had demanded a widower's pension which, as the law stands, could only be granted him if his late wife had been the main wage-earner of the two. A commission of experts set up by the government to look into the problem has now formulated a series of suggestions which are limited, in political discussion, to the concept of a so-called shared pension (*'Teilhaberente'*, Sachverständigenkommission, 1979). This means that the form of maintenance will still be attached to the status of the surviving dependent, a widowed husband or wife, rather than independently of the partner. The planned legislation aims to ease the greatest elements of present injustice by granting the surviving partner, whether husband or wife, a certain percentage (e.g. 70 percent) of the shared pension rights of both partners, but at least their own full pension. This would put a stop to the cumulation of a widow's pension together with the woman's own pension. This legislation will support the dependence of women on their husbands (for in the future, it will continue to be the woman who gives up her job for the sake of working for her husband and her children) and will further the sex-specific division of labor. It will be the women on good incomes who will lose and the housewives without children who will gain through this legislation (DIW, 1979).

It is only possible to understand this apparently anachronistic piece of legislation if one examines the political purposes of pensions in the sectors of the family and the labor market.

Marriage and dependence on the husband should be rewarded so that no further costs occur in the care of children and relatives. The costs of reproduction can thus be returned to the private sector. In the labor market, the willingness of the woman to return to or to remain in the household eases the employment situation and is one of the tactics used to obscure the level of unemployment. It is apparent that the state has taken control of economic security in old age for those in insurance schemes. It is still, however, based on a derived security which affects women, above all, and adds strength to arguments that would confine them to the family.

Old Age as a Psychic and Social Risk:
The Expansion of Social Policy
Measures for the Aged

The areas for providing the aged with assistance are set out in a welfare law, the Bundessozialhilfegesetz (federal law on social aid, BSHG), which was passed in 1961. The organs of administration are the Länder and the communities and apart from the distribution of financial support by the Sozialamt — the welfare organizations. Section 75 of the law makes a commitment to avoid and remove age-related problems and isolation. The aged should be helped to take up activities, to find companionship or to make contact with those close to them. In the years that have followed both public and private organizations have been increasingly active in the area of policy for the aged. The federal states and the communities have developed programs for the aged which are dominated by plans to develop housing, nursing homes, out-patient care and aid services in the form of counselling, activities, etc. Public and private organizations publish advice which is supposed to help avoid health and social problems in old age. The welfare organizations made education and counselling central themes for their work in the 1960s. Research and special counselling centres for the aged became institutionalized. The alternation of section 75 of the BSHG in 1974 is one consequence of this new policy for the aged which can be seen as an expansion to cover socialization functions in their widest form. The new version emphasized the preventive approach. An increase in counselling activity is demanded, there is the first mention in a legislative text of the need for preparation for old age, and there is a call for the abandonment of the idea of encouraging the aged to take up some further employment in favor of encouraging them to take up some other activity, i.e. occupational therapy (Narr, 1976, p. 43f.). In addition, this assistance should be made available to every aged person regardless of their level of income. This was a consolidation of the process by which the aged are removed from every productive function. Employment of the aged has dropped, and old people's homes now provide complete care where the aged had previously been able to cater partly for themselves. Occupational therapy was thus able to assert itself (Balluseck, 1980, p. 87).

The function of planning measures — mostly initiated by the state authorities — is to present problems as understandable and soluble and to document the state's involvement and ability to deal with the situation. The suggestions contained in such programs are all based on the current structures of the labor market, the health system and aid for the aged. The function of educational measures in adult education institutions (people's high schools or church education centers), and in day centers or clubs for the aged is to compensate for the loss of profession and/or family and consequently for the uselessness of old age. The aim is to prevent psychological and social problems and to encourage unobtrusive adjustment to this sense of uselessness (Trilling, 1981a; 1981b).

These socializing measures are a result of the division of the population into productive and unproductive elements. Increasing life expectancy and relatively secure economic perspectives call for new measures. For the aged, social control also becomes a necessity in the form of socialization. However, a lifetime of adjustment to wage-based labor and/or family life ensures that the methods used (education and counselling) do not need to be directly repressive.

The Risk of Becoming in Need of Care

In 1976, the number of those over 65 in need of care was estimated to be 804,000 (BMFJG, 1977). However, more recent examinations reveal that even ignoring those in institutions, there are over a million people over 65 in need of care in the Federal Republic of Germany (Socialdata, 1980). One figure that is known exactly is that of those in need of care receiving social aid. Within institutions, there were 145,999 recipients of social assistance over 65 in 1977. Seventy-eight percent of them were women. Outside the institutions the figure was 108,991, of whom 74 percent were women (Statistisches Bundesamt, 1979, pp. 44-49).

Those in need of care are looked after:
— in the family by relatives,
— by home nursing,
— in residential institutions of the health system or of aid for the aged.

Within the family, care is almost always provided by nonworking female relatives. Home nursing is also done by women, and in residential institutions for the aged, women account for the majority of the nursing staff. Being in need of care is therefore a female problem in two senses.

Care in the Family

The family is the cheapest institution for the care of the aged. In the Federal Republic of Germany and West Berlin, it fulfils this function in the vast majority of cases. The Bundessozialhilfegesetz recognizes the period of care for social insurance purposes for families who care for a person in need. The necessary contributions are paid by the source of social assistance, i.e. the state itself. In addition to this, some Länder have introduced an allowance for care of the needy which will be higher than the care allowance through social assistance and which is supposed to cover the costs of the nursing work involved. The allowance is, however, linked generally to low-income groups. Finally, the suggested new legislation for the maintenance of surviving dependents allows for the periods of care to be taken into consideration for the calculation of the pension of all those (male or female) who stop work in order to care for a person in need. All these measures aim at encouraging willingness to care for the aged in the family. This would greatly reduce the costs incurred by institutional care. These pieces of legislation will, above all, affect women. Theoretically it is possible for a man to return to the family in order to care for his disabled child or his old mother. In practice, however, it will be the women who are forced back into the isolation of the nuclear family and who offer themselves as cheap labor. Granting the family such an important role in the care of the aged is in itself an attempt to burden women with the social load of those in need of care.

Home Nursing

Home nursing makes it possible for the patient to remain in his own home and social environment, thus making life more tolerable in many cases. This form of care was not planned to be developed further — partly out of respect to the women who provide unpaid nursing services and partly because of the lack of interest of practising doctors in this form of care. Since 1977, however, national insurance legislation allows for certain financial relief in the case of home nursing being taken over by relatives. The period of care will be considered in the calculation of pensions. Home nursing staff and the staff of the new social units continue to be almost exclusively female. The sickness insurance organizations will only cover the costs as long as the patient is defined as in need of treatment. As soon as he is defined as in need of care, the costs must be borne by the family. The same is true of residential care.

Residential Care

The level of state influence on the institutions of the health system and of aid for the aged varies. Hospitals, as part of the health authorities' responsibilities, look to the state for their funding and thus for their level of staffing and facilities. Old people's homes, on the other hand, need only fulfil a minimum of conditions relating to room size, hygiene, etc. In both sectors similar trends can be seen in the treatment of the aged. Since the 1960s, there has been an increasing tendency to shut away those in need of care in homes, special wards, clinics and sanatoriums. This edging out of the aged and chronically sick — an approach that has existed for the past century — now appears within a new form of differentiation which involves the creation of institutions with a high staffing level for programs of rehabilitation and other, low-cost institutions for those cases which are considered to be hopeless.

Demands for change made by the welfare organizations, the public associations, but also by the new professional group of geriatric nursing staff relate to the creation of better hospitals and homes with more opportunities for rehabilitation and more effective staffing. The fact that the aged are edged out of society is left out of the discussion, and if this problem is ever mentioned, it is only in the context of the family assuming responsibility for the aged. In both cases traditional structures are maintained. The creation of better institutions (currently unviable) pushes the aged to one side, while appeals to the family force women to take on the social responsibility for the aged and the needy.

The problem of those in need of care is usually discussed under purely financial aspects and with regard to the existing structures of the health system and aid for the aged. In this way, it is not possible to define the problem adequately in terms of social policy. This would only be possible if those in need of care no longer had to be edged out of society in order to maintain the competitiveness of the wage-earners (the same argument is valid for the similar treatment of any deviant group), and if the structure of the family and the labor market no longer handed all social responsibility to women. It is also the case that the problems of those in need of care cannot be solved by social policy but must be approached through a social discourse (Habermas, 1973) on the sense of chronic suffering and the option of voluntary suicide. Such a discussion remains out of the question as long as the commitment of society to wage-based labor, competition and the sex- and class-specific division of labor carries with it the danger of a brutal reaction such as occurred during National Socialism. Human solidarity demands structures which result in a feeling of common responsibility, not simply in individual initiatives. At the moment this is impossible: women are therefore the subjects of appeals to take on nursing work, and the care of the aged is professionalized. These measures all distract from the fact that our reaction to the problem is one of helplessness, inactivity and also brutality.

Only a social policy which questions the very concepts of alienated wage-based labor and the sex-specific division of labor can motivate the lifting of a strict division of labor and thus put an end to the division into productive and unproductive social elements. This would form the basis for a discussion and initial steps to absorb those in need of care into the community.

REFERENCES

ABBREVIATIONS

BMJFG: Bundesministerium für Jugend, Familie und Gesundheit.
BSHG: Bundessozialhilfegesetz.
ND: Nachrichtendienst des Deutschen Vereins für öffentliche und private Fürsorge.

A. PERIODICALS

Altenhilfe, Berlin, 1974-1980.
Nachrichtendienst des Deutschen Vereins für öffentliche und private Fürsorge, 1922-1978.

B. BOOKS AND ARTICLES

Arnold, Brunhilde (1979), 'Die ökonomische Natur des Alters', Dissertation, University of Bremen.

Balluseck, Hilde von (1980), 'Die Pflege alter Menschen' (Berlin, Deutsches Zentrum für Altersfragen).

Balluseck, Hilde von, Marianne Rodenstein, Michaele Schreyer and Ursula Westphal-Georgi (1981), 'Thesen zu einer feministischen Sozialpolitik', in: W. Schulte (ed.), *Soziologie in der Gesellschaft* (Bremen, Universität).

Barabas, Friedrich, Thomas Blanke and Ulrich Stascheit (1975), *Jahrbuch der Sozialarbeit 1976* (Reinbek, Rowohlt).

Bock, Gisela (1979), 'Frauen and ihre Arbeit im Nationalsozialismus', pp. 113-149 in: Kuhn and Schneider.

Braun, Heinrich (1955), 'Der Deutsche Verein im Geschehen seiner Zeit', pp. 1-131 in: Muthesius.

Brunner, Otto (1978), 'Vom "ganzen Haus" zur "Familie" ', pp. 83-91 in: Rosenbaum.

Büttner, J.S. (1884), *Die Pflege unheilbar Kranker, eine Aufgabe der kirchlichen Armenpflege* (Magdeburg, Friese).

Bundesministerium für Jugend, Familie and Gesundheit) (ed.) (1977), *Pflegebedürftigkeit älterer Menschen* (Bonn, Bundesministerium für Jugend, Familie und Gesundheit).

Bundesministerium für Jügend, Familie und Gesundheit (ed.) (1980), *Hilfen für ältere Menschen in der Bundesrepublik Deutschland* (Bonn, Bundesministerium für Jugend, Familie und Gesundheit).

Bundesminister des Innern (ed.) (1980), *Bericht über die Bevölkerungsentwicklung der Bundesrepublik Deutschland. 1. Teil: Analyse der bisherigen Bevölkerungsentwicklung und Modellrechnungen zur künftigen Bevölkerungsentwicklung* (Bonn, Bundesminister des Innern).

Caritas (1964), Sonderheft Altenbildung (Freiburg, Lambertus).

Deutscher Bundestag (1956), *Stenographische Berichte,* Band 31 (Bonn, Deutscher Bundestag).

Deutscher Bundestag (1957), *Stenographische Berichte,* Band 34 (Bonn, Deutscher Bundestag).

Deutscher Bundestag (1979), *Drucksache 8/3120: Die Lage der Familien in der Bundesrepublik Deutschland. Dritter Familienbericht* (Bonn, Universitätsdruckerei).

Deutscher Verein für öffentliche und private Fürsorge (ed.) (1930), *Sozialversicherung und öffentliche Fürsorge als Grundlage der Alten-und Invalidenversorgung*. *Schriften des Deutschen Vereins*, Heft 14 (Neue Folge) (Karlsruhe, Braun).

DIW-Wochenberichte (1979), No. 14: 'Gleichberechtigung von Mann und Frau: Ein Problem für die gesetzliche Rentenversicherung'. Bearbeiterin: Ellen Kirner.

Dreher, Wolfgang (1978), *Die Entstehung der Arbeiterwitwenversicherung in Deutschland* (Berlin, Duncker & Humblot).

Dünner, Julia (1925), *Reichsfürsorgerecht. Die Fürsorgepflichtverordnung vom 13. Februar 1924 nebst allen damit zusammenhängenden Gesetzen und Verordnung des Reichs und der Länder,* (München Beck).

Freund, Richard (1891, 'Antrag auf Einsetzung einer Kommission zur Prüfung der Frage, in welcher Weise die neuere sociale Gesetzgebung auf die Aufgaben der Armengesetzgebung einwirkt,' pp. 1-17 in: *Schriften des Deutschen Vereins*, No. 14 (Leipzig, Duncker & Humblot).

Freund, Richard (1895), *Armenpflege und Arbeiterversicherung. Schriften des Deutschen Vereins*, Heft 21 (Leipzig, Duncker & Humblot).

Frevert, Ute (1979), 'Vom Klavier zur Schreibmaschine. Weiblicher Arbeitsmarkt und Rollenzuweisungen am Beispiel der weiblichen Angestellten in der Weimarer Republik', pp. 82-112 in: Kuhn and Schneider.

Friedländer, Adele (1926), 'Die Errichtung von Altenheimen', in: *Berliner Wohlfahrtsblatt*, 2, pp. 148-149.

Gladen, Albin (1974), *Geschichte der Sozialpolitik in Deutschland* (Wiesbaden, Steiner).

Goldmann, Franz (1930), 'Siechenhäuser und Altenheime', pp. 235-318 in: A. Gottstein (ed.), *Handbücherei für das gesamte Krankenhauswesen*, Vol. II (Berlin, Springer).

Gottstein, A. (1913), 'Aufgaben der Gemeinde- und der privaten Fürsorge', pp. 721-786 in: M. Mosse and G. Tugendreich (eds.), *Krankheit und soziale Lage* (new edition, Göttingen, Kromm, 1977).

Habermas, Jürgen (1973), *Legitimationsprobleme im Spätkapitalismus* (Frankfurt, Suhrkamp).

Haensch, Dietrich (1969), *Repressive Familienpolitik* (Hamburg, Rowohlt).

Hausen, Karin (1978), 'Die Polarisierung der "Geschlechtscharaktere" — Eine Spiegelung der Dissoziation von Erwerbs- und Familienleben', pp. 161-191 in: Rosenbaum.

Heimerich, Heinrich (1924), 'Die Zusammenarbeit der öffentlichen mit der privaten Fürsorge und den Trägern der Sozialversicherung', pp. 73-84 in: D. Hirschfeld et al., *Allgemeine Fürsorge* (Berlin, Dietz [Nachfolger]).

Heinsohn, Gunnar and Rolf Knieper (1974), *Theorie des Familienrechts* (Frankfurt, Suhrkamp).

Heinze, Rolf G. and Thomas Olk (1981) 'Die Wohlfahrtsverbände im System sozialer Dienstleistungsproduktion', pp. 94-114 in: *Kölner Zeitschrift für Soziologie und Sozialpsychologie,* 33.

Krippendorf, Wilhelm (1904), *Die Pflege der Siechen und Blöden* (Weimar, Böhlau).

Krug von Nidda, C.L. (1930), 'Einleitung: Die Beziehungen zwischen Sozialversicherung und öffentlicher Fürsorge im Bereich der Tätigkeit des Deutschen Vereins für öffentliche und private Fürsorge 1880-1930', pp. 1-20 in: Deutscher Verein für öffentliche und private Fürsorge 1930.

Kuczynski, Jürgen (1963), *Geschichte der Lage der Arbeiter unter dem Kapitalismus,* Vol. 3 (1871-1900) (Berlin, Akademie).

Kuhn, Annette and Gerhard Schneider (eds.) (1979), *Frauen in der Geschichte* (Düsseldorf, Schwann).

Landeszentrale für politische Bildungsarbeit (ed.) (1964), *Terror und Widerstand 1933-1845, Mappe D: Weigerung und Protest, 15: Katholische Bischöfe gegen Willkür und Mord* (Berlin, Landeszentrale für politische Bildungsarbeit).

Lehr, Ursula (ed.) (1978), *Seniorinnen* (Darmstadt, Steinkopff).

Lenhardt, Gero and Claus Offe (1977), 'Staatstheorie und Sozialpolitik', pp. 98-127 in: Chr. v. Ferber and F.-X. Kaufmann (eds), *Soziologie und Sozialpolitik,* Sonderheft 19 der *Kölner Zeitschrift für Soziologie und Sozialpsychologie* (Opladen, Westdeutscher Verlag).

Medem, E. (1888), *Siechennot und Siechenpflege* (Wittenberg, Fiedler).

Mitterauer, Michael (1978), 'Der Mythos von der vorindustriellen Grossfamilie', pp. 128-151 in: Rosenbaum.

Muthesius, Hans (ed.) (1955), *Beiträge zur Entwicklung der deutschen Fürsorge, 75 Jahre Deutscher Verein* (Köln, Berlin, Heymanns).

Narr, Hannelore (1976), *Soziale Probleme des Alters* (Stuttgart et al., Kohlhammer).

Narr, Wolf-Dietrich and Claus Offe (1975), 'Einleitung', pp. 9-46 in: Narr and Offe (eds.), *Wohlfahrtsstaat und Massenloyalität* (Köln, Kipenheuer & Witsch).

ND, see periodicals.

Niemeyer, W. (1930), 'Die wirtschaftliche Lage der Sozialrentner in 93 deutschen Städten und 105 deutschen Landkreisen', pp. 35-186 in; Deutscher Verein für öffentliche und private Fürsorge 1930.

Paetzold, Hilarion and Bubolz Elisabeth (eds.) (1976), *Bildungsarbeit mit alten Menschen* (Stuttgart, Klett).

Polligkeit, W. (1928), *Forderungen für den systematischen Ausbau der Altersfürsorge* (Frankfurt, Deutscher Verein für öffentliche und private Fürsorge).

Rodenstein, Marianne (1978), 'Arbeiterselbsthilfe, Arbeiterselbstverwaltung und staatliche Krankenversicherungspolitik in Deutschland, pp. 113-181 in: T. Guldimann, M. Rodenstein, U. Rödel, F. Stille, *Sozialpolitik als soziale Kontrolle* (Frankfurt, Suhrkamp).

Rosenbaum, Heidi (ed.) (1878), *Seminar Familie und Gesellschaftsstruktur* (Frankfurt, Suhrkamp).

Sachsse, Christoph and Florian Tennstedt (1980), *Geschichte der Armenfürsorge in Deutschland vom Spätmittelalter bis zum Ersten Weltkrieg* (Stuttgart et al., Kohlhammer).

Sachverständigenkommission für die soziale Sicherung der Frau und der Hinterbliebenen (1979), *Vorschläge zur sozialen Sicherung der Frau und der Hinterbliebenen. Gutachten vom 21. Mai 1979, veröffentlicht durch die Bundesregierung* (Bonn, Bundesminister für Arbeit und Sozialordnung).

Schwabe, H. (1870), 'Stadt Berlin', pp. 68-88 in: H. Emminghaus (ed.), *Das Armenwesen und die Armengesetzgebung in europäischen Staaten* (Berlin, Herbig).

Schwarz, Karl (1978), 'Erwerbstätigkeit verheirateter Frauen', pp. 473-480 in: *Wirtschaft und Statistik,* Heft 8 (Stuttgart et al., Kohlhammer).

Socialdata (ed.) (1980), *Anzahl und Situation zu Hause lebender Pflegebedürftiger* (Stuttgart et al., Kohlhammer).

Statistisches Bundesamt (ed.) (1979), *Sozialleistungen,* Fachserie 13, Reihe 2,

Sozialhilfe 1977 (Stuttgart et al., Kohlhammer).

Tennstedt, Florian (1976), 'Sozialgeschichte der Sozialversicherung', pp. 385-492 in: M. Blohmke, Chr. v. Ferber, K.P. Kisker and H. Schaefer (eds.), *Handbuch der Sozialmedizin*, Vol. III (Stuttgart, Enke).

Trilling, Angelika (1981 a), 'Lernen im Alter' (Kassel, unpublished).

Trilling, Angelika (1981 b), 'Bemerkungen über die Vernachlässigung nicht etablierter Beratungsmöglichkeiten' (Kassel, unpublished).

Westergaard, John (1980), 'Sozialpolitik und soziale Ungleichheit! Bemerkungen über die Grenzen des englischen Wohlfahrtsstaates', pp. 1-23, /6-91 and 144-157 in: *Zeitschrift für Sozialreform, 26.*

Wex, Else (1929), *Die Entwicklung der Sozialen Fürsorge in Deutschland (1914-1927)* (Berlin, Haymann).

Winkler, Dörte (1977), *Frauenarbeit im 'Dritten Reich'* (Hamburg, Hoffman und Campe).

12

THE DISTRIBUTION OF BENEFITS AND SERVICES BETWEEN THE RETIRED AND THE VERY ELDERLY:
The British Case

Nick Bosanquet
The City University, London

Official statements on health services and on public spending in Great Britain rarely fail to mark the increase in the number of people aged over 75 as a fact of great significance. The government's recent statement of priorities for the National Health Service, 'Care in Action', gave a list of 'changes which will have most effect on the health and personal social services' (DHSS, 1981, p. 1). First and pre-eminent in this list was the 'increase in the numbers of very elderly people'. The most recent annual White Paper on public spending in discussing social security also mentioned that 'expenditure on the elderly shows a steady rise over the survey period' (Cmnd. 8175, 1981, p. 122). Certainly, too, such statements are correct. The number of people over 75 will increase by 21 percent between 1979 and 2000 — while numbers between retirement age and 75 will decline by 11 percent.

The general interest shown in official documents might suggest that a great deal of detailed analysis had been done on the needs of the over-75s, and on the implications of these needs for policies. It is known that the very elderly have special problems of disability. This would suggest possible conflicts of priority as between improved income support and improved services. A social security plan in which payments are related to earnings during the working life — as is the case with the new British pensions scheme — might tilt the balance of spending towards the younger retired. There could well be a much sharper difference in income between 'new' and 'old' pensioners in the future, unless benefits under the old scheme are greatly improved. All these issues would suggest a case for evaluating policies in terms of the interests of the over 75s, and for assessing the incidence of current spending. Yet rather little detailed work has been done. The general statement has not been the tip of an iceberg, with a great bulk of research not readily visible to the general public. In fact, such evaluation where it takes place has tended to be rather crude. Thus an official discussion of policy aims published in 1978 under the title, 'A Happier Old Age', said of the balance of public spending: 'By far the largest proportion goes on pensions. But services are more heavily weighted towards the very old than are cash benefits' (DHSS, 1978, p. 10). No detailed evidence, however, was given for this statement which in fact needs qualification as patterns of service change. 'A Happier Old Age' went on to give another often repeated fact, that 'the average cost of care and treatment of a person aged over 75 is seven times that of a person of working age'. The ruling generalization is that people over 75 use services and many of them.

How strong is the case for a special policy for the 'very elderly'? This chapter seeks to examine this issue by looking first at the economic and social data for Britain on the characteristics of the over 75s. How far are they a distinctive group? We look at how the balance in spending between income support and service has actually changed and at the incidence of existing spending. Finally we look at possible implications for policy.

How Distinctive are the Over-75s?

There has been growing dissatisfaction with the use of age lines in decisions about social benefits. Is there any greater logic for saying that 75 is a more satisfactory line of division than 65? We are often told that age is not a very good indicator of physical state. However, the over 75s are distinctive in one sense: a very high proportion are women. In the 65-75 age group in Britain women account for 57 percent of the total. Over 75 they make up 68 percent and over 85, 76 percent. Two out of three of the very elderly are women. The obvious comparison group is that of women aged 65-75. How far are the very elderly a distinctive group either in relation to them or to elderly people in general?

The very elderly are more likely to live on their own. This has often been pointed out: but much less remarked has been the increase in proportions living with (usually) younger relatives (see Table 1). In the 75-84 age group one in four women is living with relatives: over 85 four out of ten. For men this change comes only after 85 when one in three is living with relatives. This increase in sharing is a more distinctive feature of the over 75s than their isolation. Already between 65 and 74 four out of ten women are living on their own.

TABLE 1
Elderly People in Private Households:
By Type of Household, 1978-79 (Percentages)

Household Type	Men 65-74	Men 75-84	Men 85+	Women 65-74	Women 75-84	Women 85+
With Spouse	80	62	34	47	21	8
Without Spouse, but with Others	7	11	34	14	24	39
Living Alone	14	27	32	39	55	53
Total	100	100	100	100	100	100

Source: CSO, *Social Trends 1981*, (London, HMSO, 1980), p. 47.

People over 75 are much more likely to suffer from severe disability (see Table 2).

TABLE 2
Percentage of Men and Women with Loss
of Mobility in Each Age Group (Percentages)

	Age 65-74	Age 75-84	Age 85+
Men who are:			
Bedfast Permanently	-	-	1.8
Housebound Permanently	1.5	7.3	14.5
Need Help Going Out	2.3	4.2	16.4
Women who are:			
Bedfast Permanently	-	1.0	1.9
Housebound Permanently	2.0	7.0	18.8
Need Help Going Out	6.6	14.2	30.5

Source: Hunt (1978), p. 69.

From 65-74 two in 100 elderly women are either bedfast or housebound. From 75-84 this increases to eight in 100 and over 85 to 21. About one in two of the over 85s either cannot go out or needs help to do so. This is probably a more useful indication of disability than self-reporting of illness. Taking the over 75 group as a whole, there is a very clear difference both with the elderly in general and with women aged 65-74. The over 75s are also much more likely to suffer from mental deterioration (see Table 3).

TABLE 3
Prevalence of Organic Brain Syndromes by Sex (Percentages)

	Men	Women
65-	3.9	0.5
70-	4.1	2.7
75-	13.2	7.9
80+	6.2	20.9
All Ages	6.2	6.3

Source: Report of the Royal College of Physicians Committee on Geriatrics, 'Organic Mental Impairment in the Elderly: Implications for Research, Education and Provision of Services', *Journal of the Royal College of Physicians,* Vol. 15, No. 3, 1981, p. 8.

The income pattern of the nonmarried over 75s is not very different from that of younger retired (see Table 4). For women the proportion in different bands of income shows only modest change before and after 75. The proportion in the lowest income band increases from about one-quarter to about one-third.

TABLE 4
Total Net Income of Nonmarried Persons, 1976

	Men (%)			Women (%)		
	65-74	75-84	84+	65-74	75-84	85+
Under £749	18.7	15.1	20.0	24.9	31.8	35.2
£750-£999	39.6	38.1	45.7	42.0	44.5	40.5
£1,000 or not stated	41.7	46.8	34.3	33.1	23.7	24.1

Source: Hunt (1978), p.25.

Other evidence suggests that there are much sharper differences between the married and the nonmarried than any differences that might exist by age. About 12 percent of the married as compared to 32 percent of the nonmarried have incomes low enough to receive supplementary benefit. Single women are most likely of all to be receiving supplementary benefit and least likely to be getting occupational pensions. There is also some evidence on changes in equivalent income. This suggests some rise in poverty over 75. Thirty-eight percent of households with a head aged 65-74 were in the lowest quintile of equivalent income distribution: over 75 this proportion rises to 53 percent. But this change is likely to reflect the changing balance between men and women rather than a true age differential. There is much greater difference by age in ownership of assets than in income. The very elderly are much less likely to own a washing machine or a refrigerator.

The housing situation of the elderly is rather different from that of younger people. They are much more likely to live in privately rented accommodation and more likely to lack amenities such as an indoor lavatory. But the main difference on both tenure and amenities is between the over-65s and the rest. There are few significant differences between the very elderly and the younger retired. The position is complicated by regional variation, with especially poor conditions in Greater London. The very elderly in the North are rather better housed than the younger retired in London.

Use of health and social services does show a distinct pattern. The high level of disability results in home visits both from doctors and from district nurses. Twenty-seven percent of the bedfast and housebound had regular visits from their doctors at least once a month. One-third of them received visits from a district nurse at least once a month. Among social services, the home help service gives unusual assistance to people over 75. 15.8 percent of people aged 75-84 were getting home help compared to 4.4 percent of the younger retired. The use of day centers, on the other hand, shows some fall with age, as does the use of free passes on public transport (Hunt, 1978).

The great majority of those in long-stay care in hospital, nursing home or residential home are over 75. Overall, about 5 percent of the population over 75 are in such care. The proportion has shown some decline over the past five years, as numbers have increased but few extra places opened. A higher proportion of severely handicapped people is now living in the community.

Can it be argued, in summary, that the elderly are a distinctive group? The case is much clearer in terms of the evidence on disability and on household type. The over 75s are more likely to be physically and mentally disabled and more likely to live in joint households with younger relatives. They are also more likely be in long-stay homes, or hospitals. The social data on income and housing do not suggest, however, any very sharp distinction. The single elderly (and single elderly men are in fact little better off than single women) tend to have the same sort of income and live in the same sort of housing whether they are 66 or 86. They live in similar social conditions but face increasing disability and difficulty in maintaining an independent life. In general their degree of dependence on younger relatives seems to have been underestimated.

Changes in Expenditure

It is usually argued that improvements in pensions would be of particular importance to the younger retired while improvements in services would have relevance to the very elderly. The evidence presented so far suggests reasons for modifying this common conclusion but not for abandoning it completely. It is probably true that modest improvements in the real value of pensions would not be seen as their highest priority by very elderly disabled people. However, there are some services, such as subsidized travel on public transport and day centers, which would probably rank even lower down their scale of priorities. It may be useful to divide the service category more finely between those services which are and those which are not of importance to the very elderly. Thus the district nursing and home help services are clearly of great importance to the very elderly.

The social security budget is often seen as having grown relentlessly and is often written about as a potential threat to other forms of spending. There is of course no one budget for the elderly within the British system: an increase in spending on social security does not mean a reduction in spending on services. In fact, some of the most important services are run by local government while social security is a matter for the central government. Nevertheless, the pressures from the increasing social security budget may grow in the future.

Over the second half of the 1970s there were few signs that spending on social security has grown faster than spending on services. The evidence presented in Table 5 suggests that spending

TABLE 5

Percentage Changes in Spending on Cash and Care, 1970/1-1979/80 at Constant 1980 Prices: England

	Social Security *	District Nursing	Home Helps	Local Authority Residential Care	Day Care	Geriatric In-Patient and Out-Patient Care
1970/1-1975/6	+ 37.0	+ 41.5	+ 87.7	+ 66.8	-	+ 34.7
1975/6-1979/80	+ 13.5	+ 19.2	+ 10.7	+ 16.0	+ 49 0	+ 8.6

* Figures are for United Kingdom.
Source: DHSS and Cmnd. 8175 (1981).

TABLE 6
The Effects of Taxes and Benefits on Income: Selected Households 1979 (£ sterling)

	One Adult Retired: All Age Groups	Two Adults Retired: All Age Groups	Head Over 75
Original Income	484	1,058	996
Benefits in Cash			
Age Related	1,018	1,629	1,278
Other	268	301	288
Gross Income	1,770	2,988	2,562
Direct Taxes	−99	−211	−218
Disposable Income	1,671	2,777	2,343
Rates and Indirect Taxes	−343	−621	−448
Benefits in Kind			
NHS	384	599	714
Housing Subsidy	119	108	117
Other	3	10	14
Final Income	1,834	2,874	2,740

Source: Cols. 1 and 2), CSO, 'The Effects of Taxes and Benefits on Household Income 1979', *Economic Trends*, No. 327, January 1981, pp. 124-125; (Col. 3), CSO.

on a number of services grew at about the same rate as spending on social security. In the earlier part of the decade the comparison is more favourable to services. The district nursing service showed especially rapid growth after 1975, with spending going up by a fifth. Of course this was also a time of rapid growth in the number of potential consumers. The numbers of people over 75 went up by 11 percent in the second half of the decade alone. However, the record is somewhat better than has generally been thought, both in terms of balance and of growth. The real cost of some of the services did increase over the period. There has been a particularly striking change for local authority residential care since 1975 where the number of places remained constant while spending in real terms rose by 16 percent.

The Central Statistical Office (CSO) in Britain attempts to estimate the effects of taxes and benefits on various kinds of household. It has kindly provided some special figures for households where the head is over 75. They are of limited use for this particular purpose, unfortunately, because social services are not allocated between households. They mainly confirm (see Table 6) the importance of the National Health Service to these households.

Finally there is one kind of payment which is on the boundary between 'cash' and 'care'. This is the attendance allowance. This is paid where there is a need for constant supervision or help with bodily functions by day or night. Expenditure on these allowances has risen from nil in 1970 to £146 million in 1975 and £207 million in 1979-80. The current rates of payment are £21.65p or £14.45p a week. Of 304,000 people getting these allowances about 106,000 are over 75. This is less than the take-up that might have been expected given the numbers of very elderly with severe handicaps living with relatives. Thus the numbers of bedfast or housebound elderly women living in private households is at least 200,000 and yet only 82,000 attendance allowances are being claimed by women. However, the benefit has certainly made a positive contribution and one that has been strongly concentrated on the very elderly. Only 54,000 allowances were being paid to people between 65 and 74.

Conclusions

Is there a case for special policy towards the over-75s — and if so should it involve a shift of balance between cash and care? These questions have to be set in a more general context of debate about the performance of the British government system. During the 1970s there was an increasing tendency to meet new requirements through cash or through services provided by voluntary agencies. Thus the attendance allowance supplied help which could in principle have been given by increased services. The Family Fund run by the Joseph Rowntree Trust was used to help children with severe handicaps after the thalidomide tragedy.

The choice between cash and care has been very much complicated by the division between central and local government, and by growing concern about the real cost of services. The predominant official view is that local government is inflexible and has difficulty in concentrating services on those in the greatest need. Given that local government provides many of the key types of service this change of attitude has made it even more difficult to provide a balanced approach. At the same time 'the relative price effect' has been operating more strongly to raise the real cost of services and there have been growing difficulties in their staffing and management. Services have begun to be increasingly bureaucratic, leading to problems in getting flexibility and change in service pattern.

Against this background our examination of how changes in spending have affected the over-75s must be seen as showing some relatively encouraging trends. Spending on services has expanded at least as fast as spending on social security, and some of the biggest increases have been in services which are relatively efficient both in themselves and in their concentration on the over-75s. Thus the district nursing and home help services still depend mainly on the commitment and common sense of the individual worker, working in a community setting. They have been affected by bureaucratization far less than some of the other services. Given that political interest is concentrated almost solely on improving pensions the record in services must be seen as a relatively encouraging one.

However, there are still many deficiencies affecting the over-75s, such as the low quality of long-term residential care, the lack of services for the mentally ill, the low take-up of the attendance allowance, and the failure to develop 'psycho-geriatric' services in the community.

A special policy for the over 75s is not about any one sweeping policy solution but about detailed work in a number of policy areas. The essential task is to improve support both to the very elderly living on their own and to those who are living with younger relatives. We should identify those services which are of special use to the over 75s and concentrate both on increasing them in amount and on improving access to them. The district nursing service, the home help service, the attendance allowance, and community services for mentally infirm elderly people would seem to be four key areas where there is scope for development. But perhaps the highest priority of all is for research into the preferences and needs of the very elderly and the relatives looking after them. It may be, for example, that new programmes to give short-term relief to relatives are particularly needed. The old general dilemma of services versus income support is less important in practice than the issue of access to certain specific types of service.

REFERENCES

Cmnd,8175 (1981), *The Government's Expenditure Plans* London, HMSO. p. 122.
DHSS (1987), *A Happier Old Age* London, HMSO 1987, p. 10.
DHSS (1981), *Care in Action* London, HMSO 1981, p. 1.
Hunt, A.(1978), *The Elderly at Home* London, OPCS, p. 119.

NOTES ON CONTRIBUTORS

Donald J. Adamchak is assistant professor of sociology and director of the Population Research Laboratory, Department of Sociology, Anthropology and Social Work, Kansas State University, Manhattan. He is author of several articles, including: 'Social Scarcity, Ideology and the Migration Turnaround', *Quarterly Journal of Ideology*, 1982 (with William C. Flint); 'A Note on Percent Neonatal-Post-Neonatal Mortality and Infant Mortality Rates as Correlates of Socioeconomic Development', *Population Review*, forthcoming; 'Emerging Trends in the Relationship Between Infant Mortality and Socioeconomic Status', *Social Biology*, 26, 1 (1979), pp. 16-29.

Nick Bosanquet is lecturer in economics at the City University, London. His publications include: *A Future for Old Age* (Temple Smith, 1978); 'Hospital Spending in Real Terms and Public Choice', *British Medical Journal*, 1981; 'Sir Keith's Reading List', *Political Quarterly*, 1981; and, as editor (with Peter Townsend), *Labour and Equality* (London, Heinemann, 1980). Formerly research director of the Briggs Committee on nursing and a member of the Jay Committee.

Carroll L. Estes is professor of sociology and chairperson, Department of Social and Behavioral Sciences, University of California, San Francisco, and director of the Aging Health Policy Center in the School of Nursing at the University of California, San Francisco. Her most recent book is *The Aging Enterprise* (1979). She is currently writing two other books, one (in collaboration) is forthcoming: *Fiscal Austerity and Aging* (SAGE 1983); the other focuses on the *Political Economy of Health and Aging*.

François Ewald is assistant professor, Collège de France (Paris). Her publications include: *Politiques du risque* (The Policies of Risk) (forthcoming, Paris, Grasset); *L'accident nous attend au coin de la rue* (The Accident is Waiting for Us on the Street Corner) (Paris, La Documentation Française, 1982); *La généralisation de l'assurance à la fin du 19ème siècle* (The Generalization of

Insurance at the End of the 19th Century) (Paris, Rapport au Ministère du Travail, 1979); and several articles and essays on the genealogy of insurance, formulations of risk and the sociology of law.

Eugene A. Friedmann is professor of sociology and department head, Department of Sociology, Anthropology and Social Work, Kansas State University, Manhattan. He is author, with Robert Havighurst, of *The Meaning of Work and Retirement* (Chicago, University of Chicago Press, 1954). He has also written several essays and articles, including 'The Impact of Aging Upon the Social Structure of the United States', in Clark Tibbitts (ed.), *Handbook of Social Gerontology* (Chicago, University of Chicago Press, 1960); with Harold Orbach, 'Adjustment to Retirement', in Silvano Arieti (ed.), *American Handbook of Psychiatry* (2nd ed., New York, Basic Books, 1974); 'Changements des rapports entre travail et loisirs dans une perspective de retrait', *Gérontologie et Société*, 10 (September 1979), pp. 6-19; and with William Lane, 'Academics and Retirement: The Changing Nature of the Retirement Experience', *Educational Considerations*, VIII, 1 (1980), pp. 9-14.

Danilo Giori, associate professor of sociology at the universities of Cagliari and Milan, has written articles on the elderly. He is author of *Essere vecchi* (To be Old) (Venice, Marsilio Editore, 1978) and *Vivere la vecchiaia* (Living Old) (Rome, Serelli Editore, 1982). He is on the board of editors of *Unita Sanitaria* (Sanitary Unit), a review of medical sociology.

Anne-Marie Guillemard is associate professor at Université Paris VII and member of the Centre d'Etude des Mouvements Sociaux, Centre National de la Recherche Scientifique, Paris. Author of *La Retraite une Mort sociale* (Retirement, Social Death) (Paris, Mouton, 1972) and *La Vieillesse et l'Etat* (Old Age and the State) (Paris, Presses Universitaires de France, 1980), she has also written several articles on the life style of retired people and on the making of old age policies. She is currently president of the Research Committee on Aging of the International Sociological Association.

Ephraim H. Mizruchi is professor of sociology at Syracuse University. He was recently director of the Policy Center on Aging of the Maxwell School of Citizenship and Public Affairs, Syracuse University. He is the author of *Success and Opportunity: A Study of Anomie* (New York, Free Press, 1964), and *Regulating Society: Marginality and Social Control in Historical Perspective* (New York, Free Press, 1983). He is co-author of *Stratification and Inequality* (New York, Macmillan, 1976) and editor and co-editor of a number of other books. His articles have appeared in the *American Sociological Review, Sociological Quarterly* and other scholarly journals. He is a contributor to a number of books including *The New Sociology: Essays in Honor of C. Wright Mills* (New York, Oxford University Press, 1964).

John Myles is an associate professor in the Department of Sociology at Carleton University, Ottawa. He is currently completing a book entitled *The Aged in the Welfare State: The Political Economy of Public Pension Policy* (forthcoming, Little Brown). His interests also include the role of state policy and transfer payments on inequality ('Income Inequality and Status Maintenance: Concepts, Measures and Methods', *Research on Aging* (1981) and comparative class politics ('Differences in the Canadian and American Class Vote: Fact or Pseudofact?', *American Journal of Sociology* (1979).

Chris Phillipson is senior research fellow in the Department of Adult Education, University of Keele. He is author of *Capitalism and the Construction of Old Age* (London, Macmillan Press, 1982) and has published articles on women in retirement, pre-retirement education, community work with the elderly, and the politics of aging.

Rolande Trempé is professor of contemporary history (history of labor and the labor movement) at the Université de Toulouse, Le Mirail, France. She is author of *Les Mineurs de Carmaux, 1848-1914* (The Carmaux Miners, 1848-1914) (Paris, Editions Ouvrières, 1971, 2 vols.), and 'Les industries d'un pays rural' (Industries in a Rural Area), in *Histoire du Languedoc de 1900 à nos jours* (Toulouse, Privat, 1980). She has also written several articles on the miners' union movement.

Hilde von Balluseck is professor of gerontology at the Fachhochschule für Sozialarbeit und Sozialpädagogik, a college for the vocational training of social workers in West Berlin. Her special fields of work and interest are: deviance and social control, social politics for the aged, women's research. Her most relevant publications are: *Abweichendes Verhalten und Abweichendes Handeln* (Deviant Behavior and Deviant Action) (Frankfurt, Campus, 1978); *Die Pflege alter Menschen. Institutionen, Arbeitsfelder und Berufe* (The Care of the Elderly: Institutions, Areas of Work, Professions) (Berlin, 1980).

Alan Walker is lecturer in social policy at the University of Sheffield, England, and secretary of the Research Committee on Aging of the International Sociological Association. He is author of *Unqualified and Underemployed* (London, Macmillan, 1981), editor of *Public Expenditure and Social Policy* (London, Heinemann, 1982) and of *Community Care* (Oxford, Martin Robertson/Basil Blackwell, 1982) and co-editor of *Disability in Britain* (Oxford, Martin Robertson, 1981). He is currently engaged in research into the family care of elderly people.

Volumes in the
SAGE Studies in International Sociology
Book Series